**Transcripts of Journey to Recovery with Joe M. and
The Big Book Comes Alive
Recorded in Laughlin, Nevada,
August 1988**

Disclaimer:

- **Copyright notice**: Alcoholics Anonymous, Copyright © 1939 (expired), 1955 (expired), 1976 by Alcoholics Anonymous World Services, Inc. All rights reserved.

- On August 22, 2004 Charlie P. (in a telephone conversation) gave his complete permission for these transcripts to be posted on the Internet, for the use of all members of Alcoholics Anonymous.

- These transcripts are not meant to be a replacement for the Big Book, but are an aid in the study of the program of recovery, found in the Big Book of Alcoholics Anonymous.

- Direct quotes from the Big Book are found in *Italics* and are set off by quotation marks. It is the transcriber's good faith belief that their use is consistent with the fair use clause of the copyright law.

- Any text that has been highlighted, underlined, formatted, boxed or referenced was done so at the discretion of the transcribers for their own clarification or enhancement, and has been posted here as is. Text found in parentheses may or may not be Joe or Charlie's own words.

- Though every effort was made for a direct translation of the tapes, some words may have been transcribed incorrectly or left out.

Trademark notice: Alcoholics Anonymous®, The Big Book®, and A.A.® are registered trademarks of A.A. World Services, Inc.

Transcript of Joe and Charlie Big Book Study - Laughlin, Nevada August 1998

J & C   If we're going to study the Big Book Alcoholics Anonymous, which of course that's what we're here for this weekend, I think it would be well if we would go back and look at just a little bit of the history behind the book, be able to see what happened to some of the first people that put this thing together and by looking at that history then it's going to make it a lot easier to understand the book itself as we go through that. And what we like to do to look at some of the history is to go to the forward of the 2nd Edition, Roman Numeral XV and we'll start with the last paragraph on that page so everybody that's got your books if you're ready, Roman Numeral XV and the last paragraph on that page, Joe.

One of the things that has helped me over the years in studying Bill's writings and he does this in most all of his writings, you can follow along with what he does and it'll help you understand some of his writings. For instance he'll always tell us what the problem is, then he'll tell us the solution to that problem, and then he'll give us a practical program of action to implement the solution that he just described. He does that in most all cases of his writings so that kind of helped me, in understanding how Bill writes. So the bottom of page, on Roman Numeral page XV,

Big Book p. xv, par. 4   "The spark that was to flare into the first A.A. group was struck at Akron, Ohio, in June 1935, during a talk between a New York stockbroker and an Akron physician."

J & C   Now we now that New York City stockbroker to be this fellow named Bill Wilson. I think we're treating Bill pretty good when we call him a New York stockbroker. He really wasn't, he was a New York City stock speculator. He made his living out of selling fast-talking to slow thinking people. I don't want take anything away from Bill because he's a great man, but I think we all need to realize that he's a real alcoholic just like all the rest of us, and understanding that it'll make it easier to understand the book, because after all, Bill is the primary author of the book. The Akron physician is this fellow named Dr. Bob Smith.

Big Book p. xv, par. 4   "Six months earlier, the broker had been relieved of his drink obsession by a sudden spiritual experience, following a meeting with an alcoholic friend who had been in contact with the Oxford Groups of that day."

J & C   A little later on we're going to get into Bill's story and we're going to see in Bill's story where he had, what he always called, a vital spiritual experience in the Towns Hospital in December of 1934. Now prior to him having that spiritual experience, certain things had to take place in Bill's life. And one of the things was that this meeting with the alcoholic friend took place in the later part of November 1934 and this was a fellow named Ebby Thatcher. And Ebby Thatcher came with Bill and sat down in Bill's kitchen and he gave Bill what turned out to be two vital pieces of information. He said Bill,

people like you and I who have become absolutely powerless over alcohol,
if we're going to have to recover from that condition, we're going to have to have the aid of a power greater than human power.

He said the doctors, and the ministers and the psychiatrists have tried to help people like us but human power doesn't seem to be able to do the job. And he said, we'll have to have the aid of a power greater than human power. And he said I've been attending meetings with a group of people called the Oxford Groupers and they told me if I could have a spiritual experience*, that during that spiritual experience I would be able to find that power, and I would be able to recover from alcoholism. He said also they have given me a practical program of action (now the 12 Steps).

They GUARANTEED me if I would follow that program of action: (1) I would have the spiritual experience*,
(2) I would find the power and
(3) I would be able to recover from alcoholism.

And he said, look at me Bill; it's been two months since I've had a drink. Now Bill knew about Ebby Thatcher, and he knew how Ebby drank. In fact Bill had always said, if I ever get as bad as Ebby Thatcher I'm going to quit drinking. And here's Ebby sitting in Bill's kitchen and Bill is about two thirds drunk and Ebbys been sober for two months. This made a great impression on Bill when he told him of the solution, the vital spiritual experience*, and he told him of the practical program of action necessary to have that spiritual experience. But that isn't everything Bill had to know. Let's go a little further.

Big Book * "... a profound alteration in his reaction to life." See Appendix II Spiritual Experience, Big Book pg. 569. alcoholism who is now accounted no less than a medical saint by A.A. members, and whose story of the early days of our Society appears in the next pages. From this doctor, the broker had learned the grave nature of alcoholism."

J & C   Again as we get into Bill's story, we'll be able to see how as far back as the summer of 1933, Bill was placed in the Towns Hospital, for withdrawal from alcohol by Dr. Silkworth. And after he had been in there a few days and his mind kind of cleared up Dr Silkworth sat down with Bill and began to explain to him his ideas about this thing concerning alcoholism. And he said Bill

the problem

I do not believe that alcoholism is a matter of willpower; I do not believe it's a matter of moral character, and I don't think sin has got anything to do with it.
I believe people like you are suffering from an illness, and he said it seems to be a very peculiar illness; it's **a two-fold illness, an illness of the body as well as an illness of the mind.**

And he said I think what has happened to people like you is

you've become absolutely **physically allergic to alcohol**.
And it seems to me as though anytime you put any alcohol whatsoever into your system,
it develops an actual **physical craving** which makes it virtually impossible for you to stop drinking after you have once started.
And he said because of that allergy which produces that physical craving
you'll never be able to safely drink alcohol again.

And he said you also have developed what we refer to as an **obsession of the mind**.
And he said an obsession of the mind is an idea that overcomes all other ideas to the contrary.

He said it really doesn't make any difference how badly you want to stop drinking. From time to time

your obsession of the mind to drink will be so strong that it will overcome any ideas not to drink
and your mind will actually lead you to believing it's okay to take a drink.
And he said then you'll take that drink, and then you'll trigger that allergy and you'll be unable to stop.

He said you can't safely drink because of your body,
you can't stay sober because of your mind,
therefore you've become absolutely powerless over alcohol.

Now Bill knew that in the summer of 1933, **BUT KNOWING THE PROBLEM DIDN'T SOLVE IT,** because shortly after that his mind told him it was okay to drink. And he took a drink, and triggered the allergy and drank for another year.

In the summer of 1934 he was placed back in the hospital again to be withdrawn from alcohol by Dr. Silkwood. And this time Dr. Silkworth pronounced him incurable, and told Bill's wife Lois that this guy is either going to die from DT's or he's going to be completely insane from a wet brain and you're going to have to lock him up or hire a bodyguard if you expect him to live. And Bill overheard that and he said this time fear sobered him for a bit. But then on Armistice Day 1934 his mind told him it was okay to drink. And he took a drink and triggered the allergy and couldn't stop drinking. It's ONLY AFTER Ebby came to see him and gave him the solution to that problem and gave him a program of action that Bill was able to recover. So basically he had to know three things,

(1) **HE HAD TO KNOW THE PROBLEM** he got that from Dr. Silkwood, (p. 7, par. 2),
(2) **HE HAD TO KNOW THE SOLUTION** (p. 12, par. 4; p. 27, par. 5),
(3) **AND THE PROGRAM OF ACTION**   that came to him from Ebby (Oxford Group) (p. xvi, par. 1-2)

THEN BILL WAS ABLE TO HAVE HIS SPIRITUAL EXPERIENCE AND RECOVER FROM ALCOHOLISM.

to regain health of body and mind

And Ebby began to take Bill to these Oxford Group meetings after that and it says,

Big Book p. xvi, line 9   "Though he could not accept all the tenets of the Oxford Groups, he was convinced of the need for moral inventory, confession of personality defects, restitution to those harmed, helpfulness to others, and the necessity of belief in and dependence upon God."

J & C   Which were the tenets of the Oxford Group, which were later on expanded into the Twelve Steps of Alcoholics Anonymous.

Big Book p. xvi, line 9   "Prior to his journey to Akron, the broker had worked hard with many alcoholics on the theory that only an alcoholic could help an alcoholic, but succeeded only in keeping sober himself."

J & C   After Bill got out of the hospital that last time he began to try to help other people. He began to go out and save them up out of the gutters and take them to these Oxford Group meetings. He began to go into the bars and drag them off a bar stool and take them to the Oxford Group meetings. Most of them didn't want to go but he was taking them anyhow. He was trying to sober up the world; he had lots of enthusiasm. But after a few months of trying to do this why, nobody was staying sober but Bill. And he went to Lois and said Lois I'm trying to help these people, these alcoholics stay sober, and nobody seems to want to stay sober. And she said why don't you go talk to Dr. Silkwood and see what he has to say. So he went over to talk to Dr. Silkwood and told him the same story. And Dr. Silkwood said, yes, I've heard some of the shenanigans you're pulling out there on the streets. He said you know Bill, you're staying sober, so obviously <u>trying to help other people is helping you stay sober</u>. And he said, you're talking to those drunks about that great spiritual experience that you've had, and a drunk just won't accept that. He said why don't you do for them what I did for you. Why don't you

[the problem]
(1) talk to them about the illness of alcoholism,
(2) talk to them about the physical allergy, and the obsession of the mind. (two-fold illness)

<u>Show them through your experience how that worked for you</u> and if they will accept that, then maybe you can
(3) talk to them about spiritual matters.

He said Bill; every alcoholic I know has two questions: 1. Why can't I drink like I used to without getting drunk all the time, and
2. Why can't I quit drinking now that I want to?

[the problem]
(1) Explain to them the exact nature of the illness,
(2) tell them about the physical allergy of the body and the obsession of the mind (two-fold illness), you'll get their attention.
(3) Then <u>after you get their attention</u> you can talk to them about spirituality.

TELL THEM WHAT THE PROBLEM IS FIRST. Now our book says,

Big Book, p. xvi, line 18   "The broker had gone to Akron on a business venture which had collapsed, leaving him greatly in fear that he might start drinking again. He suddenly realized that in order to save himself he must carry his message to another alcoholic. And that alcoholic turned out to be the Akron physician."

J & C   And we all know the story of Bill going to Akron. He and some other guys had put a business deal together. They were going to take over one of the companies there in Akron just through a proxy fight. And while there the whole thing blew up in the face, and his friends all deserted him and left him there in Akron, standing in the lobby of the Mayflower Hotel. Low, sad and depressed, counting the money in his pocket realized he didn't even have enough money to pay his hotel bill. He happened to look through a door off the lobby, into the bar. And I would assume probably the lights were low in the bar, the music was probably playing in the bar, the laughter was great and the smoke was thick, and Bill's mind said I believe I'll go in there and be with people of my kind and I'll feel better. And as he started through the door his mind began to think about taking a drink.

And Bill suddenly realized that if he went in that bar he was going to end up drunk. But he remembered how back in New York City, <u>every time he had tried to help another alcoholic, even though he had failed with them, every time he had tried he himself had felt better</u>. So he said to himself, what I had better do is find me a drunk here in Akron to talk to. Made a few phone calls and came in contact with a lady named Henrietta Seiberling. And Henrietta said, yeah, I know a guy that you can talk to. She said, let me call him and see if I can't set up a meeting for you. So she calls Dr. Bob's house and got hold of Anne Smith, Bob's wife. And said there's a fellow here from New York City that says he may have a possible means that Dr. Bob could recover from alcoholism. Can you bring Dr. Bob over for a visit? And Anne said well I'd like to but she said you know this is the day before Mother's Day, and he brought me home a potted plant, and it's sitting on the table and he's potted underneath the table. She said let me wait until the morning and see if I can get him to come over. So of course the next morning as soon as Dr. Bob woke up she set in on him to go over to Henrietta's and see this guy, and to talk to this guy from New York City. Now you know Dr. Bob didn't feel very good the next morning. Hung over and felt bad and he said I'm not going. And Anne kept after him and kept after him and kept after him and finally, finally Dr. Bob said I'll go over there and give that guy fifteen minutes of my time, and then I'm coming back home. So Anne took him over there, and Bill and Bob went into a room by themselves and they stayed in that room for literally hours. And Dr. Bob came out of that room and he said this is the first man I've ever met that knows what he's talking about when he talks about alcoholism. Let's see what happened to him

Big Book, p. xvi, par. 3   "This physician had repeatedly tried spiritual means to resolve his alcoholic dilemma but had failed."

J & C   Bill was surprised to find out Dr. Bob was already in the Oxford Groups. He knew more about the solution: the spiritual experience and the program of action than Bill knew, but he had never been able to apply it to the depth necessary to recover, cause he didn't know what was wrong with him. You see he thought it was willpower. He thought it was moral character. He thought it was sin. Why would he not, that's what everybody had told him up until that time? And what really interested him was the message that Bill had to carry regarding the problem, not the solution, not the program of action, but what alcoholism really consists of.

Big Book, p. xvi, par. 3   "But when the broker gave him Dr. Silkworth's description of alcoholism and it's hopelessness, the physician began to pursue the spiritual remedy for his malady with a willingness he had never before been able to muster. He sobered, never to drink again up until the to the moment of his death in 1950."

J & C   Bill went in there this time, for the first time he began to talk to Dr. Bob about the allergy of alcoholism. He told him that every time that he would go down by the bar and had every intention to have a drink or two, he would drink more than he intended to, he'd drink more that night or the next day and he'd be off and running again. And he said this Dr. Silkworth had told him that that was a physical allergy that caused him to want to crave more drinks after he took a drink and Dr. Bob said well yes I drink just like that, you really know what your talking about, that's the way I drink too. I would want to have one or two drinks, the next thing I know is I'd drink three, four, five, ten, or fifteen or twenty and didn't know how I got started. He said, you call that a physical allergy that? He said that's right. And he said, another thing he said, when I'm not drinking when I'm sober, I have these thoughts that I want to drink all the time, it's always on my mind, and Dr. Silkworth said, that's the obsession of the mind that would obsess for the idea to drink. And Dr. Bob said, well I have those same kinds of thoughts; you really know what you're talking about. So they reached a rapport through the illness of alcoholism. And he explained it at great detail, and Dr. Bob said that's me, that's just the way I drank. You really know what you're talking about. So they had some identification going.

Now this is the first time that Bill had tried this. Everybody back in New York City, he'd always talked to them about the solution: the great spiritual experience, the big white flash he'd had in the Towns Hospital. When he sat down with Dr. Bob, he didn't talk to Dr. Bob at all about Dr. Bob's drinking either. I'm sure that's what Dr. Bob expected to hear. Everybody else had talked to him about his drinking, but Bill said, let me tell you about my drinking. And through the sharing of his story, talking about his own allergy, Dr. Bob could see himself immediately in it. Through the sharing of his own story, talking about his obsession of the mind, Dr. Bob could see himself immediately in it. And he could see where he had become absolutely powerless over alcohol. And for the first time he was completely defeated when it comes to alcohol. Then he began to apply the little program of action to a depth he had never been able to do before.   Then he had a spiritual experience and he recovered from alcoholism too.

| to regain health of body and mind | Step 1 |

"... a profound alteration in his reaction to life."
See Appendix II Spiritual Experience, Big Book pg. 569.

Big Book, p. xvi, par. 3   "This seemed to prove that one alcoholic could affect another as no nonalcoholic could."

J & C   **Through the sharing of our story with a new person, we can affect them as no non-alcoholic could because we have immediate identification**
  (1) about the physical allergy,
  (2) about the obsession of the mind,
  (3) about the way we think and the things that we do.

Big Book, p. xvii, par. 1   "It also indicated that strenuous work, one alcoholic with another, was vital to permanent recovery."

J & C   Remember Bill was about to get drunk., and he really didn't go see Dr. Bob to sober up Dr. Bob. He went to see Dr. Bob to keep Bill Wilson from drinking. So it proved that night that working with another alcoholic was vital for our own recovery too. Now immediately, one of the Oxford Group tenets was you got to give it away if you're going to keep it. So immediately they made a decision that we're going to have to find us another alcoholic to talk to. Dr. Bob called the Akron City Hospital where he was actually working at that time. Talked to the head nurse and said do you have an alcoholic down there that we can come and talk to? We believe we've found a way to help him overcome alcoholism. She said, oh yeah, we've got a real one down here. He just blacked both eyes of one of the nurses, said we've got him tied down in bed. And Dr. Bob said put him in a private room, we'll be down in the morning to see him. And she said okay, and by the way Dr. Bob, have you tried this on yourself?

So the next morning they go down to see this fellow. He's named Bill Dobson, and you see the picture in AA rooms all over the world of the man on the bed. And this is Bill and Bob sitting there talking to Bill Dobson. Now they didn't talk to Bill Dobson about Bill Dobson's drinking.

    They talked to him about their own drinking.
        And through the sharing of their stories Bill Dobson could immediately see what his problem was.
        See he'd never known about the allergy and the obsession of the mind.
        He could accept the fact that he was absolutely powerless over alcohol, and
        he would have to have the aid of a power greater than himself in order to recover.

    They began to talk to him about the need for the spiritual experience.
        How they had found that necessary to apply those things in their lives in order to recover.
        They told him how they applied the little program of action and the results that they got.

    Two days later Bill Dobson said to his wife get my clothes out of the closet, I'm going home.
        And he gets up and he dresses and he goes home and he starts applying the program of action.
        And low and behold he had a vital spiritual experience and he recovered from alcoholism also.

Now this makes three of them. In the summer of 1935 in Akron they all three know the problem, they all three know the solution, they've all three applied the program of action, they've had a spiritual experience* and they have recovered from alcoholism

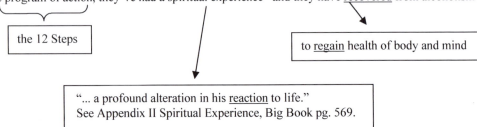

"... a profound alteration in his reaction to life."
See Appendix II Spiritual Experience, Big Book pg. 569.

Big Book, p. xvi, line 8   "This work at Akron continued through the summer of 1935. There were many failures, but there was an occasional heartening success."

J & C   You know we always give credit to Bill and Bob and the first one hundred, which rightly we should. But if we were to go back and think about that summer of 1935 these guys really, they didn't have much idea about what they were doing. They had found a few simple things that had worked for them. And they would try this on many, many different people that summer. And if it worked then they would keep it and if something didn't work they might discard that, learning as they went through that summer working with people. I know one of Dr. Bob's favorite things was to fill them up with sauerkraut juice mixed with honey. He knew that there was vitamins in that sauerkraut juice that would help the body, and of course the honey was a form of energy. And they tried that amongst many a different things. And every once in a while, one of these guys would fall over dead. I can almost see Bill turn to Bob and say, oh shit, let's don't do that again. I think maybe we ought to give credit to those they failed with that summer too. They probably learned more from their failures than they did from their successes.

Big Book p. xvii, line 11   "When the broker returned to New York in the fall of 1935, the first A.A. group had actually been formed, though no one realized it at the time."

J & C   You know this little group of alcoholics that was going to the Oxford Group; you know they were having troubles with the Oxford Group because the Oxford Groups had four absolutes. And the drunks were having trouble being absolutely anything, as we well know, they couldn't practice that, and it seemed like that these drunks liked to stand off in the corner someplace and drink coffee and smoke cigarettes and tell stories, not necessarily mix in with the other Oxford Group meeting members, so they began to call them the Drunk Squad of the Oxford Group. And that's what they liked, to separate themselves from the normal Oxford Group members.

Big Book p. xvii, par 3   "*A second small group had promptly taken shape at New York.*"

J & C   When Bill went back to New York City, he began to apply there what he had learned in Akron. Instead of talking about spirituality, he talked to the new people there about the **exact** nature of the illness and sure enough he got their attention. Some of them began to respond and a second little group started in New York City. And besides there were scattered alcoholics who had picked up the basic ideas in Akron or New York and were trying to form A.A. groups in other cities.

Big Book p.. xvii, line 19   "*By late 1937, the number of members having substantial sobriety time behind them was sufficient to convince the membership that a new light had entered the dark world of the Alcoholic.*"

J & C   In the summer of 1937 Bill was back in Akron, again on a business venture, and he decided to go by and see Dr. Bob and see how things were going in Akron. And they sat down in Dr. Bob's kitchen and they counted the number of people they knew that were staying sober, based on these three little pieces of information, and they found approximately 40 people sober.

And I think it's the first time that they really began to realize; maybe we really have found the answer to this thing called alcoholism. If we've found the answer then we need to get it to as many alcoholics as we possibly can. So the question immediately becomes well what's the best way to do that and maybe this is the beginning of the group conscious, cause Bill and Bob decided they didn't want to make that decision themselves, it was too important. And they called a meeting of the Oxford Group there in Akron and at that meeting that night there was eighteen people there, some alcoholic, some non-alcoholic, and the topic of conversation was, how can we best carry this message of recovery to the greatest number of people. Now they decided that night to do three things.

(1)   In those days you could hardly get an alcoholic in a hospital for detoxification. Any doctor that put one in there had to lie about their condition. Alcoholism wasn't very popular in the 1930's, that's for sure. So they decided, now remember this is in the midst of the depression now in 1932, nobody has a dime hardly at all, and they decided what they needed to do was to build a chain of hospitals stretching all the way across the United States where any alcoholic that needed it would be able to have detoxification. I would assume Dr. Bob was going to be the head doctor.

(2)   They also felt that this little message of recovery they had was so vital that not everybody could be entrusted with carrying it correctly. So they decided they needed to hire a group of individuals, train them and you know let them spread out across the United States more or less as missionaries to carry this message of recovery. I would assume Bill Wilson was going to be the head missionary too.

(3)   And then they said you know the Oxford Groups have written a lot of books, spiritual in natural and they've been very popular. Back in the 1930's people read a lot of books, this was in the days before television. They're really was a time before television, believe me there was. And they felt that if they could come up with a book on alcoholism, what it is, and the solution to it and a way to bring that about. The first comprehensive book on alcoholism the world had ever seen, that then surely this book would become one of the world's greatest best sellers, and they can take the profits from the book and build the hospitals and train the missionaries.

That was one reason behind the book. But I think

> the main reason behind the book was that they had already noticed
> carrying this message one on one, one person to another
> that it already had begun to be changed.

And you know how people are, when we hear something good well we like to repeat it. But we'll usually add just a little bit to it, and then the next one will add a little more, and a little more, and a little more, and after a little while it doesn't resemble the first thing. And they said

>what we really need to do is take these three pieces of information about
>the problem, the solution and a program of action
>put it down in a written form where it would no longer be changed, no longer be garbled,
>and any alcoholic anywhere in the world in the future would have this same information,
>it would be pure.

And they made the decision that night to write the Big Book, "Alcoholics Anonymous". Now thank God only one of the three things they decided that night came true. They never did get to build the hospitals because the book didn't make very much money in the beginning. They didn't get to hire and train the missionaries. But they did get to write the book. (p. xvii, line 25)

Big Book p.. xvii, line 19 "This determination bore fruit in the spring of 1939 by the publication of this volume. The membership had then reached about 100 men and women."

J & C   And after they wrote the book they sat down one night at a meeting and they were trying to determine what they were going to call the book. They needed a title for the book so someone said, well let's call it "The Way Out", that sounds like a pretty good name for a book. They did some research on that some later and they found out there were some 10 or 12 other books called

"The Way Out", so they discarded that. Somebody else suggested, well let's call it, "Comes the Dawn", now that sounds like a pretty good title for a book, and they discussed that a while and kicked that around and decided not to do that. Somebody said, let's call it "A Hundred Men", now that really sounds like a good name for a book. Well then a woman joined the group and they couldn't call it "A Hundred Men and A Women", so they discarded that idea. Bill suggested, hey let's call it "The Bill W. Movement", they discussed that about 5 minutes and kicked that out. And then one evening someone suggested, that we're alcoholics and we want to remain anonymous, how about "Anonymous Alcoholics", or "Alcoholics Anonymous", that caught on. And that's what they called the book, "Alcoholics Anonymous". And the first "Alcoholics Anonymous" that the world had ever seen was a book called "Alcoholics Anonymous". It says here,

Big Book p. xvii, line 27   "The fledgling society (this drunk squad of the Oxford Group),
"... which had been nameless now began to be called Alcoholics Anonymous, from the title of its own book.."

J & C   So we have two Alcoholics Anonymous don't we. We have a book entitled, "Alcoholics Anonymous", and then we have a fellowship entitled "Alcoholics Anonymous". Two A.A.'s and we still have that today. And I think this is very important for us to think about. This group of people who had been nameless, they had been known as the Drunk Squad of the Oxford Groups, wrote a book and in that book they put their program of recovery and they called the book, "Alcoholics Anonymous". And after the book was published they then decided to call themselves "Alcoholics Anonymous".

Now in 1939,

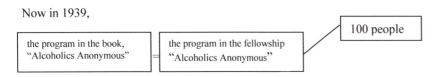

were exactly the same. The book then began to go out across the United States and the first person out here in California got a copy of this book.

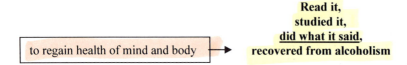

started a group called "Alcoholics Anonymous". The first person in Arkansas got a copy of this book.

**Read it,
studied it,
did what it said,
recovered** ◄——— to regain health of mind and body

started a group called "Alcoholics Anonymous". Now the growth of the fellowship began to come from the book, Alcoholics Anonymous. Now as the fellowship began to grow and get bigger and bigger and bigger, they began to notice something that the first 100 didn't have. They began to notice the great power of a fellowship of people who had escaped from a common problem. Now the first one hundred didn't have that; they only had one hundred people period.

But the fellowship, as it grew and got bigger and bigger and bigger they began to experience the power of fellowship, they then began to question the need for the severity of the program in the book. And they said

> Do you mean that we really have to turn ALL of our will and our life over to the care of God, as we understand him?
>   Can we give him the drinking and keep the rest?
> Do you mean we are going to have to share ALL of our life story with another human being?
>   Hell God already knows about it, we know about it, why tell somebody else?
> They began to say you mean we have to have God remove ALL of our character defects?
>   Hell we won't have any personality left if he does!
> And they began to talk about, do you mean we have to make amends to ALL those people we've harmed?
> And they began to say such things as, well maybe we don't need to do every bit of that.
> Maybe me could take some of it, and leave some of it?
> Maybe we can do it cafeteria style? Pick what we want, and leave that that we don't want?

And along about that time came the great advent of the treatment centers. Now please don't get us wrong, we have nothing against the treatment center. They serve a worthwhile purpose. But in the treatment centers people begin to hear some other type of words and some other languages. They begin to go into a group therapy thing and they begin to sit around the tables and talk about their problems and they begin to develop such terms as the dysfunctional family. And they begin to use such words as chemical dependency, and they began to talk about significant others, and they began to discuss meaningful relationships and they begin to talk about dysfunctional sex, and they begin to talk about this and they begin to talk about that. And the program in the treatment center wasn't like the program in the book, "Alcoholics Anonymous". Well naturally the new people from the treatment centers coming into A.A. wanted to talk about what they knew to talk about is what they had learned in other places.

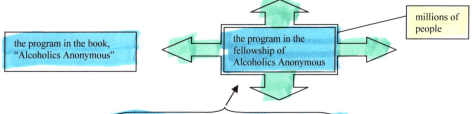

And slowly, slowly, slowly, the program in the fellowship began to change. And as the years went by, it began to change more and more and more, until today sometimes you go to an A.A. meeting and if they didn't read the preamble before the meeting, you wouldn't know what kind of meeting you're in, because they talk about everything except alcoholism and recovery there from it. We like to refer to those meetings as group depression meetings. You go in there feeling pretty good. Half way through the meeting you might as well just go ahead and blow your brains out…hell it's not even worth living any longer.

So what we're going to be talk about this weekend is not the program in the fellowship of Alcoholics Anonymous today.

We're going to talk about the program in the book, "Alcoholics Anonymous,"
that the first one hundred used, which has never been changed.
**The program in the fellowship has definitely changed.
The program in the book has never changed.**

Let's go to Roman numeral xx, let's see how effective this thing used to be, when the program in the book and the program in the fellowship were the same.

Big Book p. xix, last line "*While the internal difficulties of our adolescent period were being ironed out, public acceptance of A.A. grew by leaps and bounds. For this there were two principal reasons:* the large numbers of recoveries, and reunited homes. *These made their impressions everywhere. Of alcoholics who came to A.A.* and really tried,

> (1) *50% got sober at once and remained that way;*
> (2) *25% sobered up after some relapses, and*
> (3) *among the remainder, those who stayed on with A.A. showed improvement.*

Other thousands came to a few A.A. meetings and at first decided they didn't want the program. But great numbers of these --about two out of three--began to return as time passed."

J & C   If my math is correct that's 75% of those people who came to A.A. in the early days and worked the program that's in the book stayed sober, eventually. I know in my area, I don't know what it's like in you're area, but we can't talk about 75%. We can't talk about 50%. We can't talk about 25%. I doubt if we can talk about 10%, truthfully. And the reason for that I believe is that the fellowship of Alcoholics Anonymous got away from the program that's in the book called Alcoholics Anonymous and that worked. And so what we're going to do this weekend as Charlie said, we're going to talk about the fellowship that's in the program called Alcoholics Anonymous, and we're going to ask each and everyone of you to go back to your groups and listen to the conversations that you hear around the tables and see how closely it tallies with the program that's in the book called Alcoholics Anonymous. And if it doesn't we suggest you do something about it. That's our charge to you this weekend.

A lot of we older members of Alcoholics Anonymous tend to blame this problem on the newcomer. The newcomer comes in here, and they want to talk about the only thing they know to talk about. And too many we older members have said well we can't identify with those people anymore, so we're just going to stay home. And when we do, we've abdicated our responsibility for Alcoholics Anonymous, we've turned it over to the sickest of the sickest, who are the newcomers, and then we stand back and say look what they're doing to our A.A. Now I think that's our responsibility, to be sure that every newcomer that walks in the door, and we tell them, that stuff you've learned, wherever you've learned it, is probably good information, but that is not A.A. information, here's A.A. information. And we start talking about the program of recovery in the book, "Alcoholics Anonymous". And

>we take them (newcomers) by the hand, and we lead them through this program of recovery,
>so they can have a spiritual awakening also.
>I think they call that sponsorship, and that's sorely, sorely lacking in A.A. today.
>And I think that's our responsibility, it's not the responsibility of the new people;
>It's the responsibility of we older members.
>
>And we need to stand up and stand pact,
>and insist that in our meetings we talk about alcoholism and recovery there from;
>the program in the book.

And I'll just bet you we can see more people recover from alcoholism. Probably never will get back to 75%, but we can certainly do better than we're doing today.

Now we're not going to preach anymore. That's all the preaching for this entire weekend I guarantee you. Hope you don't' believe that.

Now that we know a little bit about the history, let's go back to the Table of Contents (Roman numeral v) let's look at it for just a moment. Let's see if we can't see the same pattern in this book that the first one hundred used. Do all of you have one of these little folders like this? Okay, we're going to put a picture up here on this screen, I know some of you will hardly be able to see it at all from this location, but you'll have a picture in that book which will match it if you can't see it.

BIG BOOK GOALS
TABLE OF CONTENTS

	GOAL 1 Problem	**GOAL 2** Solution	**GOAL 3** Action Necessary for Recovery
	DRS. OPINION Chapter 1 – Bill's Story	Chapter 2 – There Is A Solution Chapter 3 – More About Alcoholism Chapter 4 – We Agnostics	Chapter 5 – How It Works Chapter 6 – Into Action Chapter 7 – Working With Others
	STEP 1	STEP 2	STEP 3 4 5 6 7 8 9 10 11 12
	POWERLESS	**POWER**	**HOW TO FIND POWER**

I'm in the printing business and I have been all of my life and I print books like this and I've been in conversation with many people and when I started reading this book Alcoholics Anonymous I guess I must have had brain damage or something, but it never dawned on me that this book was laid out in any particular way. After all a bunch of old alcoholics wrote it so what would they know about laying out a book I thought, so I didn't pay any attention to that. Come to find out though this book had lots of good information lots of good help with laying out this book.

This book is laid out in a particular manner to bring about certain ideas.
Each chapter is very, very important. Each page is very, very important. Each paragraph is very, very important.
One paragraph leads to the next and the information in that paragraph on that page leads to the next.
And that's the way it goes in this book Alcoholics Anonymous, everything is important,
and it's laid out in a certain sequence to bring about certain ideas.

Most books have two particular goals, especially this one does.

And the 1st goal in this book **it tells us what the problem is**, and that's the goal number one. And they're going to use

>The Dr.'s Opinion, and
>Chapter 1 - Bill's Story   basically to tell us what the problem is.

And then the 2nd goal is going to be the solution; they're going to give us **the solution to the problem** that they described. And they know we're going to have problems with that solution just like they did. So they're going to talk

>Chapter 2: There Is A Solution
>Chapter 3: More About Alcoholism

>The solution has to do with spiritual matters and they know we're going to have some of those problems.
>So they wrote down

>Chapter 4: We Agnostics   for those of us who had problems in that area.

And the 3rd goal is **actions necessary for recovery** and we're going to begin with

>Chapter 5: How It Works
>Chapter 6: Into Action,
>Chapter 7: Working with Others

So this book is laid out in particular reasons to bring about certain ideas all the way across, all the way through the book. And that helped me in studying the book.

I hear people today talking about going to a Step Study Meeting. And they're always referring to studying the steps out of the Twelve and Twelve and if you'll notice these chapters correspond with the steps also. And any time you're studying the Big Book, you're studying the steps of Alcoholics Anonymous.

In that Dr.'s Opinion & Bill's Story, we're going to see nearly all the information, a little bit of it in Chapter 2 and Chapter 3 but most of it will be in The Dr.'s Opinion and Bill's Story. We'll be able to see everything that we need to in order to see what our problem really is, and we'll **be able to see where we are absolutely powerless over alcohol and our lives have become unmanageable**, and really that's Step **1**.

Step 1   If we're going to boil it down to just one word would be powerless.
        Then when we can see that powerless condition,
        Then obviously the answer to that is going to be power and remember Ebby told Bill
            it has to be the aid of a power greater than human power.

So through Chapters 2, 3 and 4,
        we're going to be able to see that power,

and we're going to get some new information about spirituality so
we'll be able to come to believe that maybe that power could help us also.

And there where you'll do Step 2. That's the power;

We came to believe that a power greater than ourselves could restore us to sanity.
I know we're powerless, and we know we need the power, and the only other thing we need to know is how do you find that power. And that's what Chapter's 5, 6, and 7 are about. There we will see the last 10 steps of Alcoholics Anonymous.

And if we follow them (The Steps)
we will have a spiritual awakening,
we will have found the power,
and we're no longer powerless over alcohol.

I read this book for years before I saw that sequence. The same identical sequence that Bill and Bob and the first one hundred had to know.

What is the problem?	Step 1	(The Doctor's Opinion)
		(Chapter 1 - Bill's Story)
What is the solution?	Step 2	(Solution)
		(Chapter 3 - More About Alcoholism)
		(Chapter 4 - We Agnostics)
What is the program of action necessary to find it?	Steps 3-12	(Chapter 5 - How It Works)
		(Chapter 6 - Into Action)
		(Chapter 7 - Working with Others)

And we'll begin to study the book in this manner. It becomes a very fascinating book; to see how each chapter ties into the next chapter to convey these certain ideas in the proper sequence.

J & C   Table of Contents. Okay, let's go over for just a few moments to the Preface, Roman numeral xi. And the second paragraph on Roman numeral xi,

Big Book p. xi, par. 2   *"Because this book has become the basic text for our Society and has helped such large numbers of alcoholic men and women to recovery, there exist a sentiment against any radical changes being made in it. Therefore, the first portion of this volume, describing the A.A. recovery program, has been left untouched in the course of revisions made for both the second and the third editions."*

J & C   And I think there's two ideas there. First when we see the words "basic text." I think we're alerted to the type book we have in front of us. All kinds of books in the world today. You got novels, novels written on fact, novels written on fiction. Biographies, autobiographies, concordances, many kind of books. But we also have a book called a textbook, and many of us don't have very fond memories of textbooks. Every time I saw the word textbook all I could thing about was cheat, I don't know why. Remember about how back in school when we used a text book, we had to read and study and do things you didn't want to do, take tests and all that kind of jazz. Lots of work involved in it. And for some people in A.A. today the very idea of a textbook just completely turns them off.

But if you would take a textbook in it's simplest form--really all it is, is a means of taking information from the mind of one human or a group of human beings, put it down in the written word then transfer that information to the mind of another human being who's using the text book. And that's all teaching is. A lot of people today say you can't teach in A.A., I don't see why you can't. Teaching is nothing more than transferring information from the mind of one person to the mind of another, increasing the knowledge of the one who's being taught. We all teach everyday and we're all being taught everyday. I don't see how in the world we could ever sponsor and help anybody if we couldn't teach them what we already know. And that's what a textbook does too. A textbook usually assumes that the reader of the book will have very little knowledge of the subject matter. It normally starts at a very simple level. Then as the knowledge of the reader increases, the material presented becomes more difficult.

The idea of a textbook on mathematics. Let's say my friend Joe here knows nothing at all about mathematics. He can't add, he can't subtract, he can't do any of those things. Oh, he can count. In fact he can probably count to twenty-one if he's standing there naked and got everything where it belongs, he might make 21. Twenty and a half actually. If I handed him a textbook on mathematics and I said, Joe, I want you to go to Chapter Five and work the algebra problems. Now being a good fellow he would go to Chapter Five and look at them but he can't even add and subtract, they just look like marks on paper to him. But if I said, Joe, Chapter 1 in this textbook on mathematics deals with the value of numbers and addition and subtraction. If you'll read it and study it, and let me help you, by the time you're through with Chapter One you'll know how to add and subtract and sure enough he learns how to do that. And then I say now let's go to Chapter Two. Based on what you've learned in One, you can go to Chapter Two and learn how to multiply and divide and sure enough he does that. And then I say, now you can go to Chapter Three and you can learn fractions and decimals and we gradually prepare his mind for the new information in Chapter Five. I think

the greatest mistake being made in A.A. today,
the newcomer comes to the door
we hand him the book
and we say go to Chapter Five and do what it says and you'll be okay

And they go to Chapter Five and they run into a series of algebra problems.

Step One says, "We admitted we were powerless over alcohol -- that our lives had become unmanageable."
The newcomer says, man I'm not powerless over anything.
They have no idea what we mean by that statement (because we've directed them to Chapter 5 (Step 3).

Step Two says, "We came to believe that a power greater than ourselves could restore us to sanity".
The newcomer says, don't tell me I'm crazy. Yeah, I do stupid things when I'm drunk, but when I'm sober I'm like other people.
They have no idea what we mean by that statement.(because we've directed them to Chapter 5 (Step 3).

But if you're not powerless and you're not nuts, then you don't need (Chapter 5) Step Three to be thinking about turning your will and your life over to the care of something you don't understand in the first place. We present them with an impossible situation.

If we can do nothing else this weekend, I hope we're going to be able to get over (realize) the idea of the value of

The Doctor's Opinion and the first four chapters.
There is where we learn what the problem is.
There is where we learn what the solution is.
That prepares us for Chapter 5. <u>You see Chapter 5 starts with Step 3.</u>
It's very difficult to start with (Step) 3, unless you've got (Step) 1 and (Step) 2 behind you.

Hopefully we'll be able to see that. I think the other thing that is so important,

Big Book p. xi, par. 2   *"...there exists a sentiment against any radical changes being made in it."*

J & C   The first edition of the Big Book, "Alcoholics Anonymous", and by the way this happens to be a 2nd printing of it. You'll notice how big this 2nd printing is. The actual lettering size is the same as your book today, but you'll also notice it that it had very wide margins on the pages. The alcoholic mind says the bigger the book, the better it'll sell. And that's why they call it a Big Book. They printed it on the thickest, cheapest old paper they could find. Cheap paper is thick, it's real thick, and you'll notice how thick this book actually is. It doesn't say a bit more than the book does today, but you know actually the thicker it is, certainly the more money it's worth. I think I can see their ideas behind some of this. What really amazes me is you notice the color on the dust jacket. I can just see some alcoholic in New York City walking down the street with this under his arm trying to remain anonymous. The brighter the color the quicker it catches the eye, and the better it.... I can see Bill Wilson all through this book, real _____.

The first printing came out in 1939. By 1955 the fellowship had changed. The stories in the back of the book were there for the newcomer to be able to identify with. In '55, since bottom had come up, age had come down, more and more women coming in, they said we need to change those stories in the back of the book. So in 1955 they deleted some stories, added some more, came out with a second edition, but the recovery section remained the same. 1976 they did the same thing. Deleted some stories in the back of the book, added some more, came out with a third edition, but the recovery section remained the same.

Now, I think what's so important for me today is whether I'm reading a first, second, or third edition--we have never changed the recovery section. I wonder why we've never found it necessary to change it. Because it works, doesn't it, yeah you betcha. And why does it work? Three reasons I think.

1. Alcoholics haven't changed a bit. They still get drunk, they get in jailhouses, they get in divorce courts, they get in knife fights, they get in gun battles, they get in car wrecks, they get in penitentiaries, they get in cemeteries. They're still doing the same dumb things today that they did back in 1939. Haven't changed a lick.

2. Alcohol hasn't changed. The names have changed. The bottles have changed. The colors have changed. But alcohol is the same thing today it was in 1939.

3. Human nature never changes. It's the same today as it was in 2000 years ago. And <u>that's what this book deals with. It deals with alcoholics, alcoholism and human nature.</u> Therefore, we've never found it necessary to change it. I think that's probably one of the greatest miracles of Alcoholics Anonymous. You know how we love to change things. Everybody that's ever read it's certainly has re-written it at least twice in their minds. Collectively though, we've never found it necessary. Joe?

Let's go to the Foreword to the First Edition, Roman numeral page xiii . It said,

Big Book p. xiii, par. 1   "We, ..."

J & C   and I think that's probably the largest word in Alcoholics Anonymous. <u>We</u> can do what <u>I</u> can't do.

Big Book p. xiii, par. 1   *"We, of Alcoholics Anonymous, are more than one hundred men and women who have recovered from a seemingly hopeless state of mind and body."*

J & C   They're already beginning to tell us again what the problem is, it says <u>a seeming hopeless state of mind and body</u>, and a little later on tonight we'll learn to separate those two ideas, the body from the mind, and to talk about them in great detail. And it says,

Big Book p. xiii, par. 1   <u>*"To show other alcoholics precisely how we have recovered is the main purpose of this book."*</u>

J & C   You'll notice that the words, "*precisely how we have recovered*" is in italics. Charlie would have you to believe that that it's squiggly writing, it isn't, it's italics. Squiggly writing. Anytime you see squiggly, you got me doing it now, any time you see italics in this book it becomes very, very important, probably ought to read it again. And it says "precisely". Later on in the book we're going to find words such as specifically, exactly, with clear-cut directions. So this book is not a book on just about how to recover from alcoholism,

<u>this book is going to tell us</u>
<u>precisely, specifically, exactly, with clear-cut directions</u>
<u>on how to recover from alcoholism.</u>

<u>And if I want to recover from alcoholism, guess what,</u>
<u>I need to do it precisely, specifically, and exactly, and try to follow the clear-cut directions best I can,</u>
<u>otherwise I may not recover from alcoholism.</u>

I think we see a couple of things here that's extremely important. First, "We are more than one hundred men and women". Most books that I read have been authored by one person, and when I read a book authored by one person, if I see something in there I don't agree with it, with my keen intellectual alcoholic mind I usually say who in the hell are they to think they're smarter than I am. And I just ignore it. But I've got to realize with the Big Book, that if I'm going to argue with it, I'm going to be arguing with one hundred people, not one.

The first forty said, Bill we want you to write the book, you know more about it than anybody else, you've been sober longer than anybody else, which by the way was just a little over 3 years at that time. But they said Bill this is not to be your book; it's to be our book. And as you write those chapters we want to see them, and we will add to, delete from, and change around whatever we want to. When we're through with it, it'll be the collective knowledge, experience and wisdom of all forty of us. By the time the book was published that forty had changed to one hundred. So if I'm going to argue with it today, I'm going to be arguing with one hundred men and women, not just one person.   And it's going to be one hundred men and women who have recovered from a seemingly hopeless state of mind and body.   Which brings in the word recovered. I hear people argue about this all over the world.

Can you recover from Alcoholism?
Well the book says you can.
It said the first one hundred had recovered from a seemingly hopeless state of mind and body.

Now I'll never be cured of alcoholism, I will always have the physical allergy, I'll never be able to safely drink alcohol again. But before I came to A.A., not only could I not drink it safely, but I couldn't keep from drinking it. And the resulting fact was I lived in an absolutely hopeless state of mind and body. And I came to A.A. and I applied the program of action in this book and I no longer live in that hopeless state of mind and body. I still can't drink, but by golly I can stay sober. Now I'll never be cured of alcoholism, but I have recovered from the state of mind and body known as alcoholism. And you're going to see the word recovered and recovery all the way through the book several times. I think that's important.

The other thing that is so important is to show other alcoholics precisely how we have done that. You know if I, if I went to an A.A. potluck meeting and let's say you've made a strawberry cake, which happens to be my favorite kind of cake. Just in case you ever make, ever make me one that's the kind I like, and I bite into that cake, and God it's just perfect. The texture's right, the taste is right, everything is just right about it. And I say, who made this cake? You'd probably say, I did. And I'll say, will you tell me how and you say, yeah I'll be glad to.   And you'll sit down and write out for me a <u>precise, specific, clear-cut set of directions</u> on how to make that cake. You'll tell me the ingredients to put in it, the quantity of the ingredients, the sequence in which to mix them together, the temperature at which to bake it, and how long to bake it.

Now, if I take your instructions in my kitchen and I follow them precisely as you made them out, when that thing comes out of the oven and cools off and I bite into it, I think I can expect it to taste exactly like your cake tasted. But if I get your directions in my kitchen and my keen, intellectual, alcoholic mind starts working, it may say, well I'm not sure about six eggs, maybe we oughta just put four in there. Instead of two cups of sugar, I believe it would be better with three. Instead of baking it at 375, surely four and a quarter would be better. Instead of baking it for eighteen minutes, I need to bake it for twenty-five. Now when it comes out of the oven and I bite into it, you betcha I'm going to be biting a piece of cake. But I wonder how closely it would resemble your cake, which was my reason for making it in the first place.

A precise, specific, clear-cut set of directions, on how to recover from alcoholism.

We've been around A.A. long enough to know and clearly understand you can't make anybody do anything that they don't want to in A.A. The only one requirement for membership in Alcoholics Anonymous is a desire to stop drinking. You can stand up in an A.A. meeting and say I don't like you people at all, can hardly drink your lousy old coffee, and every time I read your Twelve Steps I vomit, but I'm going to be a member of A.A. because I've got a desire to stay sober and nobody can say a word about that. But that's dealing with membership and the fellowship of Alcoholics Anonymous.

If you want to recover from alcoholism there are some things you're probably going to have to do
And that's what this book deals with. It doesn't deal with membership and the fellowship.
It deals with recovery from alcoholism.

And if we were to do as these first one hundred did,
then surely we can expect to receive what they got,
recovery from a hopeless condition of mind and body known as alcoholism.

Big Book p. xiii, par, 1   "For them, we hope these pages will prove so convincing that no further authentication will be necessary. We think this account of our experiences will help everyone to better understand the alcoholic. Many do not comprehend **that the alcoholic is a very sick person**. And besides, we are sure that our way of living has its advantages for all."

J & C   And that statement, "many do not comprehend that the alcoholic is a very sick person", very important to me. Cause when I come to Alcoholics Anonymous I used to stand in the back of the room and I looked down at my feet and I was ashamed, and I had

become everything I detested in a human being. Certainly thinking that I had an illness of alcoholism was not one of my thoughts. My thought was something like this, 'I feel like a no good rotten SOB and I'm guilty of everything in the world, so I must be a no good rotten SOB', and I thought that was what alcoholism was; turns out that it wasn't. You know I've been married and divorced to two women, seven times. Would you repeat that? Yeah, two of them seven times. Phyllis only admits to two of them but I divorced her once and it wasn't even my turn. She was three, the first one was four, the second was three. I'm not sure that's a record, but I'll bet it's getting pretty close to it, what do you think. I've heard some people beat that one. But my first wife she was a great old gal and I used to drink and go places, I was one of those traveling drunks you know, and didn't come back right away either. They used to have a statement around my group that said, 'He who leaves and does not return, stays gone a long time', and that was me. And from time to time I'd get drunk and go places and I'd come home as if I'd never been away.
And when I got home I looked out in my yard and all my stuffs laid out in the yard. And you all know what I mean by stuff don't ya? Dirty under shorts, dirty shirts, un-ironed clothes, you know they never throw out anything that's cleaned and ironed, I don't know why that is. They'd file for divorce on me and put a restraining order, make off with the money, make me madder than hell.

And I'd say, after all I'd done to them, after all I'd done for them, they treat me like that. So one time I was gone a while and I decided, I was trying to get back home you know and I was serious so I went to the preacher that my first wife was going to at that time and I had a little conversation with him. And he said Joe, what seems to be your problem he asked me. And <u>I didn't know what the problem was</u>, if I knew well I would have told the man cause I was serious and I said well I'll tell you what I think the problem is, and it's her. If you lived with her, you'd drink too I said. Well he gave me a prescription, a solution. He said you must, and boy did he emphasize that word, you must have faith in these things and he laid them out for me. Well I couldn't have any faith in those things, you know why? Because I didn't even believe them. How can you have faith in something that you don't even believe? <u>Thank God for the second step so I could come to believe</u>, but that was to happen some time later.

So later on I met and married my other wife. We met in a bar, The Zebra Lounge; I can almost smell it now. And we were introduced and she looked at me, she said you know Joe you look like my third husband. I said my God how many have you had and she said two. We'll I liked her right away. And we started drinking and having fun and doing all those things, and then it wasn't long after we got married well she started throwing my stuff out in the yard, filing for divorce, getting a restraining order. Well this time I went to a psychiatrist and set down and talked to him, paid him seventy-five dollars an hour and he said
Mr. McCoy, for seventy-five dollars an hour they'll call you mister. He said Mr. McCoy what seems to be your problem, well <u>I didn't know what the problem was</u>, so I told him what I thought it was, it was her and her, if you lived with those two you'd drink too I said. Well he gave me a prescription, he thought I had a valium deficiency, he didn't mention not drinking so I took the valium and continued to drink and I got into real trouble now, I mean really trouble. I got to where I didn't know the difference between my job and the bar, I didn't know the difference between my wife and your wife, and my wife and my girlfriend. I got everything all mixed up, got into a lot of trouble. So

      by the time I come to the doors of Alcoholics Anonymous I had become everything I detested in a human being.
                  I did not like who I had become and I was very, very sick.
        It wasn't until after I got into listening to, and the description of Dr. Silkworth's opinion on alcoholism
           that I began to understand what I had here, and it wasn't that I was a no good rotten SOB,
              <u>I had an illness called alcoholism, a physical allergy coupled with an obsession of the mind.</u>

and somehow or other that information helped me overcome some of these ideas that I had. And as I look back now and I know more about this, you know the very first sixteen printings of this book, "Alcoholics Anonymous", The Dr.'s Opinion is on Page 1. 1955 in the second edition, they moved the Dr.'s Opinion out of the Page 1 and put it into the Roman numeral sections. And you all know we don't read the Roman numeral section do we? Who does? And I think that most of us in Alcoholics Anonymous got away from the idea of the Dr.'s Opinion and just looked at Bill's Story, page 1. But

<mark>the information in The Dr.'s Opinion is so important to me and to the fellowship of Alcoholics Anonymous because the rest of the book is going to tell us how to recover from the condition of the body and the mind that Dr. Silkwood described.</mark>

      And I said, I was alcoholic for about two years and I didn't even know what an alcoholic was really.

We start looking at what the problem actually is. And most of us are absolutely amazed to find out what the problem is because most of us felt before we came here that it was a matter of willpower. And after all we had enough willpower that we ought to be able to control our drinking. And we found out that willpower didn't work and we assumed that we were just crazy. Or maybe we thought it was moral character, and maybe we thought we were just sinful rotten people. Now why wouldn't we think that, that's what everybody had told us up to this point? Throughout the history of human kind, they've been trying to find out for thousands of years what alcoholism is.

<u>You know you really can't do anything about a problem, until you understand the problem.</u>

And most of the people that tried to determine what alcoholism is were not alcoholics to start with. And they were the ones that said it was a lack of will power. They said if you'll just use your will power like we do you wouldn't drink that way. They're the ones said it was moral character, they're the ones who said it was sin. We alcoholics didn't say those things; hell we just kept on drinking and let them worry about what it is. Alcoholism is not anything new. You will find references to alcoholism as far back as human history has recorded. And one of the oldest recordings of human history is to be found in the bible. And in the book of Proverbs in the bible there's some information there about alcoholism.

Now, the book of Proverbs was written by a fellow named Solomon. And you all remember Solomon was a very, very wise, very learned individual. He might have been the first social worker the world had ever seen. Yeah, whenever people had a problem they went to Solomon to get the answer for it. And apparently somebody asked him one time about alcoholism, cause he describes us in the Proverbs (23:29). He said,

Who has woe? Who has sorrow? Who has wounds without cause?
Who has redness of eye?   They that tarry long at the wine.

J & C   Everybody was a wino in those days; they didn't have the hard stuff like we got it today. He said,

You will be as one who stoopeth in the midst of the sea.

J & C   Remember how you used to lay down in bed and that old bed start moving around on you.

Or that sleepeth at the top of a tall mast.

J & C   You know the way a mast sways back and forth. And he said,

You will say they have beaten me and I felt it not.

J & C   And he surely knew some of us men, he said,

And thine eyes shall behold strange women.

J & C   Alcoholics really haven't changed very much have they?

And thine heart shall utter perverse things.

J & C   Like trust me honey, please trust me. He said, and yet,

They will arise in the morning and seek it yet again

Almost a perfect description of alcoholism as we know it today, but he didn't have an answer for it, cause he didn't know what caused it. And we've had medical people; spiritual people throughout our history try to determine what alcoholism is. There was a doctor named Dr. Trotter that lived in England long time ago, and he said that I believe alcoholism is an illness, but he couldn't explain what it was, therefore they didn't have an answer for it. There was a doctor who lived here in the United States named Dr. Benjamin Rush. He's one of the signers of the Declaration of Independence, he wrote a paper on alcoholism, described the alcoholic, and he said he felt it was an illness too. But he couldn't name what it was, he couldn't determine it, so he had no solution.

It's only in this century that we have been able to find out what alcoholism is and then once we found out what it is then we could find a solution to it. And I don't think we alcoholics today who are in A.A. realize how lucky, lucky we really are, to be living in the period of time where we found out what alcoholism is and we found out the solution to it. And as I look at our history, which we're going to be doing a lot of this weekend, I'm convinced in my mind that God got tired of seeing people like us die from alcoholism and he took various different people from around the world and gave us these pieces of information that allows us to recover from that condition today. And I think one of the first persons that he used was this little doctor called Dr. Silkworth. When Dr. Silkworth was in medical school he became very interested in the alcoholics. But when he got out of medical school he learned like most doctors did it was very difficult to make a living working with alcoholics. Most doctors do not like to work with alcoholics, they said then and they say today that an alcoholic will not tell you the truth. That's certainly true isn't it? And they said they will not do what we tell them to do. And that's certainly true isn't it? But they said the main reason we don't want to work with them is they won't pay their bills. So Dr. Silkworth, in order to find a way to make a living had to go off into another field, but always interested in we alcoholics. And he became very successful in his field.

But in the late 1930's, 1920's we had of course the great stock market crash and Silky had everything he owned invested in the stock market, and he lost it just like everybody else did. Lost the good job he had and he had to find a job somewhere, and Charlie Towns from the Towns Hospital who Silky had met before through his interest on/in alcoholics offered him a job. He said why don't you come to work here and I'll pay you thirty dollars a week and room and board and you can help me in working with other alcoholics/working with alcoholics. So Silky went to work in the Towns Hospital in 1930, and he began to work with people like us and began to see us come into the hospital, terrible, terrible, physical and mental condition. And he begin to withdraw us from alcohol, build the body up, and etc., and 60 or 90, 30/60/90 days later he would see us leave the hospital in reasonably good shape and then a month or two or three or four later he'd see us come back in, in worse shape than we were before, continually going in and out, in and out, in and out, in and out. He also noticed some people that he worked with who drank like we drank, but did not go in and out, in and out, and in and out. He also noticed other people who drank moderately and safely, and he began to say there's something different about these alcoholics. There's something different about the body. Apparently alcohol does something to them that it doesn't do to normal people. And he began to develop this little idea that

<u>when you put alcohol in your body it produces an actual physical craving that makes it impossible for us to stop drinking.</u>

But he also said even in those days,

that's not the real problem of the alcoholic, he said
<u>the real problem is that the alcoholic cannot keep from drinking.</u>

He said people who are heavy drinkers, people who are moderate drinkers, if they want to quit drinking they just quit, and it don't bother them at all. But he said

it seems as though the alcoholic, after they quit, the mind begins to play tricks on them,
and begins to think about one or two drinks and how it makes them feel.
And he said that idea becomes so powerful that it overcomes the idea that they can't drink,
and they take a drink and end up drunk every time.
He said now if you can't drink safely,
and if you can't keep from drinking,
then you're powerless over alcohol

Now we don't know whether Bill Wilson was the first one he told that to or not, but we know Bill was probably the first one to act on that information. Then after Bill got sober, and after Dr. Bob got sober, and after Bill Dobson (A.A. Number Three - p.182 Big Book) got sober and after the first 40 got sober based on that information and decided to write the book, they went to see Dr. Silkworth and said will you let us put that information in the book so that other alcoholics can see what their problem is too. And they said will you write some of it for us, and the Doctor said yeah, you can use it and I'll write some of it under one condition, that we will call it "The Doctor's Opinion". He said I can't prove it, there's no facts behind it, so we'll just have to call it an opinion. And he said, by the way, don't use my name. He said they'll throw me completely out of the medical profession if you use my name on this deal.

In 1956 when they came out with a Second Edition, 1955 and 1956 they came out with a Second Edition, by that time the Medical Association, the American Psychiatric Association had recognized the fact that Alcoholism is an illness. And Dr. Silkworth said in the Second Edition, you can put my name in it now. So for the Second and Third you've got Silkworth, but in here you don't. Let's look at what the Doctor had to say for just a little bit. Let's go to Roman number page twenty-four, that's xxiv, I didn't know that when I got sober. He said,

Big Book p. xxiv, par. 2 "The physician who, at our request, gave us this letter, has been kind enough to enlarge upon his views in another statement which follows. In this statement he confirms what we who have suffered alcoholic torture must believe---that the body of the alcoholic is quite as abnormal as his mind."

J & C   Now we know

>there's no 'must' in the fellowship of Alcoholics Anonymous,
>but there are a lot of 'musts'* in this book called, "Alcoholics Anonymous"

and there's one of the first ones,

>"We must believe---that the body of the alcoholic is quite as abnormal as his mind."

Now this is the first time we can find anywhere in written history, the reference to the fact that the body is affected as well as the mind. Everything up until this time, they had talked about the mind only. Weak will, moral character, sin and etc. But here we see a statement that says the body is quite as abnormal as the mind. I think he's telling us two things,

1. That the body is affected also, and I think he's also saying
2. The mind is abnormal, when it comes to alcohol.
   We react to it different physically and also mentally in an abnormal manner.

And we'll talk about both of those; the first one we're going to look at is the body. It said

Big Book p. xxiv, par. line 13 "It did not satisfy us to be told that we could not control our drinking just because we were maladjusted to life, that we were in full flight from reality, or were outright mental defectives. These things were true to some extent, in fact, to a considerable extent with some of us. <u>But we are sure that our bodies were sickened as well. In our belief, any picture of the alcoholic, which leaves out this physical factor, is incomplete</u>.

The doctor's theory that we have an allergy to alcohol interests us. As laymen, our opinion to its soundness may, of course, mean little. But as ex-problem drinkers, we can say that his explanation makes good sense. It explains many things for which we cannot otherwise account."

J & C   Now, if the purpose of a textbook is to transfer information from the mind of one human being through the written word to the mind of another human being, then it stands to reason that the transference of that information is going to be based upon the understanding of the words that are used. If the writer of the book uses a certain word and understands it this way (<), the reader of the book reads that word and understands it this way (>), a different understanding then the information that comes through is going to be garbled and incomplete information. And there seems to be a few key words in the Big Book, that many of us have had difficulty with, and I think the first word we've had a real problem with is this word,

>Allergy

Well most of us when we come here we assume already we know what an allergy is, I know I did.
I knew if you were allergic to something and you got around it or you ate it or you drank it or something like that, that there would be some physical manifestation or indicator of that allergy.
For instance if you eat strawberries and you're allergic to them you'll break out in a rash, the rash being the manifestation of that allergy.

> you don't see our allergy you feel it, and only we alcoholics feel it.

If you're allergic to milk and you drink it you'll have a bad case of dysentery, the dysentery being the manifestation of that allergy.
If you're allergic to certain plants such as ragweeds, and you get around them, your eyes, nose, itch, water, and you start sneezing. The itchy, watering eyes, nose and the sneezing, that's the manifestation of that allergy.
So I knew if you were allergic to something there would be something there that you could see.

So they came to me and they said Charlie, <u>you got an allergy to alcohol and you'll never be able to safely drink it again.</u>
And I said how in the hell can I be allergic to alcohol; I'm drinking a quart a day.
How can you possibly drink that much of something you're allergic to?
And I said besides that when I drink alcohol I don't break out in a rash, and I don't have a bad case of dysentery.
Once in a while I might depending on what I had been drinking, but usually I didn't. Nor did it make my eyes, nose, itch, water, and cause me to sneeze. And I said I don't understand what you're talking about, you need to explain that to me.
And they said well you don't need to understand; they said all you gotta know is you can't drink it.

Well today I think I know why they told me that, I don't think they understood it a bit better than I did.

And I went from person to person to person to person, trying to get somebody to explain this allergy to me, and all they would say is what difference does it make, forget the damned allergy, don't drink and you'll be all right, keep coming to meetings.
Now if you're an alcoholic like I am with a keen, intellectual, alcoholic mind and you got a question like that dangling out here in front of you, if you don't get the answer to it, sooner or later it's going to drive you out of your mind. And one day in sheer desperation I went to a source of information that has never failed me since that time. I went to the dictionary and I looked up the word allergy and I found several different definitions of it (the way you do with any word depending on how you use it). But I think I found the one that fit me exactly when it said,

<u>An allergy is an 'abnormal' reaction to any food, beverage, or substance of any kind.</u>

An abnormal reaction. So I began to look back over my drinking history to see where I was abnormal, and to my amazement I found out, I don't know what's normal and what's abnormal.

> The only difference between normal and abnormal is how the majority of people react to substances of any kind.

The only thing I knew about drinking was the way I drank and the way those people drank who drank with me. If they didn't drink like I did, we didn't drink together.

So to find out what's normal to see if I'm abnormal, I have to go to the normal, social, temperate moderate drinker; those that drink alcohol and do not get in trouble with it. And I asked them to describe to me how they feel when they take a drink. And they said we come home from work, tired, tense, wrought up from the day's work, we can have a couple of drinks before dinner.

We begin to get a relaxing, comfortable feeling. We'll go ahead and have dinner, and we probably won't drink any more that night. Well, I don't feel that way when I drink alcohol. Whenever I take a drink of alcohol it passes over my lips, my lips begin to tingle immediately. Hits my teeth and they kind of chatter up and down. Strikes my tongue, and I can feel it begin to grow, and expand and swell. Hits my cheeks and they kind of flutter in and out. At the same time it's passing through my sinus cavities up into my forehead and I begin to get a feeling up here in my forehead, which is absolutely, indescribably, wonderful. Now, I didn't swallow the damn stuff yet, I just got it in my mouth. When I swallow that alcohol and it starts down through my esophagus, great things begin to take place. The first thing that happens is my chest begins to grow and expand, and gets bigger and bigger. Hits my stomach and just literally explodes like a bomb. Immediately I feel it racing through my arms, and they get longer and longer; hits my hands and fingers and they begin to tingle and vibrate. The same time it's racing through my arms it's racing through my legs, their getting longer and longer, I'm getting taller and taller and it hits my feet and toes and they get a hot, intense burning, exciting get up and go somewhere and do something feeling. I don't understand a comfortable, relaxing feeling when you have a drink. These people told me something that blew my mind for me. They said Charlie, whenever we have a couple of drinks we begin to experience a feeling of dizziness, a feeling of being out of control, and they said we don't like that feeling. Therefore, one or two drinks is all we want to drink. How many times have you and I tried to get them to drink more and they said oh, no, no, I feel this already, or oh, no, no, no, this is making me dizzy, I don't want anymore. So today I realize that's the normal reaction to alcohol**.** You see for most people when they put alcohol in the system it hits the stomach, it immediately goes into the bloodstream, immediately goes to the brain. And
for a normal drinker it acts as a downer, it's a sedative.

It's supposed to give them a slightly tipsy out of control feeling. Now when it goes into my stomach, into my bloodstream, into my brain, instead of me getting a slightly tipsy out of control feeling,
alcohol for me (the alcoholic) acts as an upper, its a stimulant,

and my brain gets a very exciting, in control feeling. They have two drinks and they want to go to bed. I have two drinks and by God I want to go to town, immediately. I react to it differently mentally.

And another thing they told me is that when we have a couple of drinks not only do we get a slightly tipsy out of control feeling, they said we begin to experience a feeling of nausea, they said we don't like that feeling and therefore one or two drinks is all we want to take. How many times have you tried to get them to drink more and they say oh, no, no, this is making me sick, I don't want anymore of it. That's the normal reaction to alcohol.

Alcohol is a toxic substance; a destroyer of human tissue
When you put it in your body, your mind and body is supposed to react to it with nausea
and say puke it up and get it out of here.
When I put it in my body, instead of my body experiencing the feeling of nausea,
my body experiences an actual physical craving which demands more of the same.
Their body said puke it up, mine said put some more in here.
<u>So not only do I react to it differently mentally, but I also react to it differently physically.</u>

Now the only difference between normal and abnormal is what the majority of people do. If the majority, nine out of ten, react that way, one out of ten reacts the way I do, then

<u>my reaction is considered to be abnormal,</u>
<u>therefore I'm considered to be allergic to alcohol.</u>
<u>You can't see it, you can only feel it, and only alcoholics feel it.</u>

You see I kept looking for the rash; I kept looking for the dysentery. No you don't see our allergy, you feel it and only we alcoholics feel it. Joe.

End of Tape 1

Charlie said you can get to trouble going to town. That's the trouble with trouble; it always starts off as fun, isn't it? How many of you went off to get drunk and to get into trouble. I would go out and get drunk and have a little fun. And that's the trouble with trouble it always starts out as fun, at least that's the way it did with me.

You know I just love to watch normal, social, temperate, moderate drinkers. Fascinating to watch them, saw one on the airplane yesterday. Yeah, yeah, he ordered a drink, got him a mixer with it and he put his mixer in this glass with ice in it, poured his little bottle in there. They buy little-bitty bottles on airplanes. I think it costs them four dollars today and hell there's not a drink in that bottle period but anyhow that's what they get. And he poured it in there and then he took a little stick, and he went through a stirring ceremony. I don't know much about stirring when it comes to drinking but he stirred and he stirred and he stirred, and after a while he laid his little stick down and you know what he did then? He picked up his magazine and started reading his damn magazine. I'm sitting there watching him saying drink the damn stuff what the hell did you get it for. That's what we call alcohol abuse. Now that may be normal but I call that sick to drink like that. So I think I'll read this again,

Big Book p. xxiv, par.3 "The doctor's theory that we have an allergy to alcohol interests us. As laymen, our opinion as to its soundness may, of course, mean little. But as ex-problem drinkers, we can say that his explanation makes good sense. It explains many things for which we cannot otherwise account."

J & C   And the explanation for this explains many things for which I could not otherwise account. It explained to me why I would go down by the bar with every intention of having two and the next thing I know it's midnight or one or two or three o'clock in the morning or the next day or the next week and I'd wonder what in the hell happened. I just went down there to drink two. Well this idea about this allergy to alcohol interested me; it explained many things, which I couldn't otherwise account. Now let's go to Roman numeral page xxvi. A good textbook will never tell you anything for what it doesn't give you more information to back it up. He's talked here about the allergy, now let's go over to Roman numeral xxvi, first paragraph; let's expand on that just a little bit.

Big Book p. xxvi, par. 2   "'We believe, and so suggested a few years ago, that <u>the action of alcohol on these chronic alcoholics is a manifestation of an allergy</u>*; "

J & C   I used to hate that word, they'd call me a chronic alcoholic and I hated it. I don't particularly like it today, but I found out too that chronic just means something that you do over and over and over, so therefore I was a chronic drinker or a chronic alcoholic.

Big Book p. xxvi, par. 2   "... <u>is a manifestation of an allergy*; that the phenomenon of craving is limited to this class and never occurs in the average temperate drinker. These allergic types can never safely use alcohol in any form at all</u> and once having formed the habit and found they cannot break it, once having lost their self-confidence, their reliance upon things human, their problems pile up on them and become astonishingly difficult to solve.

J & C   You know this manifestation of allergy that Charlie talks about, the phenomenon of craving after we take the few drinks.

<u>We don't have the craving before we take the few drinks.</u>
<u>It's only after we take the few drinks that the phenomenon of craving develops,</u>
<u>and then we have to have more and more and more, and</u>
<u>only alcoholics have that</u>

Non-alcoholics do not crave alcohol after they take a drink, they just don't. The get all they want to drink every time they drink which is two or three maybe and that's all they want cause they don't have this phenomenon of cravings but alcoholics have.

* An allergy is an abnormal reaction to any food, beverage, or substance of any kind.

The action of strawberries on one who is allergic to strawberries, is manifested by a rash.
The action of milk on one who is allergic to milk is manifested by dysentery.
The action of ragweed on one who is allergic to ragweed, is manifested by itchy, watery eyes, sneezing and etc.
<u>The action of alcohol on one who is allergic to alcohol, is manifested by, and he refers to it as the phenomenon of craving.</u>

He uses the word phenomenon cause he didn't understand it.
So what it is, is manifested by an actual physical craving in the body
  that demands more of the same after we have started.
And the word craving is very, very important.

> The Allergy is manifested by a physical craving,
> which is triggered by the first drink
> You can't see it, you can only feel it
> and only alcoholics feel it

Now I hear people today say well I came to A.A. and I craved a drink for four years. No, in the context of the Big Book that's the wrong use of the word craving. They might have needed a drink or wanted a drink, desired a drink.

The only way an alcoholic can crave alcohol is to first put it the body,
then the physical craving develops and then we can't stop and we end up drunk.

So in the "recovery section (Roman numeral section +1st 164 pages) of the book - <u>when you see the word 'craving' it's always referring to the body</u>, never to the mind,   <u>we'll use the word 'obsession' for the mind,</u> the word craving is for the body.

Now he goes on a little further over on Roman numeral xxviii and he talks about five different kinds of drinkers. Then he drives this idea of the phenomenon of craving home being an allergy one more time. Let's look at these five drinkers. He says the classification of alcoholics, this is on Roman numeral page xviii,

Big Book p. xxviii, par. 3   "The classification of alcoholics seems most difficult, and in much details outside the scope of this book. There are, of course, the psychopaths who are emotionally unstable. We are all familiar with this type. They are always "going on the wagon for keeps." They are over-remorseful and make many resolutions, but never a decision."

J & C   We call that Type 1.

Big Book p. xxviii, par. 4   "There is the type of man who is unwilling to admit that he cannot take a drink. He plans various ways of drinking. He changes his brand or his environment."

 J & C   That's Type 2.

Big Book p. xxviii, line 15 'There is the type who always believes that after being entirely free from alcohol for a period of time he can take a drink without danger.'

J & C   Type 3.

Big Book p. xxviii, line 18 'There is the manic-depressive type, who is, perhaps, the least understood by his friends, and about whom a whole chapter could be written.'

J & C   Now that's Type 4. Now I've always thought I was the next one, type five.

Big Book p. xxviii, par. 5   "Then there are types entirely normal in every respect except in the effect alcohol has upon them. They are often able, intelligent, friendly people."

J & C   God I like that, wasn't that good. Any more type fives in the room tonight? Yeah, a whole bunch of them. Now, he makes his point one more time.

Big Book p. xxviii, par. 6 "All these, and many others, have one symptom in common: <u>they cannot start drinking without developing the phenomenon of craving. This phenomenon, as we have suggested, may be the manifestation of an allergy which differentiates these people, and sets them apart as a distinct entity</u>. It has never been, by any treatment with which we are familiar, permanently eradicated. The only relief we have to suggest is entire abstinence."

J & C   Now I think what he said is this, that if all we alcoholics in this room tonight should take a drink, God forbid that happen, but if we did, we would not all react just exactly the same. In just a little bit one of us would be crying in our beer, oh, boo hoo hoo, the world's not treating me right. In just a little bit, one of 'em be up here on this stage, whooping and hollering and dancing, and cutting up and having a hell of a good time. In just a little bit there'd be two over in that corner getting in a fight just sure as anything. Look over here and there'll be a couple, one putting the make on the other, we tend to do that too when we drink. We would do many different things, but if we're a real alcoholic there's one thing that every one of us would do, we would start looking for a second drink. The phenomenon of craving has taken over now, the allergy has manifested itself, and now we can't stop. Got to have a third drink and a fourth and a fifth, and a sixth, and an eighth and a tenth and on and on until we're drunk, sick and in all kinds of trouble.

**Now it really doesn't make any difference whether we're born with it,
or whether we drank ourselves into it**.

I was born with it I'm sure. The first drink I took at age fourteen the allergy presented itself that night and I got drunk. Every time I drank I got drunk. I drank twenty-six years I don't ever remember taking one drink of anything that had alcohol in it, it always led to two, to three to six to eight to ten, etc. Some of you, I'm sure, drank with safety for several years, but somewhere you crossed the line and the same thing began to happen to you after several years of drinking that happened to me from the very beginning, but what difference does it make. The fact is that that's the way we are tonight. I know that's the way we are tonight too because if we were not that way tonight, we wouldn't be in this room tonight. If you and I could drink without getting drunk, where would we be? We'd be out there drinking without getting drunk but you see we can't do that. That's what we've got in common in the fellowship of Alcoholics Anonymous, is

We can't drink without getting drunk | wanting more, wanting another |

Now back in the 1930's this was the Doctor's Opinion. In the 1930's they knew very little about metabolism. Today they know lots about,

Metabolism.
1) Today they know that if you put anything in your system such as a piece of bread or a piece of beefsteak, that the mind and body recognizes what that is.
2) Certain organs in the body begin to produce some things called enzymes.
3) They attack that food and begin to break it down and separate it into useable and non-useable items.
4) What the body can use such as the proteins, the amino acids, the vitamins the body will retain,
5) What it can't use it will dissipate through the urinary and intestinal tract,

they call that metabolism. Today they have proven that The Doctor's Opinion is no longer just an opinion, it's actual truth. And we're going to look at a little picture here for just a minute, and I want to stress that this is not A.A. information. A.A. won't get involved into why we're allergic, because that might bring controversy. But this information presented to us a few years ago by members of the medical profession, is so interesting and has such depth and meaning for people like us, I think we would be remiss if we didn't look at it. So let's look at it for just a moment.

In the center of that picture there's nine people there that drink safely. They are at ease with alcohol. They take a drink or two, the mind and body senses it, the enzyme production starts, and the enzymes attack the alcohol,

(1st Stage)   breaks it down into acetaldehyde,
(2nd Stage)   then to diacetic acid,
(3rd Stage)   then to acetone.
(final Stage) In the final stages it becomes a simple carbohydrate made up of water, sugar, and carbon dioxide.
- The water would be dissipated through the urinary and intestinal tract.
- The sugar is calories, energy, empty calories, none of the amino acids, none of the vitamins, but a form of energy. The body will burn them; store the excess as fat to be used at a later date.
- The carbon dioxide will be dissipated through the lungs.

> this is how alcohol is processed through the body of the non-alcoholic

In the normal social drinker this takes place at the rate of approximately one ounce per hour. Now I know it'll vary with different people, but the average is one ounce per hour. And if they don't drink more than an once per hour forever they can't get drunk. Their body metabolizes it and burns it up and gets rid of it at that rate. Very seldom do you see a social drinker drinking more than an once per hour. If you're with one of them and they're drinking more than an ounce an hour, you better get out of the way. Cause they're going to puke on you after a while. They'll either go to sleep or they'll puke on you, one of the two, every time.

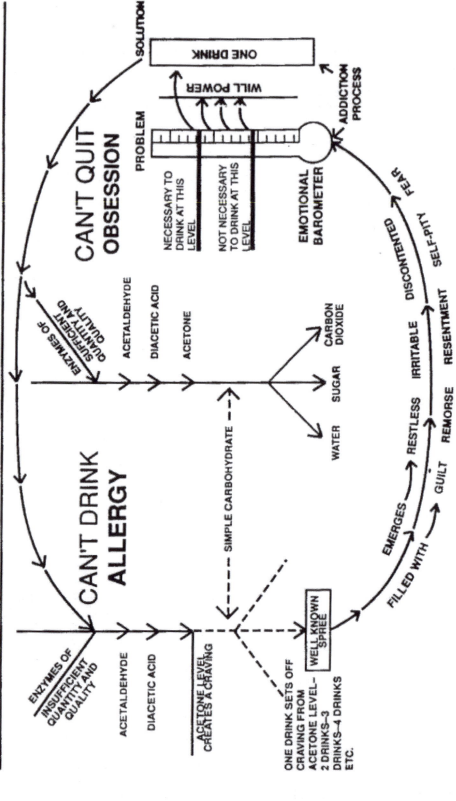

The left-hand side is the one who does not drink safely, or he's at disease with alcohol. And if you want to use the word disease that's all it means, something that separates you from the norm.

When alcoholics put it in our body, the same thing happens. The enzymes attack the alcohol,

(1st Stage)   break it down to acetaldehyde,
(2nd Stage)   then to diacetic acid,
(3rd Stage)   then to acetone.
(final stage) - - - - - - - - - - -

> this shows how alcohol is not completely processed through the alcoholic's body, and the resulting havoc it creates.

It seems as though, in our bodies, the enzymes necessary to complete the metabolism,
breaking it down from acetone to the simple carbohydrate,
are not there in the same qualities and/or quantities as they are in the body of the nonalcoholic.
Therefore it stays in our body for a longer period of time as acetone.
<u>It is proven today, that acetone ingested into the human system that remains there for an appreciable period of time,
will produce an actual physical craving for more of the same.</u>

In a non-alcoholic's body it (acetone) goes through that stage (conversion to simple carbohydrate) so rapidly
the craving never occurs.
In our body it stays there long enough, the craving develops
and that demands a second drink.

Now just think
1) you got most of the acetone from the first (drink),   2) now you put that in from the second (drink).

<u>The acetone level goes up, and if the acetone's what causes the craving, then the craving becomes harder with a second drink.</u>
Now you put in the third,

1) you got most of the first, (drink)   2) nearly all of the second (drink)   3) and now you put in the acetone from the third (drink),

and <u>the craving goes up, and that demands a fourth.</u>

1) you got most of the first, (drink)   2) nearly all of the second, (drink)   3) that from the third, (drink)   4) and now you put in the acetone from the fourth (drink)

<u>as the acetone level increases the craving becomes harder.</u>

At midnight we're laying out in the parking lot, they've run over us and broken our leg, and they come running up to us and say can we help you, and we say, my God yes, give me another drink. You see we're craving it harder at midnight after thirty drinks than we were at 6:00 in the evening after 2 drinks. That explains to me why I never got enough. Hell I drank twenty-six years; I never did get all the alcohol I wanted. I got a hell of a lot more than I needed, more than I could stand, but I never got all I wanted.

Because the more you drink, the higher the craving;
the higher the craving the more you want,
the more you want
... it's just endless.

Now if this never got any worse, we could probably learn to live with this situation, but we know not only do we have an illness,

<u>we have a progressive illness that always gets worse and never better.</u>

Today we know that as we drink, the more we drink, the longer we drink, the more tissue we destroy. <u>Alcohol is a destroyer of human tissue,</u> and the more tissue we destroy it seems as though that it acts upon two organs of the body first, which are the liver and the pancreas. Now today we know that the organs of the body that produce the enzymes necessary to metabolize alcohol are the liver and the pancreas. And as we drink and as we damage them

    1) the enzyme production becomes less and less,
    2) the craving becomes harder and harder
    3) with the resultant drinking becoming worse and worse.

> 1) alcoholics don't have the quality/quantity of enzymes required to completely metabolize alcohol to begin with
> 2) because the enzymes can't metabolize the alcohol we are left with acetone sitting around in our systems
> 3) when acetone remains there for an appreciable period of time, it produces an actual physical craving for more alcohol
> 4) the alcohol we crave is a destroyer of human tissue - the more we drink, the more we destroy human tissue
> 5. the first organs to be destroyed are the liver and the pancreas which are the two organs that produce the enzymes necessary to metabolize alcohol
>
> the more we drink, the more we crave,
> the more we crave, the more we drink,
> the more we drink the more we destroy
> the more we destroy, the more we drink
> the more we drink, the more we crave ...

We know also that the body begins to shut down on the production of everything as we get older, now I wish that we're not true, but believe me it is, I'm experiencing lots of that. If I should take a drink today after twenty some odd years of sobriety, I wouldn't start where I left off twenty some odd years ago,

1) The craving would be harder,
2) the drinking would be harder, and
3) the resultant trouble would be harder
due to the aging factor

> Alcoholism is a progressive disease. This is true in many areas of our lives whether we are drinking, or sober twenty some odd years. In relation to the physical aspect, for each year that we grow a little older in sobriety, our bodies grow older too. And as the body age's, the production of enzymes needed to break down alcohol, slows down as well. If an alcoholic picks up a drink after twenty years of sobriety, the acetone that will now remain longer in his system will trigger stronger cravings than he has ever felt before. The drinking will be much worse and it will be much harder to stop if he so desires. We can't pick up where we left off; it would be as if we never stopped.

So not only do we have a physical illness, we have a progressive physical illness due to two factors:
(a) damage to the body, and also   (b) due to the aging factor.

Now that I see that, I can accept the fact that I can no longer successfully drink alcohol. Until I could see this I knew there had to be a way I could drink without getting drunk, and I damn near killed me trying to find it. But now that I can see this I can accept the fact that I can no longer safely drink alcohol.

Now if that's all that was wrong with me, and if that's all that was wrong with you, we would pass the hat, get up and go home and never have to go to another A.A. meeting. But you see that's just half of my problem; the other half is right up here in my head. If I never took the first drink this allergy couldn't hurt me.

I have a friend who's allergic to, of all things, fish. Every time he eats fish, his throat swells up, he almost chokes to death. But that's not his problem; the fact that he's allergic to fish is beside the point because if he don't eat fish that can't happen to him. But he's got something up here in his head that isn't right when it comes to fish. The switch doesn't close, or a light bulb doesn't come on or something. He's three french fries short of a Happy Meal. From time to time his mind tells him that it's okay to eat fish. And he'll eat the fish, his throat swells up, he ends up in the hospital every time. And I bet it always starts like this, 'Well I haven't had any fish in 90 days, surely I could have one piece of fish'. He says, 'it's that Orange Roughy I've been eating, if I eat nothing but Halibut it'd be okay'. Or he might even say, 'it's them damn people I've been eating fish with, if I just change my crowd'. Whatever the reason, his mind gives him permission to do so. Now I'm the same way when it comes to alcohol.

Left on my own resources,
from time to time my mind tells me it's okay to drink alcohol,
and then I take the drink and the allergy takes over.
So the real problem centers in my mind rather than my body.

Let's look at the mind for just a few minutes, and then we'll be through for the night. As Charlie said, the Doctor said,

Big Book p. xxviii, line 29   *"It has never been, by any treatment with which we are familiar, permanently eradicated. The only relief we have to suggest is **entire abstinence**."*

J & C In other words, <u>if we have an allergy to alcohol, and we crave more when we drink, he suggests we don't drink</u>. And that's the end of that.

So now we're going to talk about the most dangerous part of the illness, and <u>the most dangerous part of the illness of alcoholism is when we're not drinking.</u> You know why it's the most dangerous part of the illness? <u>Because we're thinking</u>, about drinking. So let's move back now to Roman numeral page xxvi, and we're going to start talking about the mind, two-fold illness. We talked about the physical allergy in great detail, now were going to talk about <u>the obsession of the mind</u>. It's the bottom page roman numeral twenty-six

Big Book p.xxvi, par. 5   *"Men and women drink essentially because they like <u>the effect</u> produced by alcohol."*

J & C Now many alcoholics are highly offended when you say that. They say, no, that's not the reason I drank. They say the reason I drank cause I love the taste of alcohol. I wouldn't argue with them whether they do or not. I loved the taste of cold beer, I always have all my life as far back as I can remember. I also love the taste of cold mountain spring water. I never did sit down and drink a case of cold mountain spring water. You see that beer did something for me that that spring water didn't do.

All my life as a kid growing up I was on the outside of the crowd looking in. Always wanted to be a part of, and knew I could not be. Always knew that whatever I said, whatever I did, it would be the wrong thing, people would laugh and I would be embarrassed. You ladies I couldn't even get around you, if I got around you I would be absolutely completely tongue tied, you scared me to death. One night somebody gave me a drink of moonshine whisky and all those fears disappeared. And I was allowed to ask a girl to dance with me for the first time in my life. I was allowed to take her home from the dance for the first time in my life. We got in the back seat of a '36 Chevrolet, and I was allowed to do some things I'd been wanting to do for a long, long time. I loved what alcohol did to me, for me, not to me but for me.

And if it gave me a slightly tipsy <u>out of control</u> beginnings of a nauseous feeling, I wouldn't love that,   ← this is how the 'normal, social, temperate, moderate drinker' feels when he drinks alcohol, so he only has one or two

but you see it gives me that great, exciting, <u>in control</u> feeling and allows me to function in the manner I've never been able to function before.   ← this is how the alcoholic drinker feels when he drinks alcohol, (abnormal)

Big Book p.xxvi, par. 5   *"Men and women drink essentially because they like <u>the effect</u> produced by alcohol."*

J & C I think we can all pretty well identify with <u>that effect in the beginning</u>. I certainly had <u>that same effect</u> and drank it for the same reasons, but we know that <u>alcoholism is a progressive illness</u> too, it gets worse over time.

And after a while I began to do some of those things that Charlie talked about, and I began to drink more, and more, and more, and

the effects become progressively unpleasant

I began to wake up some mornings with a little guilt, shame and remorse as a result of the things that I was doing while drinking. And that brought on more drinking, and I had to drink to get rid of those feelings, so another effect by which I drank.
And as the years and time went by and the trouble that I had in my life went by in the end I drank for the sickest effect of all, which is total oblivion. And there's only one thing wrong with oblivion though isn't there, it's you wake up, then you got to start doing it again. So there are many, many effects by which we drank, and it progressively gets worse. He said,

Big Book p. xxvi, par. 5   *"The sensation is so elusive that, while they admit it is injurious, they cannot after a time differentiate the true from the false. To them their alcoholic life seems the only normal one"*

J & C And I couldn't recognize the truth from the false because my alcoholic life had become normal to me. Everywhere I went, alcohol was involved, every bar that I went to (if) they (didn't) drank like that, the way I did, in that bar, I didn't go to those bars. That's what I was doing down there in the Zebra Lounge. You know one time I remember I woke up one morning and had a clear thought and I looked over at my wife Phyllis and I said, 'Phyllis, do you realize that most people don't drink like we do'. And you know what she said? Now I don't talk this way, this what she said, 'bullshit', yeah, that's just what she said. 'Everybody we know drinks just like we do'. You know I thought well that's true.

> So my alcoholic life had become normal.
> The abnormal had become normal.

And I couldn't hardly tell the truth from the false in that light.

Now he begins to describe how people like us feel whenever we're sober, in forced periods of sobriety.

Big Book p. xxvi, par. 5   *"They are restless, irritable and discontented ...,"*

J & C   Put a few little words in there too, say they were full of guilt, shame and remorse. And remember you know when we first got sober and we were new, they said if we didn't drink we were going to feel better? Well you're going to feel better all right; you're going to feel resentment better, you're going feel anger better, you're going to feel a lot of things better. Running around, feeling lousy as hell, wanting to feel better, knowing only one way to feel better. We begin to think about what one or two drinks will do for us. We don't think about what 20 drinks will do, or thirty, we think about what one or two will do for us.

Big Book, top of p. xxvii   *"... unless they can again experience the sense of ease and comfort which comes at once by taking a few drinks--drinks which they see others taking with impunity."*

J & C   And impunity simply means those people who are drinking and seemingly they don't have any problems.

Big Book, top of p. xxvii   *"After they have succumbed to the desire again, as so many do,"*

J & C   After we've finally given in and taken a couple of drinks.

Big Book, top of p. xxvii   *"and the phenomenon of craving develops, they pass through the well-known stages of a spree, emerging remorseful, with a firm resolution not to drink again."*

J & C   And how many times have I done that, how many times have you done that? Come off of one of those big drunks and long extended period drunks and promise them and yourself and anybody that will listen, I'll never do it again, I'm through, I promise you I'm through. And those of you who've made those promises you know that we were sincere and we meant that. He said,

Big Book, top of p. xxvii   *"This is repeated over and over, and unless this person can experience an entire psychic change there is very little hope of his recovery."*

See he's quit talking about the body now, he's talking about the psychic change, the mind. Later on in our book the psychic change is going to be described as a spiritual experience, a spiritual awakening, a personality change. All four words mean the same thing. A psychic change (without it), there's very little hope for us for recovery, so the change is going to have to be here in the mind.

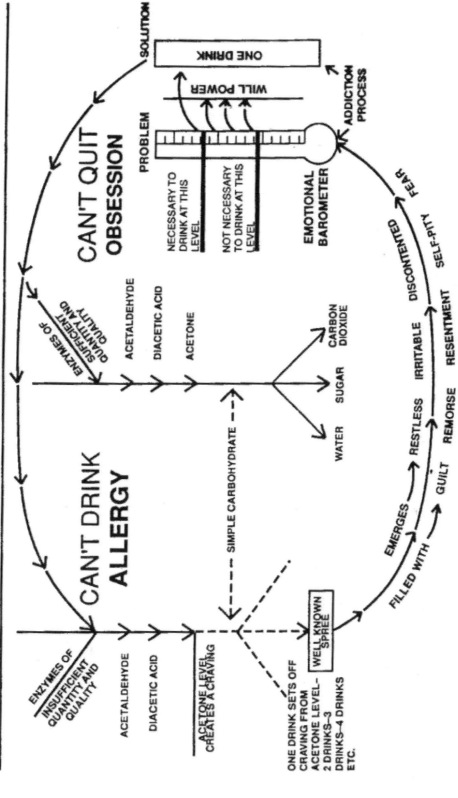

Let's look at this picture up here again for just a moment. Over here on this side (left) we can see that because of the allergy we can no longer safely drink alcohol. But as we said before, that's not going to bother us if we don't take the first drink. So apparently the problem is going to be over on this side.

<u>The real problem centers in the mind telling us we can drink,
rather than in the body that ensures that we can't drink.</u>

The Doctor told us then, and they tell us today there's nothing that can be done for that. So the only possible means of recovery will be to find a way to live where our minds don't tell us it's okay to drink. And we're dealing here with our emotions. We're dealing here with the way we think. We're dealing here with the way that we feel whenever we're sober. We are very, very complex human beings. Not only are we complex physically, but we also are complex mentally too. And all people experience emotions. All people experience from time to time anger, resentment, fear, worry, depression, excitement, elation, guilt, remorse. These are all emotions that all human beings have.

Now somewhere back in our lifetime as we begin to experience those emotions as we grow up, we start seeking a solution to them. And like me when I was a kid growing up I was just an emotional basket case, couldn't hardly function in normal society. Always scared to death, always worried, always angry, always doing things that I shouldn't do and feeling the guilt and the remorse associated with that. Now I used to think that only we alcoholics did that. But I found out today that that's normal as kids grow up, everybody experiences these kinds of feelings. And they start looking for an answer and many people find it in many different ways. Some people find that when they don't feel good emotionally that they can go out here and start working and the excess work seems to make them feel better. Some people find that when they're emotionally fouled up they can eat certain foods and that seems to make them feel better. Some people are into sexuality, that makes them feel better, and some people find that there's establishments like this building (Casino) that if you're emotionally disturbed you can do a little gambling and that makes you feel better. Now it doesn't make any difference what you find that makes you feel better. When you find the solution to that emotional problem your mind has a memory bank, it immediately records the solution. And the reason it does that is the next time you have that emotion problem you don't have to go looking for a solution, your mind feeds it back to you. Well a little gambling made me feel better, or that food make me feel better or that work made me feel better or whatever. Now that's called mental addiction and everybody has that. You know we become mentally addicted to certain types of automobiles, we become mentally addicted to our hairdressers, we become mentally addicted to certain dishwater products that we use, dish soap. You know we got a problem, we find the answer, the mind records it, feeds it back to us the next time we have the problem.

As a kid growing up I had that emotional problem and one night somebody gave me that drink of moonshine whisky and immediately those problems disappeared, and that great exciting in-control feeling came over me and I was allowed to ask that girl to dance, take her home and get in the back seat of that '36 Chevrolet. It answered my problem that night. My mind immediately recorded what it did for me. The next time I got into a solution (situation) where I didn't feel right, things were not right, my mind said if you could find a drink you'd feel better. And I found a drink of whiskey and by God the magic happened a second time. In other words, <u>alcohol became the solution to my emotional problems</u>. Now if I had been nonalcoholic and that worked for me, that would have been great, but I also had that physical allergy over there on that (left) side. And when I had the problem and I used the solution, it sure enough made me feel better BUT also <u>it triggered the allergy and I would drink more than I intended to drink and I would end up drunk</u>. And I would repeat that cycle over and over and over and over and over again,

the mind causing me to drink,
the allergy causing me to get drunk.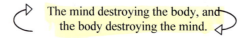

The <u>emotions</u> after coming off the drunk to feed the mind caused me to drink and
the drink then would trigger the allergy

and as time went by it got worse and worse and worse because this is a progressive illness, the drinking would become harder and harder, the trouble would become more and more. The restlessness, irritability, guilt, remorse became more and more. The emotions became worse and worse (the emotional barometer), to trigger the idea of taking the first drink**.**

<mark>The mind destroying the body, and
the body destroying the mind.</mark>

Now somewhere down the line I said to myself one day, 'Charlie, you're gonna have to do something about your drinking'.

Now I didn't say you got to quit drinking, I said you're going to have to do something about your drinking.

So the first thing we alcoholics do, to do something about our drinking is,

1) <u>We decide we're going to control our drinking while drinking</u>.

Tonight we're just going to have two beers, we're just going to have two drinks. Go to the Liquor Store and buy a half a pint cause nobody can get drunk on half a pint. And I spent 3 or 4 or 5, 6 years trying to control my drinking while drinking. Anybody in here ever try to control your drinking while drinking? Well now I can see why

that (controlled drinking) would not work because of the allergy. ⟶

> the more you drink, the higher the craving;
> the higher the craving the more you want,
> the more you want, the more you drink ...

And after 4 or 5, 6 years of trying to control my drinking while drinking I said to myself one day, 'Charlie, I don't believe you can drink anymore'. Took me a long time to realize it. And I said I don't believe you can drink anymore. So what do we alcoholics do when we finally decide we can't drink anymore?

2) <u>We trot out the most useful tool we have and we put it right there, and it's called WILLPOWER.</u>

And we say sick him will, we're through with that drinking, we'll never take another drink as long as we live. Now believe me, you people that are non-alcoholic, when we say we're going to quit drinking, that is exactly what we intend to do. You see we are strong-willed people. We can use our willpower to handle all other problems and we assume that we can use willpower here and we really intend to quit drinking. Now as the days went by, I haven't done anything about my emotions by the way,

> I'll just quit drinking,
> and as the days go by these emotions begin to build up.
> The fear, the guilt, the remorse, the shame, the worry,
> the depression, becomes worse and worse.

> the resulting effect when sobriety is based on willpower

It's not the big things in life that kill us, it's the things that all people have to go through on a daily basis in life. It's getting up every damn morning and going to work, it's a bitching wife, it's a griping husband, it's screaming kids, it's burnt bacon, it's broken shoestrings, it's flat tires. All the things that everybody has to go through and these emotions start building up (emotional barometer). Now after a while the mind says, 'a drink would make you feel better'. But remember I put willpower in here, and willpower said, 'no siree we're not going to drink, we quit', and that day we don't drink. The next day the emotions are still here and they're building up a little higher and a little higher and a little higher and it said, 'God a drink would make me feel good, and the mind said, 'no siree we've quit drinking, we ain't never going to drink again'. The next day the emotions are still here and they're building up a little higher and a little higher, and your mind begins to say, 'well hell you've been sober 90 days, you've proven you're not an alcoholic, one drink wouldn't hurt anybody'. Your mind says, 'no, we're not going to do that, we've quit drinking, hell we've sworn off, we'll never take another drink'. The next day the emotions are still here and there building up higher and higher and the mind says, 'by golly anybody's been sober 92 days owes them self a drink'. And we begin to think about that great exciting in-control feeling that comes with one or two drinks. We begin to think about the sense of ease and comfort that Dr. Silkworth talks about here.
> And as we begin to think about what alcohol is going to do for us,
> it begins to push out the idea of what it does to us.

And we begin to forget the jailhouse, we forget the last car wreck, we forget the divorce courts and the hospitalization and the mind begins to key in on one thing and one thing only, what it's going to do for us. Then when the desire to drink comes, willpower is no longer there. Cause you see the only time willpower is there is when the mind sees something wrong with what it wants to do, and just before we drink, we don't see anything wrong with drinking.

> willpower becomes non-existent, we take the drink we trigger the allergy
> we go through the well know stages of a spree
> we emerge remorseful with a firm resolution not to do this again.
>
> And we repeat that cycle over and over and over.

The body destroying the body over here (left hand side),
the mind over here causing us to drink more and more (right hand side).

if you can't safely drink because of the body
and if you can't quit because of the mind,
then you've become absolutely powerless over alcohol.

And that's our problem. Now if you're going to solve a problem you got to be able to attack it somewhere. I can't attack it over here (physical), can't do nothing about that, maybe I can attack it over here (mental).

If I could find a way to live where I could be sober and not be restless, irritable and discontented.
If I could find a way to live where I could be sober and not be filled with shame, fear, guilt, and remorse, just maybe I could find a way to live where I could have peace of mind, serenity and happiness.
Maybe I could find a way to live where I could be sober and have that great sense of ease and comfort that comes at once by taking a couple of drinks.
Maybe I could find a way to live where I don't need to take a drink in order to make me feel better, and that's called recovery.

> the program of recovery that's found in the Big Book of Alcoholics Anonymous

As we use our program, as we go through the steps,

these kinds of feelings down here begin to disappear, | guilt, remorse, resentment, self-pity, fear |

and they begin to be replaced with peace of mind, serenity, and happiness.

And under those conditions our emotions do not build up to the level that suggest we take a drink to feel better, because we already feel better. That's what the 12 steps of Alcoholics Anonymous do for us. Fellowship alone will not bring that about, the program will.

Let's read the very next statement in the Big Book,

Big Book p. xxvii, par. 2 *"On the other hand--and strange as this may seem to those who do not understand--once a psychic change has occurred, the very same person who seemed doomed, who had so many problems he despaired of ever solving them, suddenly finds himself easily able to control his desire for alcohol, <u>the only effort necessary being that required to follow a few simple rules.</u>"*

J & C   And as Charlie said, <u>those few simple rules are the twelve steps of Alcoholics Anonymous</u>. And our book says that in the Twelve and Twelve, that if you practice as a way of life will expel the obsession to drink and make the person happily and usefully whole. And that is called recovery, and that's is exactly what the twelve Steps of Alcoholics Anonymous is all about.

> Twelve Steps and Twelve Traditions
> Foreword p. 15, par. 3
>
> A.A.'s Twelve Steps are a group of principles, spiritual in their nature, which, if practiced as a way of life, can expel the obsession to drink and enable the sufferer to become happily and usefully whole.

J & C   Last night we spent quite a bit of time talking about the problem, talking about

<u>the physical allergy that ensures we can't safely drink,</u>

talking about

<u>the obsession of the mind that ensures that we can't keep from drinking</u>

and the ultimate conclusion to that was

<u>if you can't safely drink without getting drunk,
and if you can't keep from drinking,
then you've become absolutely powerless over alcohol</u>

and most certainly our lives had become unmanageable if not at that time then we just keep on drinking and after a while they will be for sure. So this morning we're going to look at an example of a guy that had that problem. A good textbook never tells you anything anyhow but what it don't back it up with more information. And we're going to look at Bill's Story this morning and Bill's Story is a classic example of an alcoholic who had the allergy and who had the obsession of the mind. Now we got to remember back in the 1930's Bill learned very early on the value of sharing your story with another alcoholic, when he went to see Dr. Bob, and immediately Dr. Bob could see his problem also. They went to see Bill Dobson and they shared their stories with Bill Dobson. Bill Dobson could see his problem through their stories, and they learned very early on that it was necessary for one alcoholic to identify with another in order to be able to get their interest and get their attention. And when the Big Book was first published they knew they wouldn't be able to sit down with the first person out here in California and share their story one on one. So the Big Book had to be complete enough to do that. So they said we'll put Bill's Story in here at the very beginning, and another alcoholic in reading Bill's Story will be able to identify with Bill. And if we can identify with Bill and see his alcoholism, see him make a recovery from that condition, we can begin to believe and we can begin to hope that we're enough like Bill Wilson and if he could recover from that condition then just maybe we could too. Now a lot of you have said we have trouble identifying with Bill Wilson cause after all he was a night school lawyer and we were not, after all he was a New York City stock speculator and we were not, and a lot of the women say we can't identify with him because he's a man, and many people say well he was an older fellow and we couldn't identify there either. **But if we look for the way Bill thinks, and the way Bill acts and the way Bill drinks, if we're a real alcoholic there's not an alcoholic in this room that can't identify with Bill Wilson.**

So as we go through Bill's Story this morning we'll look for

1. identification,
2. the progression of alcoholism
3 him drinking finally for the sickest reason of all, complete oblivion,

then well look and see how Bill recovered from alcoholism and if we've identified with him then we begin to believe that if he could do it just maybe we could it too…identification, the beginning of believe, the beginning of hope.

I too didn't think I could identify with Bill Wilson that I've seen pictures of and he was an old man I thought. Turned out **he was 43 years old when this book was written**, so a relatively young man. But as I began to study and read Bill's Story I began to see that he was a very optimist person, hardworking, had lots and lots of willpower. He was a self made man who became very successful in his own right. And through Bill's story we're going to see what he was like, then we're going to see how he learned that he was sick, and then we're going to see how he affected a recovery. So the total story of Alcoholics Anonymous is contained in Bill Wilson's story. So let's go to page one, Bill's Story. He said

Big Book p. 1, par. 1   *"War fever ran high in the New England town to which we new, young officers from Plattsburg were assigned, and we were flattered when the first citizens took us to their homes, making us feel heroic. Here was love, applause, war; moments sublime with intervals hilarious"*

J & C   Anybody ever have any moment's sublime with intervals hilarious? I have. I love the way Bill writes.

Big Book p. 1, par. 1, line 6   *"I was part of life at last, and in the midst of the excitement I discovered liquor. I forgot the strong warnings and the prejudices of my people concerning drink. In time we sailed for "Over There." I was very lonely and again turned to alcohol. "*

We landed in England. I visited Winchester Cathedral. Much moved, I wandered outside. My attention was caught by a doggerel on an old tombstone:

> "Here lies a Hampshire Grenadier
> Who caught his death
> Drinking cold small beer.
> A good soldier is ne'er forgot
> Whether he dieth by musket
> Or by pot."

J & C   Now when he says that about pot, he's not referring to this wacky weed. He's talking about a pot of beer, that's the way they used to drink it over in England at that time. He said

Big Book p. 1, par. 3   *"Ominous warning which I failed to heed."*

"Twenty-two, and a veteran of foreign wars, I went home at last. I fancied myself a leader, for had not the men of my battery given me a special token of appreciation? My talent for leadership, I imagined, could place me at the head of vast enterprises which I would manage with the utmost assurance. I took a night law course, and obtained employment as investigator for a surety company. The drive for success was on. I'd prove to the world I was important."

J & C   I already identify with Bill Wilson. **That seems to be one of the main characteristics behind every alcoholic I've ever known. The great drive for success** was on; **I'll prove to the world that I'm important also**. It seems to be the driving force behind each one of us.

Big Book p.2, par 1, line 4   *"My work took me about Wall Street and little by little I became interested in the market. Many people lost money but some became very rich. Why not I? I studied economics and business as well as law. Potential alcoholic that I was, I nearly failed my law course. At one of the finals I was too drunk to think or write. Though my drinking was not yet continuous, it disturbed my wife.*

J & C   I can identify with Bill.

Big Book p.2, par. 1, line 11   *"We had long talks when I would still her forebodings by telling her that men of genius conceived their best projects when drunk;*

J & C   I have no trouble identifying with Bill Wilson.

Big Book p.2, par. 1, line 13   *"that the most majestic constructions philosophic thought were so derived."*

J & C   I can identify with Bill. Charlie said last night we make our living selling fast talk to slow thinking people, and Bill's trying to do some of that here, but we all know that Lois didn't buy that. He said

Big Book p.2, par. 2   *"By the time I had completed the course, I knew the law was not for me. The inviting maelstrom of Wall Street had me in its grip. Business and financial leaders were my heroes. Out of this ally of drink and speculation, I commenced to forge the weapon that one day would turn in its flight like a boomerang and all but cut me to ribbons. Living modestly, my wife and I saved $1,000. It went into certain securities, then cheap and rather unpopular. I rightly imagined that they would some day have a great rise. I failed to persuade my broker friends to send me out looking over factories and managements, but my wife and I decided to go anyway. I had developed a theory that most people lost money in stocks through ignorance of markets. I discovered many more reasons later on."*

J & C   Now Bill is referring to a time back in the 1920's when the stock market was on a roll. Just about everybody that dealt with stocks was making money. All you had to do was buy them and hold unto them, let them go up in price, sell them, take your profits, buy some more. Everything was done on about a 10% margin; everything was pure speculation. Bill really became one of the first investment counselors on Wall Street. He began to say look, sooner or later this bubble is going to burst. Sooner or later we're going to have to start making our decisions based on fact rather than speculation. He went to the people who had the money and he said I don't have the money to do this but if you guys would back me financially, I'll leave New York City and I'll start visiting these companies. And I'll look at the plants and I'll talk to the employees and I'll examine the books wherever I can and I'll write up reports and send them back in here and we'll start making our decisions whether to buy or not based on fact. And they said, no, Bill, we don't need that kind of information. We're making about all the money we want to make anyhow. And you know how we alcoholics are, if we get a good idea, stubborn as hell, we're going to carry it out one way or another. He said the hell with them, I don't need them anyhow, I'll just go do this on my own. He said,

Big Book p.2, par.3   "We gave up our positions and off we roared on a motorcycle, the sidecar stuffed with tent, blankets, a change of clothes, and three huge volumes of a financial reference service. Our friends thought a lunacy commission should be appointed. Perhaps they were right. I had had some success at speculation, so we had a little money, but we once worked on a farm for a month to avoid drawing on our small capital. That was the last honest manual labor on my part for many a day. We covered the whole eastern United States in a year. At the end of it, my reports to Wall Street procured me a position there and the use of a large expense account. The exercise of an option brought in more money, leaving us with a profit of several thousand dollars for that year."

J & C   Bill and Lois, traveling on the motorcycle, living in the tent, went up and down the eastern seaboard of the United States and he wrote up reports on approximately 100 of the largest companies in the eastern states sending them to New York City. The guys that had the money saw them and say oh yeah man this is great information and immediately they put Bill on the payroll, gave him a large expense account, the exercise in option made a good profit, for the first time in his life he's got something. He came from a little town called East Dorset, Vermont, he had never had anything before in his life. Here's how he feels

Big Book p.3, par.2   "For the next few years fortune threw money and applause my way. I had arrived."

J & C   God how many of us have done the same kind of things Bill did.

Big Book p.3, par. 2, line 2   "My judgment and ideas were followed by many to the tune of paper millions. The great boom of the late twenties was seething and swelling. Drink was taking an important and exhilarating part in my life. There was loud talk in the jazz places uptown. Everyone spent in thousands and chattered in millions. Scoffers could scoff and be damned. I made a host of fair-weather friends."

J & C   And here's Bill now back in New York City on top of the heap. He's making money for himself and a lot of other people. He's drinking also but drinking is not a problem right now it's a very exciting thing and Bill is really, really, really becoming a success at what he wanted to be. We also know though that **if he's alcoholic his drinking is going to get worse because it is a progressive thing**. Let's see where he goes now from the top of the heap. He said,

Big Book p.3, par. 3   "My drinking assumed more serious proportions, continuing all day and almost every night. The remonstrances of my friends terminated in a row and I became a lone wolf."

J & C   How many of us have done the same thing. People began to say Bill, you're drinking too much. Bill, you're costing us money. Bill, why don't you cut back? Bill, why don't you quit? **And once again rather than even consider that Bill said, to hell with them I don't need them. He begins to operate on his own now.** I have no problem identifying with Bill Wilson.

Big Book p.3, par. 3, line 4   "There were many unhappy scenes in our sumptuous apartment. There had been no real infidelity, for loyalty to my wife, helped at times by extreme drunkenness, kept me out of those scrapes."

J & C   Now I've always believed about everything Bill wrote, but I'm not sure about that. You see we have a book in A.A. called, As Bill Sees It, and in AlAnon they have a book called, As Lois Remembers. A whole lot different. They're not exactly the same either. Let's go over to page 4, 1st paragraph. Now here's old' Bill he's making lots of money, he's doing well, he's got lots of willpower, lots of hope for the future, hardworking, optimistic, a self made man. On page 4 it says,

Big Book p.4, par. 1   "Abruptly in October 1929 hell broke loose on the New York stock exchange. After one of those days of inferno, I wobbled from a hotel bar to a brokerage office. It was eight o'clock five hours after the market closed. The ticker still clattered. I was staring at an inch of the tape which bore the inscription XYZ-32. It had been 52 that morning. I was finished and so were many friends. The papers reported men jumping to death from the towers of High Finance. That disgusted me. I would not jump. I went back to the bar."

J & C   Bill had a solution to that didn't he.

Big Book p.4, par. , line 11   My friends had dropped several million since ten o'clock so what? Tomorrow was another day. As I drank, the old fierce determination to win came back."

J & C   How many of us have done the same thing. Just come out of the jailhouse, the divorce court, the hospital, or wherever, low, sad, depressed? Stop off in the bar have a couple of drinks and as the alcohol courses through our veins we say, we'll show them. By God they're not going to treat us that way. And we're off and we're running again, **that old fierce determination to be somebody to show them.**

Big Book p.4, par. 2   "Next morning I telephoned a friend in Montreal. He had plenty of money left and thought I had better go to Canada."

J & C   Now Bill was a drunk, he wasn't stupid; he knew where the money was so he went to Canada.

Big Book p.4, par. 2, line 3   "By the following spring we were living in our accustomed style. I felt like Napoleon returning from Elba. No St. Helena for me! But drinking caught up with me again and my generous friend had to let me go. This time we stayed broke."

J & C   Now **we see our drinking progressing** to the point where we can no longer even hold a job.

Big Book p.4, par.3   "We went to live with my wife's parents. I found a job; then lost it as the result of a brawl with a taxi driver. Mercifully, no one could guess that I was to have no real employment for five years, or hardly draw a sober breath. My wife began to work in a department store, coming home exhausted to find me drunk. I became an unwelcome hanger-on at brokerage places."

J & C   Where he used to be the fair-haired boy, where he used to make lots of money for lots of people, he goes in there now and they say, Bill, we'd rather you didn't come in here today. Your about half drunk and you don't look good and your smelling bad, you're embarrassing us in front of our customers, please move right on down the street. Certainly, **certainly we can see the progression of alcoholism. We've gone from excitement to now then we've gone to the point where it controls us completely**, no longer hold a job, **nobody wants us around anymore**. It starts to get worse,

Big Book p.5, par.1   "Liquor ceased to be a luxury; it became a necessity."

J & C   Now we're drinking for an entirely different reason. **We're drinking now because we absolutely have to drink in order to live. No fun left anymore, no excitement, drinking in order to be able to live."**

Big Book p.5, par. 1,line 2   "Bathtub" gin, two bottles a day, and often three, got to be routine. Sometimes a small deal would net a few hundred dollars, and I would pay my bills at the bars and delicatessens. This went on endlessly, and I began to waken very early in the morning shaking violently. A tumbler full of gin followed by half a dozen bottles of beer would be required if I were to eat any breakfast. Nevertheless, I still thought I could control the situation, and there were periods of sobriety which renewed my wife's hope."

J & C   Remember last night Dr. Silkworth said **we really cannot differentiate the true from the false. To us what we're doing is normal.** We see that Bill's life is going to hell in a hand basket already. Bill can't see that. He thinks that he **can still control the situation.** Let's see were he goes on control. Things were real bad in Bill's life but it says,

Big Book p.5, par. 2-3   "Gradually things got worse. The house was taken over by the mortgage holder, my mother-in-law died, my wife and father-in-law became ill. Then I got a promising business opportunity. Stocks were at the low point of 1932, and I had somehow formed a group to buy. I was to share generously in the profits. Then I went on a prodigious bender, and that chance vanished."

J & C   This is a story within itself. The people that had the money knew how good Bill was at putting these deals together. And they came to Bill and said Bill we've got a proposition for you. We've got an opportunity to not only to make money for us, but to make money for you. And if you can stay sober we'd like for you to handle this thing. And Bill said, don't you worry about that drinking, he said, I'm through with that drinking, you'll not have to worry about that. And he worked for a matter of months putting this deal together and a few days before it was to be successfully completely, one night they're all sitting around in the hotel room talking about this and somebody passes around a bottle of Applejack. This was during the days of prohibition. It came to Bill, and he said, no thank you, I'm not drinking anymore. After a while it came back to him, and the guy next to him said, Bill, you don't understand what this is. He said, this is the finest Applejack in the world, it is called Jersey Lightening, you better have a drink. Bill's mind said, hmm I've never tasted any Jersey Lightening. No more thought than that he reached out, grabbed the bottle, took a drink, triggered the allergy, couldn't sober up and blew the whole deal. Now the importance in it lies with the next statement. He said,

Big Book p.5, par. 4   "*I woke up. This had to be stopped. I saw I could not take so much as one drink. I was through forever. Before then, I had written lots of sweet promises, but my wife happily observed that this time I meant business. And so I did.*"

J & C   For the first time Bill could differentiate the truth from the false. For the first time he could truly see what alcohol was doing to him. **And he did just like all the rest of us, he trotted out his willpower and he said, sick him will.** We're through with that drinking, we'll never drink as long as we live. Now they try to tell us we are weak willed people, don't you believe that, we are strong willed people. Weak willed people do not become alcoholics; first time they vomit they quit drinking. An alcoholic knows there's got to be some way to drink without puking, we damn near kill ourselves you know, we got lots of willpower. You see Bill doesn't know what we learned last night. **Anytime there's a battle going on between the willpower and the obsession of the mind, the obsession of the mind is stronger than willpower and it always wins**, that's how strong it is. Let's see what happened to him on willpower. He said,

Big Book p.5, par. 5   "*Shortly afterward I came home drunk. There had been no fight. Where had been my high resolve? I simply didn't know. It hadn't even come to mind. Someone had pushed a drink my way, and I had taken it. Was I crazy?*"

J & C   You see if his willpower's not working then he begins to question his sanity. Am I crazy is that it?

Big Book p.5, par. 5, line 5   "*I began to wonder, for such an appalling lack of perspective seemed near being just that. Renewing my resolve, I tried again. Some time passed, and confidence began to be replaced by cocksureness. I could laugh at the gin mills. Now I had what it takes! One day I walked into a cafe to telephone. In no time I was beating on the bar asking myself how it happened. As the whisky rose to my head I told myself I would manage better next time, but I might as well get good and drunk then. And I did.*"

J & C   Anybody in here identify with Bill Wilson? He said

Big Book p.6, par. 1   "*The remorse, horror and hopelessness of the next morning are unforgettable*"

J & C   Can you guys hear him from the back? Can you hear back there okay? Okay. My voice is a little low here this morning. Okay where am I. Laughlin, Nevada. I got a wonderful memory it's just short.

Big Book p.6, par. 1   "*The remorse, horror and hopelessness of the next morning are unforgettable. The courage to do battle was not there. My brain raced uncontrollably and there was a terrible sense of impending calamity. I hardly dared cross the street, lest I collapse and be run down by an early morning truck, for it was scarcely daylight. An all night place supplied me with a dozen glasses of ale. My writhing nerves were stilled at last. A morning paper told me the market had gone to hell again. Well, so had I. The market would recover, but I wouldn't. That was a hard thought. Should I kill myself? No not now. Then a mental fog settled down. Gin would fix that. So two bottles, and oblivion.*"

J & C   See Bill questioned, **he used his willpower and that didn't work, he begin to question his sanity and that didn't work, and then he began to contemplate suicide,** and then he was drinking for the sickest effect of all total oblivion. And that's where we find Bill at this time. He said,

Big Book p.6, par. 2   "*The mind and body are marvelous mechanisms, for mine endured this agony two more years. Sometimes I stole from my wife's slender purse when the morning terror and madness were on me. Again I swayed dizzily before an open window, or the medicine cabinet where there was poison, cursing myself for a weakling. There were flights from city to country and back, as my wife and I sought escape. Then came the night when the physical and mental torture was so hellish I feared I would burst through my window, sash and all. Somehow I managed to drag my mattress to a lower floor, lest I suddenly leap. A doctor came with a heavy sedative. Next day found me drinking both gin and sedative. This combination soon landed me on the rocks. People feared for my sanity. So did I. I could eat little or nothing when drinking, and I was forty pounds under weight."*

J & C   Here we find Bill drinking for oblivion, not eating very often. I can identify with Bill. He's dying of malnutrition, and I can identify with Bill because when I was drinking those last years of my drinking occasionally I'd eat a bologna sandwich cause I knew you were supposed to eat something rather than just drink and that's what Bill was doing at this time, dying of malnutrition.

Big Book p. 7, par. 1   "*My brother-in-law is a physician, and through his kindness and that of my mother I was placed in a nationally-known hospital for the mental and physical rehabilitation of alcoholics."*

J & C   This is the Towns Hospital in New York City and this is the summer of 1933.

Big Book p. 7, par. 1, line 4   "*Under the so-called belladonna treatment my brain cleared."*

J & C   Belladonna was a drug that they used to fool the body into thinking it had alcohol in it, it was used for withdrawal purposes. It's what they use Valium for today.

Big Book p. 7, par. 1, line 5   "*Hydrotherapy and mild exercise helped much.*"

J & C   Hydrotherapy is water treatment; we saw some of that in a treatment center in Australia back in the 1980's. They would put the alcoholic on a gurney, roll him into the shower room and they had showerheads all the way around the shower room alternating hot and cold water. Be in there for about thirty minutes. Doesn't cure alcoholism, but it makes a clean drunk out of you I'll guarantee you that. Those guys would come out of there and their skin all wrinkled up and shriveled up. He said,

Big Book p. 7, par. 1, line 6   "*Best of all, I met a kind doctor"*

J & C   Now this is Dr. Silkworth.

Big Book p. 7, par. 1, line 7   "*who explained that though certainly selfish and foolish, I had been seriously ill, bodily and mentally."*

J & C   Silky sat down with him and explained his ideas about the **physical allergy and the obsession of the mind**. And here's the effect it had on Bill. He said,

Big Book p. 7, par. 2   "*It relieved me somewhat to learn that in alcoholics the will is amazingly weakened when it comes to combating liquor, though if often remains strong in other respects. My incredible behavior in the face of a desperate desire to stop was explained. Understanding myself now, I fared forth in high hope. For three or four months the goose hung high. I went to town regularly and even made a little money. Surely this was the answer self- knowledge."*

J & C   For the first time Bill understood his problem.

He knew it was not will power.
He knew it wasn't moral character and sin.

He knew it was a physical allergy coupled with the obsession of the mind, and
that's what made him absolutely powerless.

And he said, now that I know what's wrong with me I'll not have to drink any longer. Let's see where he goes from here.

The information we learned last night about the Doctor's Opinion and the illness of alcoholism is very, very important information, but you know it's just information, **it will not solve alcoholism. Just because we know what the problem is**, as Bill found out.

Big Book p. 7, par 3   "But it was not, for the frightful day came when I drank once more. The curve of my declining moral and bodily health fell off like a ski-jump. After a time I returned to the hospital."

J & C   Now this is the summer of 1934. A year later we go back into the Towns for the second time.

Big Book p. 7, par 3, line 4   "This was the finish, the curtain, it seemed to me. My weary and despairing wife was informed that it would all end with heart failure during delirium tremens, or I would develop a wet brain, perhaps within a year. We would soon have to give me over to the undertaker of the asylum."

J & C   Bill was laying in the hospital room there all sick, he overheard Lois and Dr. Silkworth talking. She said Dr. Silkworth is there any hope for him? And he said, no I don't believe so Lois, we're going to have to give him over to the undertaker or the asylum, cause there's no solution for Bill. And he said,

Big Book p. 7, par. 4   "They did not need to tell me. I knew, and almost welcomed the idea. It was a devastating blow to my pride. I, who had thought so well of myself and my abilities, of my capacity to surmount obstacles, was cornered at last. Now I was to plunge into the dark, joining that endless procession of sots who had gone on before. I thought of my poor wife. There had been much happiness after all. What would I not give to make amends. But that was over now. "

J & C   Bill was a very hardworking, optimistic individual and now we see Bill, he is hopeless, he is without hope. But we all know you can't live long without hope, you've got to have hope, but Bill is hopeless at the moment. Now let's look at this next statement very carefully. He said,

Big Book p. 8, par. 1   "No words can tell of the loneliness and despair I found in that bitter morass of self-pity. Quicksand stretched around me in all directions. I had met my match. I had been overwhelmed. Alcohol was my master."

J & C   I've never seen a better description of Step 1. No Step 1 written in those days, but surely this is where Bill took it. He admitted completed defeat, alcohol had whipped him in a fair fight. He was completely powerless over alcohol. Now if that should happen to you and I today, chances are we would say well that being the case, I guess I'd better go to AA. But Bill didn't have any AA to go to. He's in the best facility he knows that. So even though he's admitted his powerlessness, even though he's taken what we know as Step 1, the only thing he can do is leave that hospital, try to stay sober on his own.

Big Book p. 8, par. 2   " Trembling, I stepped from the hospital a broken man. Fear sobered me for a bit. Then came the insidious insanity of that first drink, and on Armistice Day 1934, I was off again. Everyone became resigned to the certainty that I would have to be shut up somewhere, or would stumble along to a miserable end. How dark it is before the dawn! In reality that was the beginning of my last debauch. I was soon to be catapulted into what I like to call the fourth dimension of existence. I was to know happiness, peace, and usefulness, in a way of life that is incredibly more wonderful as time passes. "

Near the end of that bleak November, I sat drinking in my kitchen. "

J & C   And I imagine it was a pretty bleak November. He started drinking on November the 11th, triggered the allergy, couldn't stop, been drunk now for about 3 weeks.

Big Book p. 8, par. 3, line 2   " With a certain satisfaction I reflected there was enough gin concealed about the house to carry me through that night and the next day. My wife was at work. I wondered whether I dared hide a full bottle of gin near the head of our bed. I would need it before daylight.

My musing was interrupted by the telephone. The cheery voice of an old school friend asked if he might come over. "

J & C   Now this was Ebby Thatcher. Bill and Ebby had gone to school together when they were younger, did lots of drinking together. And Bill knew about Ebby and he knew how Ebby drank. And he said he *was sober*. And if you'll notice that's in squiggly writing; squiggly writing in the Big Book is very important. This really amazed Bill, Ebby's sober. He said,

Big Book p. 9, line 1   "It was years since I could remember his coming to New York in that condition. I was amazed. Rumor had it that he had been committed for alcoholic insanity. "

J & C   The last Bill had heard about Ebby was that Ebby was going to be committed to the State Insane Asylum in the State of Vermont for alcoholic insanity. That's what they used to do with people like us before we had the treatment centers. They'd haul us in front of a judge, the judge would commit us to the state insane asylum for alcoholic insanity, for an undetermined period of time. Till you got well; you would stay there until you got well. And that's the last he'd heard about Ebby. He said,

Big Book p. 9, line 4   "*I wondered how he had escaped.*

J & C   He was amazed that Ebby was out of this treatment center, err insane asylum, excuse me... Same thing, same thing, yeah. They've renamed everything in all these things. They talk about dysfunctional families today; well mine was just crazy as hell. But Ebby come from a very prominent family in Albany, New York. In fact his father was the Mayor of Albany, very prominent family. And Ebby's drinking was embarrassing the family, so they called Ebby in one day and said Ebby you're embarrassing the family with your drinking and we would like for you to just basically get out of town and go on over there to Vermont and stay at the old summer place and we'll be over there this summer. And while you're there you might as well sober up. And if you get sober, you might as well make yourself useful and paint up and fix up the old summer place because we'll be using it. So Ebby went out, got out of town and went over to Vermont to begin to fix up the old summer place, painting and fixing it up. And one day he finished painting this wall and he looked at it and he was admiring that and he noticed that some pigeons were doing some things on the side of his wall that he didn't like. So he went in the house and got his shut gun out and began to shoot at the pigeons, blowing holes in the side of the wall. Well the neighbors they don't like that at all, so they called the police and had him arrested and they took him before the judge and they were going to commit him for alcoholic insanity. But Ebby got real lucky; two fellows interceded on his behalf. One guy's name was Rowland Hazard and the other was Cebra Graves. And they asked the judge if he might release Ebby to their care because they were going to the Oxford Group and they felt if they took Ebby to the Oxford Group meetings and if he would apply the tenets of the Oxford Group to his life, maybe he too could stay sober as they had. Well Ebby began to go to the Oxford Group meetings and he began to stay sober and a couple of months later he goes to New York to the Calvary Mission was the headquarters of the Oxford Group at that time. And he began to stay there in that mission and after a while he decided that he remembered his friend Bill, he said I think I'll go over and talk to Bill, maybe I can help Bill stay sober as these two fellows have helped me. Now Bill didn't know any of this though, he said I wondered how he had escaped.

Big Book p. 9, line 5   "*Of course he would have dinner, and then I could drink openly with him. Unmindful of his welfare, I thought only of recapturing the spirit of other days. There was that time we had chartered an airplane to complete a jag! His coming was an oasis in this dreary desert of futility. The very thing an oasis! Drinkers are like that.*
The door opened and he stood there, fresh-skinned and glowing. There was something about his eyes. He was inexplicably different. What had happened?
I pushed a drink across the table. He refused it. Disappointed but curious, I wondered what had got into the fellow. He wasn't himself. "Come, what's all this about? I queried.
He looked straight at me. Simply, but smilingly, he said, "I've got religion."

J & C   Now I'm damn glad that didn't happen in my kitchen. I have no idea what I would have done. But here's what Bill did. He said:

Big Book p. 9, par. 5-6   "*I was aghast. So that was it - last summer an alcoholic crackpot; now, I suspected, a little cracked about religion. He had that starry-eyed look. Yes, the old boy was on fire all right. But bless his heart, let him rant! Besides, my gin would last longer than his preaching.*
But he did no ranting. In a matter of fact way he told how two men had appeared in court, persuading the judge to suspend his commitment. They had told of a simple religious idea

J & C   Which is step 2

Big Book p. 9, par. 6 line 4,   *and a practical program of action.*

J & C   Which is steps 3 through 12.

Big Book p. 9, par. 6, line 5   *That was two months ago and the result was self-evident. It worked!* "

(here is the phrase that Joe and Charlie use: **practical program of action.**)

J & C   So now then Bill knows all three things. He got the problem from Dr. Silkworth, he got the Solution here referred to here as a simple religious idea from Ebby, he got the practical program of action from Ebby, so now he knows all three things. But Bill is also just like so many of us, he did not like this simple religious idea. Now Bill's thoughts and his ideas about God and about religion and etc. were enough that made him resent what Ebby had brought to him. He said,

Big Book p. 9, par. 7   "He had come to pass his experience along to me if I cared to have it. I was shocked, but interested. Certainly I was interested. I had to be, for I was hopeless.
He talked for hours. Childhood memories rose before me. I could almost hear the sound of the preacher's voice as I sat, on still Sundays, way over there on the hillside; there was that proffered temperance pledge I never signed; my grandfather's good natured contempt of some church folk and their doings; his insistence that the spheres really had their music; but his denial of the preacher's right to tell him how he must listen;

J & C   Now Bill's grandfather Grandpa Griffith raised him from twelve years on. And Grandpa Griffith believed in some power greater than human power but he wouldn't let anybody tell him how he had to believe in it. His grandpa had a great problem with the world's religions; he passed that along to Bill.

Big Book p. 10, par 1,line 9   "*his fearlessness as he spoke of these things just before he died; these recollections welled up from the past. They made me swallow hard.*
That war-time day in old Winchester Cathedral came back again."

J & C   Bill's having a problem now with this religious idea that Ebby's talking about. We've seen him take Step 1. In the next couple of pages we're going to see him take Step 2. Let's see how he came to be able to accept this religious idea. Now Bill's already took Step 1, so now he's between Steps 1 and 2, he hasn't taken Step 2 yet. He begins to ponder these things. He said,

Big Book p. 10, par. 3   "*I had always believed in a Power greater that myself. I had often pondered these things. I was not an atheist. Few people really are, for that means blind faith in the strange proposition that this universe originated in a cipher and aimlessly rushes nowhere. My intellectual heroes, the chemists, the astronomers, even the evolutionist, suggested vast laws and forces at work. Despite contrary indications, I had little doubt that a might purpose and rhythm underlay all. How could there be so much of precise and immutable law, and no intelligence? I simply had to believe in a Spirit of the Universe, who knew neither time nor limitation. But that was as far as I had gone.*"

J & C   Now here's where I really begin to identify with Bill Wilson.

Big Book p. 10, par. 4   "*With ministers, and the world's religions, I parted right there. When they talked of a God personal to me, who was love, superhuman strength and direction, I became irritated and my mind snapped shut against such a theory. To Christ I conceded the certainty of a great man, not too closely followed by those who claimed Him. His moral teaching most excellent. For myself, I had adopted those parts which seemed convenient and not too difficult; the rest I disregarded.*"

J & C   Anybody in here identify with Bill Wilson, huh? You betcha. We can see that Bill's having a terrible time with this religious idea. Now let's go down to the middle paragraph.

Big Book p. 11, par. 3   "*But my friend sat before me, and he made the pointblank declaration that God had done for him what he could not do for himself. His human will had failed. Doctors had pronounced him incurable. Society was about to lock him up. Like myself, he had admitted complete defeat. Then he had, in effect, been raised from the dead, suddenly taken from the scrap heap to a level of life better than the best he had ever known!*
Had this power originated in him? Obviously it had not. There had been no more power in him than there was in me at that minute; and this was none at all."

J & C   **This is why the identification process is so important**. Bill knew about Ebby. He knew how Ebby drank. And he knew that

if Ebby had been sober two months,
some power greater than Ebby had to be working in Ebby's life.

Whether Bill likes it or not, **is absolutely beside the point**; Ebby is living *proof* of it.

That's what you and I offer to the newcomer. When we sit there talking to the newcomer we're living *proof* that
some power greater than human power is working in our lives also.

Whether the newcomer likes it or not **is beside the point**. We are the *proof* of it. Ebby was the *proof* for Bill.

Now I'd liked to have been there that day, sitting in a corner watching them. Bill's about two-thirds drunk. Ebby has come out of the Oxford Groups and they were a group of people practicing first century Christianity to the best of their ability. The terms they used were highly religious in nature. Ebby is on fire and he's talking about God, and Bill don't like it at all. And they're sitting there arguing with each other about who God is and what He is and Bill said don't give me that religious crap. Oh yeah I believe in the Great Mind, The Spirit of Nature, but don't give me that other kind of stuff, and Ebby's trying to put it on old Bill and they're arguing back and forth, back and forth, back and forth. Let's go over to page 12, first paragraph. He said,

Big Book p. 12, par. 1   *"Despite the living example of my friend there remained in me the vestiges of my old prejudice.*

J & C   Bill still doesn't like this idea.

Big Book p. 12, par. 1, line 2   *The word God still aroused a certain antipathy. When the thought was expressed that there might be a God personal to me this feeling was intensified. I didn't like the idea. I could go for such conceptions as Creative intelligence, Universal Mind or Spirit of Nature but I resisted the thought of a Czar of the Heavens, however loving His sway might be. I have since talked with scores of men who felt the same way."*

J & C   In other words Bill was saying **there's got to be a harder way to do this, what you're saying is too simple**. Now I guess Ebby finally, finally got tired of this deal. Let's look at the next statement very carefully. If you notice it's in squiggly writing,

Big Book p. 12, par. 2   *"My friend suggested what then seemed a novel idea. He said, "Why don't you choose your own conception of God?"*

J & C   In other words, he said, Bill what are we arguing about? What difference does it make what we call Him. ***Why don't you choose your own conception of God?*** **We're no longer dealing with religion now; we're dealing with spirituality. You see, religion says, this is the way you have to believe.**

**Spirituality says it really doesn't make any difference how you believe, the only question is
are you willing to believe?**

So **we're through with religion now, we're talking about spirituality**. And here's the effect that it had on Bill.

Big Book p. 12, par. 3   *"That statement hit me hard. It melted the icy intellectual mountain in whose shadow I had lived and shivered many years. I stood in the sunlight at last.*

J & C   It took all arguments away from him. He couldn't argue with that statement.

Big Book p. 12, par. 4   *"It was only a matter of being willing to believe in a Power greater than myself. Nothing more was required of me to make my beginning. I saw that growth could start from that point. Upon a foundation of complete willingness I might build what I saw in my friend. Would I have it? Of course I would! "*

J & C   Surely, this is when Bill took Step 2. No Step 2 written in those days. But here's where he came to believe in a Power greater than himself, based on Ebby's simple little statement, <u>"Why don't you choose your own conception of God?"</u> And that statement has opened the door for countless millions of we alcoholics who were having trouble with religion. And I think **the reason it really works is we're allowed here to have our own conception of God**. And you know as I look back in my lifetime I realize I've never had any problem with my own conception of anything, you betcha. Let me believe the way I want to and I'm ready to go now. Bill is now taking a Step 2. Isn't that something? Isn't that something? When he made the statement, <u>"I saw that growth could start from that point. Upon a foundation of complete willingness I might build what I saw in my friend. Would I have it? Of course I would!"</u>

This is Bill's first reference to a wonderfully effective spiritual structure and he's going to start painting a picture in our mind using words. Eventually he'll tell us what the structure is, and show us where we'll pass through it to freedom. Now his first reference to it is, <u>"Upon a foundation of complete willingness I might build what I saw in my friend."</u>

The foundation of this structure is willingness. That came from Step 1.

   When we could see what we were doing would no longer work period, we became willing to change.

Later on we're going to see where **Believing, Step 2, is the cornerstone of that structure**. And eventually he'll tell us exactly what it is. A beautiful way to teach, painting pictures in our mind using words.

   If we are willing, and if we believe, then we've already started the road to recovery.

Bill has now taken Steps 1 and 2. Immediately Ebby starts taking him to Oxford Group meetings, but remember,

Bill's still drinking. Triggered the allergy on November 11, he can't stop.

J & C On about December the 10th probably, 1934, Bill was put back in the hospital for the third time, for withdrawal from alcohol by Doctor Silkworth. Ebby comes to visit with him**,**

1. **they begin to apply the little Oxford Group program of action, and**
2. **Bill had his spiritual experience**. (after Steps 3-12)

Let's look on page 13. Let's see if we can't see the last 10 steps of Alcoholics Anonymous. He's taken 1 & 2, let's see if we can't see the last ten. He said,

Big Book p.13, par.2 *At the hospital I was separated from alcohol for the last time. Treatment seemed wise, for I showed signs of delirium tremens.*
There I humbly offered myself to God, as I then I understood Him, to do with me as He would. I placed myself unreservedly under His care and direction. I admitted for the first time that of myself I was nothing; that without Him I was lost.

J & C **The first tenet that the Oxford Group had was Surrender**. Now Bill later on when he wrote the steps he realized that no alcoholic would like the word surrender so he changed their 1st Step into our 3rd where, **"We made decision to turn our will and life over to the Care of God as we Understand Him"**. We see him there taking the first Oxford Group tenet, which turned out to be our Step 3. He's now taken 1, 2 and 3. He said,

Big Book p.13, par. 3 *I ruthlessly faced my sins*

J & C I ruthlessly faced my sins. **Their second tenet was exam your sins**. And Bill knew that no good alcoholic's going to do that, so he changed that into **Made a searching and fearless moral inventory of ourselves**. He's taking Step 4 there

Big Book p.13, par. 3 *and became willing to have my new-found Friend take them away, root and branch. I have not had a drink since.*

J & C <u>**"... became willing to have my new-found Friend take them away, root and branch"**.</u> You'll notice friend is capitalized. This is one of the words Bill uses for God. And that little statement <u>"... became willing to have my new-found Friend take them away, root and branch"</u>, later became **Step 6 and 7.** We became willing to have God remove these things and humbly asked Him to do so. There we're dealing with six and seven.

Big Book p.13, par. 4 *My schoolmate visited me, and I fully acquainted him with my problems and deficiencies.*

J & C He's taking what we know today as **Step Five**, there in the Towns Hospital with Ebby.

Big Book p.13, par. 4   *We made a list of people I had hurt or toward whom I felt resentment. I expressed my entire willingness to approach these individuals, admitting my wrong. Never was I to be critical of them. I was to right all such matters to the utmost of my ability.*

J & C   They had an Oxford Group **tenet** called **Restitution**. And Bill knew that no self-respecting alcoholic is going to do restitution, so he took that and made two Steps out of it, **Step 8 and 9**, where **we made a list and became willing, and then made amends.** There he's dealing with eight and nine.

Big Book p.13, par. 5   *I was to test my thinking by the new God-consciousness within. Common sense would thus become uncommon sense*

J & C   That statement later became **Step 10** where **we continue to take personal inventory and when we were wrong promptly explained it, I mean admitted it.** That's the new Step 10.

Big Book p.13, par. 5   *I was to sit quietly when in doubt, asking only for direction and strength to meet my problems as He would have me. Never was I to pray for myself, except as my requests bore on my usefulness to others. Then only might I expect to receive. But that would be in great measure.*

J & C   And there we see all the elements of Step 12, **where we sought through prayer and** medica.., **meditation to improve our conscious contact with God** so on and so forth. **There he's dealing with Step 11,** I'm sorry, Step 11.

Big Book p.13, par. 6   *My friend promised when these things were done I would enter upon a new relationship with my Creator; that I would have the elements of a way of living which answered all my problems.*

J & C   It's got to be **the first part of Step Twelve... Having had a spiritual awakening as the result of these steps**.

So we see Bill in the Towns Hospital applying the Oxford Group tenets which later he made into the last ten steps of Alcoholics Anonymous. This is why he was able to say in How It Works, these are the steps we took which are suggested as a program of recovery. Bill took them in the Towns Hospital with the help of Ebby. Now let's see what happened to him

Big Book p.13, par. 6   *Belief in the power of God, plus enough willingness, honesty and humility to establish and maintain the new order of things, were the essential requirements. Simple, but not easy; a price had to be paid. It meant destruction of self-centeredness. I must turn in all things to the Father of Light who presides over us all.*

J & C   Poor old alcoholics have to give up the 2 most important things in our lives and the first thing is our alcohol and the second thing is our self-centeredness. Very difficult to do, very difficult but very simple.

Big Book p.14, par. 3   *These were revolutionary and drastic proposals, but the moment I fully accepted them, the effect was electric. There was a sense of victory, followed by such a peace and serenity as I had never know. There was utter confidence. I felt lifted up, as though the great clean wind of a mountain top blew through and through. God comes to most men gradually, but His impact on me was sudden and profound. For a moment I was alarmed, and called my friend, the doctor, to ask if I were still sane. He listened in wonder as I talked.*

J & C   You know Bill overhead Lois and Dr. Silkworth talking so he'd thought he gone crazy. He thought he'd check it out with Dr. Silkworth to see if he had gone crazy. Finally he shared with the Dr. his experience.

Big Book p.14, par. 5   *"Finally he shook his head saying, "Something has happened to you I don't understand. But you had better hang on to it. Anything is better than the way you were." The good doctor now sees many men who have such experiences. He knows that they are real."*

J & C   Now we don't know what happened to Bill that day, we were not there to see that. But we know this was probably about December the 14th of 1934. We do know that Bill didn't die until January of 1971. We do know that it was never necessary for him to take another drink from this day until the day that he died. **Something profound took place in his life that day.**

Bill always said, 'I had a vital spiritual experience as the result of these steps,

**during which old ideas were cast aside and replaced with a new set of ideas, and
I was able to live the rest of my live without drinking.'**

Now here's a guy that went in the hospital, **selfish and self-centered to the extreme, always doing what he wanted to do whenever he wanted to do it**. That was his attitude when he went in there. Let's look at his attitude now that he's had the spiritual experience

Big Book p.14, par. 6   *While I lay in the hospital the thought came that there were thousands of hopeless alcoholics who might be glad to have what had been so freely given me. Perhaps I could help some of them. They in turn might work with others.*

J & C   Bill had that **gigantic spiritual experience** and then he immediately began to think of how he can give it to other people. Something profound happened with Bill. He said.

Big Book p.14, par 7   My friend

J & C   and this time you'll notice it's a small 'f', he's referring to Ebby now.

Big Book p.14, par 7   My friend had emphasized the absolute necessity of demonstrating these principles in all my affairs. Particularly was it imperative to work with others as he had worked with me. Faith without works was dead, he said. And how appallingly true for the alcoholic! For if an alcoholic failed to perfect and enlarge his spiritual life through work and self-sacrifice for others, he could not survive the certain trials and low spots ahead. If he did not work, he would surely drink again, and if he drank, he would surely die. Then faith would be dead indeed. With us it is just like that

J & C   Thank God Bill knew that and accepted that fact cause when he was in Akron about to get drunk he remember how back in New York City even though **he'd never helped anybody else that he himself had felt better**. That's why he got hold of Dr. Bob, to try to help Dr. Bob. **Not necessarily to sober up Bob, but to keep Bill from getting drunk**. And thank God it kept him from getting drunk, and Bob sobered up and from there we have the fellowship of Alcoholics Anonymous.

Faith without works is dead.
(Chapter 6, Into Action, p. 76 & 88)

And you know just about

anybody I see drink today that's been in A.A. for any period of time,
usually they have quit working with other people.

And when they quit working with other people

1. they start thinking about self only and,
2. **after a while all the old problems come back,** and
3. **we end up getting drunk** all over again.

Always working with others will help us when nothing else will.

He said,

Big Book p.15, par. 2   My wife and I abandoned ourselves with enthusiasm to the idea of helping other alcoholics to a solution of their problems. It was fortunate, for my old business associates remained skeptical for a year and a half, during which I found little work. I was not too well at the time, and was plagued by waves of self-pity and resentment. This sometimes nearly drove me back to drink, but I soon found that when all other measure failed, work with another alcoholic would save the day. Many times I have gone to my old hospital in despair. On talking to a man there, I would be amazingly lifted up and set on my feet. It is a design for living that works in rough going.

J & C   We took a design for living that works in rough going and turned it into a non-drinking society I'm afraid. This is a design for living.

And the work is really, really hard, but the pay is really, really good too.

We've managed to stay sober, isn't that something? Now if we're a brand new alcoholic out here in California, no fellowship around us, the first contact we've ever had is this book called Alcoholics Anonymous, and we've

1. read the Dr.'s Opinion, we've been able to **see what our problem is**.
2. read Bill's story, we've been **able to identify with another alcoholic**.
3. seen him go from
    a) fun **drinking** to
    b) drinking **because of absolute necessity** going finally
    c) to the sickest of all, **complete oblivion.**
4. seen him **recover from that condition**

and surely, surely we can say to ourselves

we're enough like this guy that if he can recover just maybe we could too.

The beginning of belief, the beginning of hope.

End of Tape 2

> regained health of mind and body

J & C   By now we could probably hardly wait to see what really did take place in Bill's life and how he <u>recovered.</u> And I don't think it's by accident the very next chapter is titled, 'There is a Solution'. There is a solution to the thing that Bill has really described in his own story here and to what Dr. Silkworth has talked to us about. Now

<u>if our problem is (being) powerless which we should be convinced of that by now</u>

<u>then obviously the answer is going to lie within power.</u>

And in this chapter there is a solution. We're going to talk about two powers. We're going to talk about

(1) <u>the power of the fellowship</u>   and we're going to talk about   (2) <u>the power of the vital spiritual experience</u>

And if we, who are powerless, could get both of these powers in our lives, then maybe we could overcome alcoholism also.

On page 17, for those who are powerless he writes <u>the prescription.</u> Here he talks about the two powers. Ebby presented Bill with a solution and now Bill is going to present us with a solution in the same way. He said there is a solution. A friend of mine back home said there's many different types of solutions are there are people in A.A. And if you look at the chapter heading on, page 17, he'll tell you how many solutions there are,

"There is a solution", (ONE)

J & C   He said, "We", and there's that big word again.

Big Book p. 17, par. 1   *"We, of Alcoholics Anonymous, know thousands of men and women who were once just as hopeless as Bill. Nearly all have recovered. They have solved the drink problem.*
We are average Americans."

J & C   Today we can say that we're average citizens of the world because by last count (1988) there was, A.A.'s in 154 countries around the world.

Big Book p. 17, par. 2   *"All sections of this country and many of its occupations are represented, as well as many political, economic, social, and religious backgrounds. We are people who normally would not <u>mix</u>."*

J & C   And I think that we're probably the most <u>mixed</u> up group of alcoholics in the world here this morning here in Laughlin, Nevada. You know if we didn't have "Alcoholics Anonymous" to talk about or drinking or recovery there from, I wonder what we would drink about/talk about. There's hardly anything... I told you I had a good memory it's just short. We wouldn't have anything to talk about. It says,

Big Book p. 17, par. 2   *"We are people who normally would not mix. But there exists among us a fellowship, a friendliness, and an understanding which is indescribably wonderful."*

J & C   And I hear that this morning and before the meeting all the talk and the laughter and the goings on, that's the fellowship of Alcoholics Anonymous, the spirit of Alcoholics Anonymous, and I got sober on the spirit of Alcoholics Anonymous. That was the only thing keeping me here. So it's a powerful thing, the fellowship of Alcoholics Anonymous, kept me sober for quite some time.

> the fellowship can keep you sober for quite some time, but it can't keep you sober forever (without the program in the book)

Now he's going to describe this fellowship of Alcoholics Anonymous. By talking about something he already assumes that we know about it, he thinks that we already know about it and all great teachers have always done this. When they want to teach you something new, they talk to you first about something you already know and use that as an example to teach you something new. You know we had a great teacher that lived 2000 years ago and he was really good at this. When he wanted to teach something to the shepherds, he'd tell them a story about sheep. But if he wanted to teach the same thing to the fisherman he would change the story, this time it would be about fish. Then when he went to the farmer he talked about cattle and grains. All good teachers do this. Bill is going to use the example of the great passenger ship. He said,

Big Book p. 17, par. 2   *"We are like the passengers of a great liner the moment after rescue from shipwreck when camaraderie, joyousness and democracy pervade the vessel from steerage to Captain's table."*

J & C   Bill is referring to a time in the Thirties when your mode of transportation from one continent to another was by the great ocean liners. And on those great ocean liners they had what they called the steerage section. And people who were immigrants and didn't have very much money they usually booked passage in the steerage section. Way down in the bowels of the ship, with very little fresh air, dormitory style living, I call it the cheese sandwich section, not very good down there. If you had a little more money though and you wanted better accommodations you could pay for fourth class and come up a deck to two. Maybe you could go third class and come up another deck or two. Maybe you could go second class and come up another deck or two. And each time the accommodations and the food were better. If you had enough money you could go in what they call first class. In first class they had big fine staterooms, they had great dining rooms, they had good food, fine waiters, access to fresh air all the time. But that still wasn't the most elite place on the ship. If you had the right kind of money, old, old money, old money, if you had the right religion, the right ethnic background, the right everything, you might be invited to dine at the Captain's table. Just a few select people could do that. And at the Captain's table you had the best of everything; the best service, the best food, the best everything. Now it's a long, long way from the Captain's table to the steerage section.

And in the journey across the ocean, those two people should never have met each other. If fact most of those ocean liners even had separate stairwells. So the first class people never even had to see those who rode in the steerage section. They had nothing whatsoever in common. Then I think about the Titanic. When the night it hit the iceberg and these two guys are standing there at the rail of the ship and one of them got his tuxedo on, his shiny shoes and his little bow tie and everything that goes with it. Standing next to him is the guy from the steerage section. Got his old work overalls on, his old brogans, never wore a tie in his life. These guys have nothing whatsoever in common with each other until they jumped overboard. And when they jumped overboard, and their butts hit that cold water, they had something in common. How in the hell do we save ourselves? And they grabbed on to each other and held on to each other, and I doubt very seriously if the man from the Captains table asked for a financial statement from the man from the steerage section. And when these two guys were rescued and got back on another ship or back on land there was a feeling amongst them, which was indescribably wonderful. This has always been true

When people escape from a common peril
there is a feeling that ties them together and it's one of the greatest feelings in the world
and that's what we've got in the fellowship of Alcoholics Anonymous.
We don't care who you are.
We don't care where you came from.
We don't care how much money you got.
We don't care what your education is.
We don't care what your ethnic background is, what your religion is or anything else.

All we want to know is, are you an alcoholic?
And if you are, there is a feeling amongst us, which is indescribably wonderful.
<u>Even though we are so different from each other, we are still bound together</u>.

Now watch him, he's going to give us a warning.

Big Book p. 17, par. 2   *"Unlike the feelings of the ship's passengers, however, our joy in escape from disaster does not subside as we go our individual ways."*

J & C   These two guys when they finally got back on shore, they looked at each other and said well we really don't belong together, and they separated probably never to meet again. But we will always be alcoholic, and this feeling we have for each other never goes away and we find it again in city, after city, after city, and country after country.

One of the greatest things I've been able to experience in my lifetime is to go to an A.A. meeting in a foreign country and feel just exactly as good as I did at home. Even though I don't know those people <u>we are bound together because we're alcoholics</u>.

Big Book p 17. par. 2   *"The feeling of having shared in a common peril **is one element** in the powerful cement which binds us. But that in itself would never have held us together as we are now joined."*

J & C   In other words, this feeling we have for each other in the fellowship of Alcoholics Anonymous is one of the things that bind us together. But then he said, that itself is not enough.

Big Book p. 17, par. 3   *"The tremendous fact for every one of us is that we have discovered <u>a common solution</u>. We have a way out on which we can absolutely agree, and upon which we can join in brotherly and harmonious action. This is the great news <u>this book</u> carries to those who suffer from alcoholism."*

J & C   <u>Not the news of the fellowship</u>, but <u>the news of the common solution</u>. And later on we're going to see where

<u>the common solution
is the spiritual experience
brought about through the program of action.</u>

This is <u>the prescription</u> that J & C refers to on page 1 of this script	if we can get the power of the fellowship - which supports us and helps us, and if we can get the power of the spiritual experience - which changes us, <u>and add the two together</u> then that will be enough power to overcome our powerlessness over alcohol and we can recover from that condition.

I think one of the greatest tragedies that I see in the world today, and there's lots of tragedies going on in the world today, one of the greatest that I see is we people who are in the fellowship of Alcoholics Anonymous are spending literally hundreds and hundreds of thousands of dollars, hundreds and hundreds and thousands of men and women work hours, trying to attract other alcoholics to the fellowship of Alcoholics Anonymous, when

we've got thousands and thousands (of alcoholics) who are already members of Alcoholics Anonymous
who are sitting around dying from untreated alcoholism,
because they are doing nothing about the common solution.

And the reason they're doing nothing about the common solution is   <u>nobody's telling them about it.</u>
<u>nobody's talking about it,</u>
<u>nobody's saying look, here's the</u> **program of action**.
<u>nobody's saying, let me take you by the hand and walk   with
you so you can have a</u> **spiritual experience**.

And <u>they're fellowship only,</u> and after a while they go back to drinking and they say well, A.A. don't work for us.
No, they didn't work for A.A.; they didn't do the program.

> the fellowship can keep you sober for quite some time, but it <u>can't</u> keep you sober forever (without the program in the book)

And again   it's not their fault,
             it's our fault
             we're not insisting that new people work the program of Alcoholics Anonymous and
             we're letting them die around us.

Thousands of us are dying everyday who are already members of the fellowship of Alcoholics Anonymous

It's our responsibility to see that every newcomer knows about page 17 and knows

             there are two powers: a) the power of the fellowship, and
                                      b) the power of the spiritual experience.

And we're not going to recover without both of them.
Now we might stay sober for a while, but
we're not going to recover from alcoholism without both of them.

A good textbook never tells you anything but what it doesn't back it up and prove it. The first half of this chapter is designed to show you and I why fellowship alone is not sufficient.

The last half of this chapter is used to show us the solution to alcoholism, the vital spiritual experience. Let's look for just a few minutes at why fellowship alone is not sufficient and then we'll take a break. Go to page 20,

Big Book p. 20, par. 2   *"You may already have asked yourself why it is that all of us became so very ill from drinking. Doubtless you are curious to discover how and why, in the face of expert opinion to the contrary, we have recovered from a hopeless condition of mind and body. If you are an alcoholic who wants to get over it, you may already be asking What do I have to do? It is the purpose of this book to answer such questions specifically."*

J & C   Remember last night we talked about precisely, specifically, with clear-cut directions. Well here's one of those words.

Big Book p. 20, par. 3   *"We shall tell you what we have done. Before going into a detailed discussion, it may be well to summarize some points as we see them."*
How many time people have said to us: "I can take it or leave it alone. Why can't he?" "Why don't you drink like a gentleman or quit?" "That fellow can't handle his liquor." "Why don't you try beer and wine?" "Lay off the hard stuff." "His will power must be weak." "He could stop if he wanted to." "She's such a sweet girl, I should think he'd stop for her sake." "The doctor told him that if he ever drank again it would kill him, but there he is all lit up again."
Now these are commonplace observations on drinkers which we hear all the time. Back of them is a world of ignorance and misunderstanding. We see that these expressions refer to people whose reactions are very different from ours."

J & C   And we're going to look at two kinds of drinkers that these expressions that Joe just read, would refer to them.

Big Book p. 20, par. 6   *"Moderate drinkers have little trouble in giving up liquor entirely if they have good reason for it. They can take it or leave it alone."*

J & C   Remember we talked about them last night. They have a couple of drinks; they get a slightly tipsy out of control beginnings of a nauseous feeling? Alcohol is no big deal for them. If they have any problems with it, they simply leave it alone. Those expressions that Joe read would certainly refer to the moderate drinker.

Big Book p. 20, par. 7   *"Then we have a certain type of hard drinker. He may have the habit badly enough to gradually impair him physically and mentally. It may cause him to die a few years before his time. If a sufficiently strong reason ill health, falling in love, change of environment, or the warning of a doctor becomes operative, this man can also stop or moderate, although he may find it difficult and troublesome and may even need medical attention."*

J & C   We call this guy the heavy or the hard drinker. They drink like we alcoholics drink, but they are not alcoholic. If a good enough reason presents itself to them, they'll do one of two things. They may learn to moderate their drinking; they do not have the physical allergy. They may quit drinking entirely and stay quit; they do not have the obsession of the mind. They drink like us, but they're not alcoholic. You and I see them all the time. They're the guy that said when I was in the service I was an alcoholic also. And when I got out of the service I got married, went to church, quit drinking, don't see why in the hell you can't. No, they're not alcoholic. The expressions that Joe read in the beginning refer to the heavy drinker.

Big Book p. 21, par. 2   *"But what about <u>the real alcoholic</u>? He may start off as a moderate drinker;*

J & C   Which many of us did.

Big Book, p. 21, par 2   *"he may or may not become a continuous hard drinker;*

J & C   Some of us stayed periodic.

Big Book, p. 21, par 2   *"but <u>at some stage</u> of his drinking career <u>he begins to lose all control of his liquor consumption</u>, once he starts to drink."*

J & C   Now then we're going to describe the real alcoholic, and when you see a description in there that fits you, would you please raise your hand. We'd like to see if we're in a room full of real alcoholics.

Big Book p. 21, par. 2   *"but at some stage of his drinking career he begins to lose all control of his liquor consumption, once he starts to drink."*

J & C   Charlie talked last night about; he talked last night about <u>crossing over that line</u>. He talked last night about crossing over that line, but I don't know what line he was talking about, but I know one thing; I was drunk when I went over it.

Big Book p. 21, par. 3   *"Here is the fellow who has been puzzling you, especially in his lack of control. He does absurd, incredible, tragic things while drinking.   He is a real Dr. Jekyll and Mr. Hyde.   He is seldom mildly intoxicated.   He is always more or less insanely drunk."*

J & C   Anybody like that in here? You betcha.

Big Book p. 21, par. 3   *"His disposition while drinking resembles his normal nature but little."*

J & C   I always get good looking and out of debt as soon as I start drinking.

Big Book p. 21, par 3   *"He may be one of the finest fellows in the world.   Yet let him drink for a day, and he frequently becomes disgustingly, and even dangerously anti-social."*

J & C   We got any of those people in here?

Big Book p. 21, par 3   *"He has a positive genius for getting tight at exactly the wrong moment, particularly when some important decision most be made or engagement kept."*

J & C   Anybody in here like that, always getting drunk at the wrong time. Now everybody holds their hand up here on this one.

Big Book p. 21, par 3   *"He is often perfectly sensible and well balanced concerning everything except liquor, but in that respect he is incredibly dishonest and selfish. He often possesses special abilities, skills, and aptitudes, and has a promising career ahead of him."*

J & C   Anybody like that in here? I've never heard anybody but an alcoholic say that though. I've never heard an AlAnon say it yet.

Big Book p. 21, par 3   *"He uses his gifts to build up a bright outlook for his family and himself, and then pulls the structure down on his head by a senseless series of sprees."*

J & C   Anybody like that in here?

Big Book p. 21, par 3 "He is the fellow who goes to bed so intoxicated he ought to sleep the clock around. Yet early next morning he searches madly for the bottle he misplaced the night before."

J & C   Any bottle hiders in here?

Big Book p. 22, par1 "If he can afford it, he may have liquor concealed all over his house to be certain no one gets his entire supply away from him to throw down the waste pipe."

J & C   Anybody spread them around wherever you might be? Phyllis and I used to by a lug of whiskey, which is 3 fifths; one to share, and one to hide from each other.

Big Book p. 22, par1 "As matters grow worse, he begins to use a combination of high-powered sedative and liquor to quiet his nerves so he can go to work."

J & C   Anybody ever have to have a little something in the morning?

Big Book p. 22, par 1 "Then comes the day when he simply cannot make it and gets drunk all over again. Perhaps he goes. to a doctor who gives him morphine or some sedative with which to taper off. Then he begins to appear at hospitals and (treatment, uh excuse me), sanitariums."

J & C   I never did taper off, I always tapered on for some reason.

Big Book p. 21, par 2 "This is by no means a comprehensive picture of the true alcoholic, as our behavior patterns vary. But this description should identify him roughly."

J & C   Now if our government has ever done anything right in the field of alcoholism, it's the education of the public as to what alcoholism is and what it isn't. Because of that a lot of the stigma has been removed from alcoholism. Many, many people are getting to us today before they have to do everything here that describes the real alcoholic. And I'll guarantee you if you're alcoholic you found yourself in there somewhere; at least one of them are going to fit you. In my case practically every one of them, one in particular. Seven years after I got sober I sold a forty-acre, forty-five thousand boiler chicken operation. For years after that, every once in a while I would run into the guy that bought it and sometimes he would way and smile and say, hey Charlie, we have found another one. And he was referring to partially empty vodka bottles. Behind corner posts, under rocks, hollow trees, falling out of feed bins. And he found them for years in there. Now here's the question,

Big Book p. 22, par. 3 "Why does he behave like this? If hundreds of experiences have shown him that one drink means another debacle with all its attendant suffering and humiliation, why is it he takes that one drink? Why can't he stay on the water wagon?"

J & C   The moderate drinker can. The heavy drinker can. Why can't the alcoholic?

Big Book p. 22, par. 3 "What has become of the common sense and will power that he still sometimes displays with respect to other matters?
Perhaps there never will be a full answer to these questions. Opinions vary considerably as to why the alcoholic reacts differently from normal people. We are not sure why, once a certain point is reached, little can be done for him. We cannot answer the riddle. We know that while the alcoholic keeps away from drink, as he may do for months or years, he reacts much like other men. We are equally positive that once he takes any alcohol whatever into his system, something happens, both in the bodily and mental sense, which makes it virtually impossible for him to stop. The experience of any alcoholic will abundantly confirm this.
These observations would be academic and pointless if our friend never took the first drink, thereby setting the terrible cycle in motion. Therefore, the main problem of the alcoholic centers in his mind, rather than in his body.

J & C   Would you read that again please?

Big Book p. 23, par. 1, line 3 "Therefore, the main problem of the alcoholic centers in his mind, rather than in his body."

J & C   Now we must remember that always, just before we take the first drink, we are stone cold sober. Or stark raving sober one of the two. And

> the real problem centers in our mind telling us we can drink while sober,
> rather than in the body that ensures that we can't drink.

Big Book p. 23, par 1   *If you ask him why he started on that last bender, the chances are he will offer you any one of a hundred alibis. Sometimes these excuses have a certain plausibility, but none of them really makes sense in the light of the havoc an alcoholic's drinking bout creates. They sound like the philosophy of the man who, having a headache, beats himself on the head with a hammer so that he can't feel the ache. If you draw this fallacious reasoning to the attention of an alcoholic, he will laugh it off, or become irritated and refuse to talk.*
Once in a while he may tell the truth

J & C   And as strange as it may seem there are times we alcoholics tell the truth – not very often – but once in a great while.

Had a lady who was in Al-Anon came to me one time and her husband was still drinking and she said, "Charlie, all he does is lie, lie, lie." She said "How can you tell when one of you guys are lying." And I said "Lady, watch him closely, and if you see his lips moving he's probably lying to you all right". And then I said "Do you want me to tell you how to keep him from lying?" and she said "Yeah yeah" and I said "Don't ask him those stupid questions …he has no more idea than you do". Now here's the truth.

Big Book p. 23, par 2   *And the truth, strange to say, is usually that he has no more idea why he took that first drink than you have. Some drinkers have excuses with which they are satisfied part of the time. But in their hearts they really do not know why they do it. Once this malady has a real hold, they are a baffled lot. There is the obsession that somehow, someday, they will beat the game. But they often suspect they are down for the count.*

J & C   Now there is the word obsession.   Remember that

> <u>An obsession of the mind is an idea that overcomes all ideas to the contrary.</u>
> <u>An obsession of the mind is an idea that is so strong it can make you believe something that is not true.</u>

That great obsession of every alcoholic is
- someday, somehow we are going to find some kind of liquor that we can drink without getting drunk.
- someday somehow we are going to find a group of people that we can drink with
- someday somehow we are going to find a place…

> And that idea is so strong; it makes us believe that it is OK for us to drink.
> We take a drink, we trigger the allergy and we end up drunk.
> So the real problem centers in our mind telling us we **can** drink
> rather than in our body which ensures that we can't.

I've never heard anybody yet say "I'm gonna go have 2 drinks and go to the jailhouse tonight." We always say we are going to have 2 drinks and have fun. And we have the 2 drinks and then we go to the jailhouse. So the real problem is right up here, rather than down here.

Big Book p. 24, par 2   *The fact is that most alcoholics, for reasons yet obscure, have lost the power of choice in drink. Our so-called will power becomes practically nonexistent. We are unable, at certain times, to bring into our consciousness with sufficient force the memory of the suffering and humiliation of even a week or a month ago. We are without defense against the first drink.*

J & C   Can't remember the jailhouse, can't remember the divorce court, can't remember what alcohol had done **to** me, can only remember what it has done **for** me. And that will drive me back to drinking. I always said that I don't want for memory it's just short. Just can not remember those things that alcohol had done to me.

Big Book p. 24, par 1   *The almost certain consequences that follow taking even a glass of beer do not crowd into the mind to deter us. If these thoughts occur, they are hazy and readily supplanted with the old threadbare idea that this time we shall handle ourselves like other people. There is a complete failure of the kind of defense that keeps one from putting his hand on a hot stove.*

J & C   You know if you've put your hand on a hot stove and it's burned you badly, chances are you will always remember that. Chances are you will never go put your had on a hot stove again to see if it will burn you the second time.

Now I remember as a kid growing up back in the depression years and there's a few of you in here old enough to remember that too. Back in the 1930's we didn't have very much. We didn't have hot and cold running water, we didn't have forced air heat. Joe said his family was not so poor they had to live in a tent but he said by God if we'd have had the money we'd have lived in a tent. That's about how bad it was.

But I remember in those days, even though you didn't have anything, you were very poor people, cleanliness was still next to Godliness. And every Saturday night everybody in the family had to take a bath. Now whether you needed a bath or not is besides the point, you still had to take one. And one night in the middle of the winter, mother had heated the bath water on the old heating stove in the living room, put it in the Number 3 Zinc washtub sitting being that stove. Now every kid in the family takes a bath in the same water…I'm the baby of the family. By the time it got to me the crud would be about an inch think on it. Mother said "Get in there and get yourself clean" and I thought to myself how in the hell do I get clean there but I didn't dare say that to her. You didn't talk to your parents that way in the 1930s. I scraped the crud back, I got in the tub, began to wash myself heating stove standing here red hot…somehow I managed to lean over and stick my rear against that hot stove. Burned a blister on my rear end about as big as my hand, hurt me worse than anything had ever hurt me before. And do you know that I have never had an obsession of the mind to stick my ass on a hot stove since then. I have never jerked my britches down, backed up to a stove and said burn me again.

Now alcohol has burned me over and over and over and over and over just as bad as that stove ever burned me and for some strange reason my mind cannot remember that. Left on my own resources I start thinking about drinking and after a while I think about only what it's going to do for me. That great sense of ease and comfort, that great exciting in control feeling that comes from the first couple of drinks and my mind keys in on that. I forget about the jailhouse, the hospitals and the divorce courts and I don't see a thing in the world wrong with taking a drink. And I take a drink, and I trigger the allergy and I end up drunk…over and over and over again.

Big Book p. 24, par 4   *When this sort of thinking is fully established in an individual with alcoholic tendencies, he has probably placed himself beyond human aid, and unless locked up, may die or go permanently insane*

J & C   Now if we've placed ourselves beyond human aid, then the fellowship of Alcoholics Anonymous will not bring about recovery. Because the fellowship is made up of a group of human beings who are just as powerless over alcohol as I am. So there has got to be a solution to that condition that we've just talked about and page 25 gives it to us.

Big Book p. 25, par 1   *There is a solution.*

J & C   OK guys, here we go. We're gonna start getting well now. Better come on in. Let's go to page 25. Let's begin to look at the solution we could see that the fellowship gave us enough power to support us for a while. But we were told that the fellowship enough was not sufficient. And then it explained why fellowship alone was not sufficient. So now on page 25 we'll start looking at the real solution to alcoholism.

Big Book p. 25, par 1   *There is a solution. Almost none of us liked the self- searching, the leveling of our pride, the confession of shortcomings which the process requires for its successful consummation. But we saw that it really worked in others, and we had come to believe in the hopelessness and futility of life as we had been living it. When, therefore, we were approached by those in whom the problem had been solved, there was nothing left for us but to pick up the simple kit of spiritual tools laid at out feet. We have found much of heaven and we have been rocketed into a fourth dimension of existence of which we had not even dreamed.*

J & C   And you notice up there it says

Big Book p. 25, par 2   *The great fact is just this, and nothing less: That we have had deep and effective spiritual experiences* which have revolutionized our whole attitude toward life, toward our fellows and toward God's universe. The central fact of our lives today is the absolute certainty that our Creator has entered into our hearts and lives in a way which is indeed miraculous. He has commenced to accomplish those things for us which we could never do by ourselves.*

J & C   And you notice up there it says

Big Book p. 25, par 2   *The great fact is just this, and nothing less: That we have had deep and effective spiritual experiences**

J & C   And there is a little asterisk there referring us down to the bottom of the page. It says "Fully explained – Appendix II" And later on we'll refer to it on page 27 it "For amplification - see Appendix II" And on page 47 referring to the asterisk it says "Please see Appendix II".

Must be important. Very important if they repeat it three times.

And they are talking about spiritual experiences and spiritual awakenings and in the first printing of the book they didn't have this little asterisk there and they didn't have the reference to the spiritual experience in the back of the book.

And a lot of people would write in to that little office, to Bill, and say Bill what do you mean by spiritual experience and spiritual awakenings? We're doing the same things that you are doing but we're not having the same experiences that you had. What do you mean by that?

And it was very important for me looking back at it now that I know this because I had this spiritual experience mixed up with a bunch of things that I learned when I was 7 or 8 years old. Cause when I was 7 or 8 years old I told myself, I said "Self if I ever get big enough they can't catch me I'm not going anymore". To church that is. And I got big enough they couldn't catch me and I didn't go. So when I arrived at Alcoholics Anonymous I had the spiritual knowledge of a 7 or 8 year old boy which was practically none and that that I did have was all mistaken and mixed up. And lot's of emotionalism, things that I didn't understand. The times that they would catch me and take me to that revival, they had a revival there quite often in my area in the southern Baptist. Really southern. And when I would get there and they would be preaching all day and singing songs and having dinner on the ground and prayer meetings all day long and church way into the night. Bored the heck out of me.

But one night my Aunt Much, and she's a big woman, Aunt Much, that's the reason they call her that. But Aunt Much kind of got into the spirit of this thing that night and she began to jump up and down and she began to talk in a strange language that I had never heard of before, squealing and hollering and rolling around in the sawdust. Scared the heck out of me. So when this book began to talk about spiritual experiences and spiritual awakenings I thought that was what I was going to have to have. And I was dreading it I'm telling you I was. But thank God for people like me who didn't know any better they put this information in the back of the book talking about spiritual experiences and spiritual awakenings. And this used all throughout this book. And they want to make real sure that I understand what they mean by that. So let's go back to page 569 (page 567 in the 4th edition) and see what they mean by the terms spiritual awakenings and spiritual experiences.

Big Book p. 569, par 1   *The terms "spiritual experience" and "spiritual awakening" are used many times in this book which, upon careful reading,*

J & C   And we all know that alcoholics don't do careful reading.

Big Book p. 569, par , line 3   *"shows that the personality change sufficient to bring about recovery from alcoholism has manifested itself among us in many different forms.*

J & C   OK the first paragraph we see something. We see that the term may be spiritual experience or it may be spiritual awakening and in either case it's going to be a personality change sufficient to bring about recovery. Dr. Silkworth referred to this as a psychic change. A change in the way we think and the way we feel and our attitude. So we could see several terms.

spiritual experience
spiritual awakening
personality change
psychic change
all meaning the same thing.

Spiritual experience happens suddenly, like it did with Bill and some of the people in back of the stories in the first book, and then we have the spiritual awakening, which develops slowly over a period of a long time.

Big Book p. 569, par 2   *Yet it is true that our first printing gave many readers the impression that these personality changes, or religious experiences, must be in the nature of sudden and spectacular upheavals. Happily for everyone, this conclusion is erroneous. In the first few chapters a number of sudden revolutionary changes are described. Though it was not our intention to create such an impression, many alcoholics have nevertheless concluded that in order to recover they must acquire an immediate and overwhelming "God-consciousness" followed at once by a vast change in feeling and outlook.*
Among our rapidly growing membership of thousands of alcoholics such transformations, though frequent, are by no means the rule. Most of our experiences are what the psychologist William James calls the "educational variety" because they develop slowly over a period of time.

J & C   Now Bill's was a sudden spectacular change. Some of the others in the stories in the back of the book were sudden spectacular changes. But what he's saying here is for most of us it won't happen that way. Most of us will have the educational variety and we will change as we learn and as we apply, slowly over a period of time.

Sooner or later though we awakened to the fact that we have changed also. And then we'll call it a spiritual awakening. So it really doesn't make any difference whether it's sudden and spectacular or whether it's a slow thing that evolves over a period of time. In either case it's going to be a personality change sufficient to bring about recovery.

Now I can begin to think with this, I can live with this kind of idea. But when you start talking about what Aunt Much had in the Baptist Church, I couldn't live with that idea at all. Cause I was raised in the southern Baptist Church too. And my idea of a spiritual experience was an entirely different thing. Thank God for this Appendix. It let me know what it really is. A change in my personality.

My personality is made up by the way I think, by the way I feel, my attitude and outlook upon life, people, places and things in general. That's what determines my personality. I come here restless, irritable and discontented. Filled with shame, fear, guilt and remorse. If I can change from that to peace of mind, serenity and happiness, I have undergone one hell of a change in my personality. This educational variety is the type that we are having this weekend. Right? We won't be the same after this weekend. None of us will. No.

Big Book p. 569, par. 4   Quite often friends of the newcomer are aware of the difference long before he is himself. He finally realizes that he has undergone a profound alteration in his reaction to life; that such a change could hardly have been brought about by himself alone. What often takes place in a few months could seldom have been accomplished by years of self discipline. With few exceptions our members find that they have tapped an unsuspected inner resource which they presently identify with their own conception of a Power greater than themselves.
Most of us think this awareness of a Power greater than ourselves the essence of spiritual experience. Our more religious members call it "God-consciousness."
Most emphatically we wish to say that any alcoholic capable of honestly facing his problems in the light of our experience can recover provided he does not close his mind to all spiritual concepts. He can only be defeated by an attitude of intolerance or belligerent denial.
We find that no one need have difficulty with the spiritual side of the program. Willingness, honesty and open mindedness are the essentials of recovery. But these are indispensable.
"There is a principle which is a bar against all information, which is proof against all arguments and which cannot fail to keep a man in everlasting ignorance - that principle is contempt prior to investigation."

J & C   See I knew so many things that were not true when I arrived in Alcoholics Anonymous. Lifelong theories that were not true. I lived my life based upon those things and they didn't work. And they were so true in my mind that it was almost impossible for me to learn something that was true. So I had to lay aside a bunch of old ideas to be able to accept new and I needed an open mind. In fact I need an open mind more today then I have ever needed an open mind because there is so much more to learn throughout life.

J & C   OK, now we pointed out the fact a while ago that Bill loves to teach by using examples of something we already know about to teach us something new. That's what he did when he used the great ocean liner. Another trend that Bill has, and I think it's very important for us to realize it, is like most writers he did repeat himself quite often. But every time he repeated himself he would normally find a different word that means the same thing. And if you see what he's doing you can understand him. If you don't though you'll think that he's talking about something different.

There seems to be one key word in this whole thing dealing with spiritual experience and that is the word **change**.

Let's see how many times he said change on page 569 (page 567 in the 4th edition) and how many different ways he had of saying it.

In the first paragraph he talked about a **personality change sufficient to bring about recovery**,
In the second paragraph he again mentioned personality changes but then he said **in the nature of sudden and spectacular upheavals**. An upheaval is to change something entirely.
In the third paragraph, first sentence he said **sudden revolutionary changes**. To revolutionize something is to change it entirely.
Third paragraph last sentence, he said **immediate and overwhelming "God-consciousness"**. To overwhelm something is to change it entirely.
Third paragraph last sentence, he said **vast change in feeling and outlook**.
Fourth paragraph first sentence, he said **such transformations**. To transform is to change.
Fourth paragraph about the middle of it he said **profound alteration**. To alter is to change.

So the key thing here is to change from what we were when we came here to something entirely different up here in our minds.
- To go from restless, irritable, discontented, selfish, self centered human beings, to go from that to one that has peace of mind, serenity and happiness and the willingness to help others is an entire change in the way we think.
- That's a spiritual experience.
- That's a spiritual awakening.
- That's a personality change sufficient to recover from alcoholism.
- That's a psychic change.

Now I can buy into that. To go from what we were to something entirely different in the way we think. Religion has nothing to do with this at all. We make the change through spirituality. It's seems that's the only real way that people change, is through spirituality.

They talked about change and I told you that when I got here I had become everything I detested in a human being. And I didn't like what I had become and who I was. So they talk about change and I thought they meant for me to become something that I'm not. So I looked around the fellowship of Alcoholics Anonymous and I found me some heroes. Some people that I wanted to be like and we need those heroes in the beginning. I still need my heroes. Charlie was one of my heroes. So I set about to be exactly like Charlie. I didn't like me so I wanted to be like Charlie. And I almost made it. Thank God I didn't. We only need one Charlie. But I tried to emulate and be exactly like him because I didn't like me. And that's good I needed that. So the type of change I think they are talking about today is to change from what I had become to that which God intended for me to be, just me. And that's a marvelous experience in Alcoholics Anonymous and in life. Just to become who you are and what God intended for you to be, only. And there is only one of those. Thank God. Now let's go back to page 25

Big Book p 25, par 3   *If you are as seriously alcoholic as we were, we believe there is no middle-of-the-road solution. We were in a position where life was becoming impossible, and if we had passed into the region from which there is no return through human aid, we had but two alternatives: one was to go on to the bitter end, blotting out the consciousness of our intolerable situation as best we could;*

J & C   That's Step 1, remaining powerless.

Big Book p. 25, par 3   *and the other, to accept spiritual help.*

J & C   That's Step 2, to accept the need for the power greater than we are.

Big Book p. 25, par 3   *This we did because we honestly wanted to, and were willing to make the effort.*

J & C   Now we saw where Step 1, the physical allergy, the obsession of the mind, we saw where that came from, from Dr. Silkworth in New York City. Now you would think that the idea of the spiritual experience would have come to us through religious people. Let's look on page 26 and let's see where this idea really did come from. Now we're talking here about a certain American businessman. This is this fellow names Rowland Hazard. He was the one that stepped in between Ebby and the judge

Big Book p. 26, par 1   *A certain American business man had ability, good sense, and high character. For years he had floundered from one sanitarium to another. He had consulted the best known American psychiatrists. Then he had gone to Europe, placing*

himself in the care of a celebrated physician who prescribed for him. Though experience had made him skeptical, he finished his treatment with unusual confidence.

J & C   He didn't go there for a 28-day treatment program. He was with Dr. Jung for a full year. Dr. Jung psychoanalyzed him for one day a week for 52 weeks.

Big Book p. 26, par 1   His physical and mental condition were unusually good. Above all, he believed he had acquired such a profound knowledge of the inner workings of his mind and its hidden springs, that relapse was unthinkable. Nevertheless, he was drunk in a short time. More baffling still, he could give himself no satisfactory explanation for his fall.
So he returned to this doctor, whom he admired, and asked him point-blank why he could not recover. He wished above all things to regain self-control. He seemed quite rational and well-balanced with respect to other problems. Yet he had no control whatever over alcohol. Why was this?
He begged the doctor to tell him the whole truth, and he got it. In the doctor's judgment he was utterly hopeless; he could never regain his position in society and he would have to place himself under lock and key, or hire a bodyguard if he expected to live long. That was a great physician's opinion.
But this man still lives, and is a free man. He does not need a bodyguard, nor is he confined. He can go anywhere on this earth where other free men may go without disaster, provided he remains willing to maintain a certain simple attitude.
Some of our alcoholic readers may think they can do without spiritual help. Let us tell you the rest of the conversation our friend had with his doctor.
The doctor said: "You have the mind of a chronic alcoholic. I have never seen one single case recover, where that state of mind existed to the extent that it does in you." Our friend felt as though the gates of hell had closed on him with a clang.
He said to the doctor, "Is there no exception?"
"Yes," replied the doctor, "there is. Exceptions to cases such as yours have been occurring since early times. Here and there, once in a while, alcoholics have had what are called vital spiritual experiences. To me these occurrences are phenomena. They appear to be in the nature of huge emotional displacements and re-arrangements. Ideas, emotions, and attitudes which were once the guiding forces of the lives of these men are suddenly cast to one side, and a completely new set of conceptions and motives begin to dominate them. In fact, I have been trying to produce some such emotional rearrangement within you. With many individuals the methods which I employed are successful, but I have never been successful with an alcoholic of your description."

J & C   Change…change…change…change

Asterisk, for amplification, see Appendix 2. Can you imagine this? This is the world's third most well known psychiatrist at that time. There was Dr. Freud, Dr. Adler and Dr. Jung. Rowland goes to Dr. Jung and is treated for a year. Goes out and gets drunk and comes back, begs the doctor to tell him the whole truth. He has the humility to say "Rowland, I've done all I can do for you. With my knowledge of the mind and my skills I just can't help you anymore. You're probably going to die from alcoholism." And then he could have said, "Rowland I think you're suffering from a bad Valium deficiency. Let me write you a prescription. You come back for another year." He was a good enough man not to do that. And Rowland said, "Are there no exceptions to this?" And this guy was great enough to go out of his field and say "Oh ya, ya, ya. Once in a while I've seen people like you have a vital spiritual experience. He said "I don't understand it. It's phenomena to me but I have seen it happen."

Now they tell us that Rowland tried to get to Freud first. And Freud wasn't taking any more patients. He tried to get to Adler and Adler was too busy. Jung was the third choice. Now Adler and Jung were both students of Freud. And Jung had fallen out with Adler and Jung (Freud) on one thing only. Adler and Jung (Freud) thought all answers would lie within the mind. I mean Adler and Freud. Jung thought some people might be able to be helped through spirituality. And thank God that Rowland didn't get to Freud or Adler. We'd be sitting around today psychoanalyzing ourselves rather than depending upon spirituality. And unfortunately that's what we are doing in a lot of our AA meetings. Trying to psychoanalyze rather than depend upon spirituality. And what blows my mind to think is this. We alcoholics who are so proud of our 12 steps, and rightfully we should be, I think we need to stop once in a while and remember where they came from.

- Step 1 came from a nonalcoholic neurologist in New York City named Dr. Silkworth
- Step 2 came from a nonalcoholic psychiatrist from the other side of the world named Dr. Jung
- The last ten steps came from a group of people called the Oxford groupers who were nonalcoholic practicing first century Christianity to the best of their ability.

Everything that you and I use for recovery came to us from nonalcoholics. I think we need to remember that. It might be good for our humility to do so. Joe.

Is that odd or is that God?

You know I think about Dr. Silkworth. He knew what the problem was. He observed that through working with 50,000 of us alcoholics and it became his opinion. But he didn't have a solution for it. Dr. Jung had a solution for alcoholism, the vital spiritual experience, but he didn't know what the problem was. The Oxford Group had some tenets that we could work. They had the planned program of action, so to speak, but they weren't involved in the problem nor the solution, either one. And here's a wholesale miracle that has happened from that moment until this, if you will. Prior to this he said

Big Book p. 27, par 4   Exceptions to cases such as yours have been occurring since early times. Here and there, once in a while, alcoholics have had what are called vital spiritual experiences. To me these occurrences are phenomena.

J & C   He went back and joined the Oxford Group and took the planned program of action and the tenets of the Oxford Group and he recovered and he was able to help Ebby and Ebby brought this to Bill. And Bill was over there getting all this other information gelled in the mind of Bill Wilson. One person. But the miracle is this. Back in those days it was just here and there, once in a great while. Today we can look around these rooms with each other and say to each other, here and now every time an alcoholic will apply these things to their life they too can recover and they call it Alcoholics Anonymous. A wholesale miracle has happened. I am not the miracle. The miracle is Alcoholics Anonymous. And I get to participate in it.

And I'll go see Bill now as he finishes up with Chapter 2. Probably sitting down and reviewing what he's told us up to this point. Saying to himself that in the Doctor's Opinion and my story I was able to show them the problem. In Chapter 2 I was able to show them the solution. Now let's look at a little picture for just a moment illustrating the solution before we go any further.

WHAT IS THE SOLUTION?

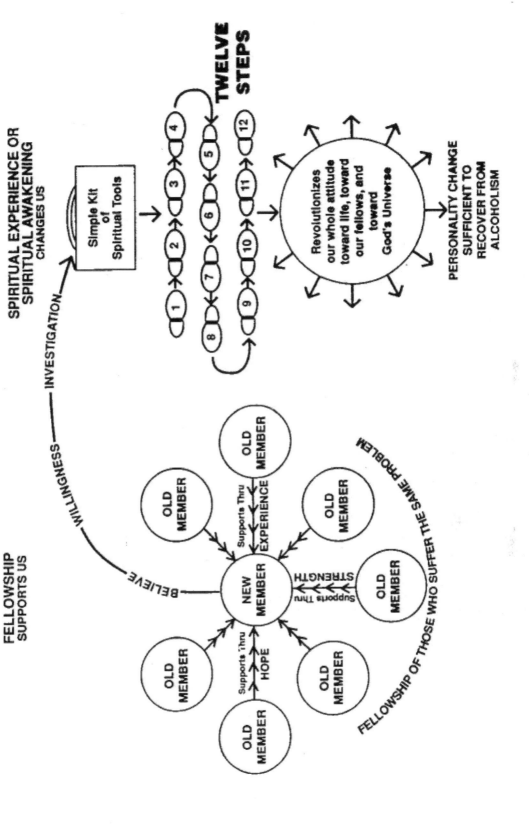

And that little picture we have up here on the screen talking about what is the solution. And on the left-hand side of the picture we see the fellowship, which supports us. Where the older members through the sharing of their experience, strength and hope with the newcomer, provides enough support for the newcomer to be able to stay sober for a period of time. And by the way it's a two way street. As we older members support the new member, then we draw strength from that too. Great strength in the fellowship. It would be almost impossible to be in AA today for very long and not begin to believe that there is some power greater than human power working within this thing. When you hear countless hundreds of people saying

- "it's only by the grace of God" or
- "because of God as I understand him" or
- "because of the power greater than I am I haven't found it necessary to take a drink in" x number of days, weeks, months, years or whatever.

You can hardly hear that over and over and over and not begin to believe there is some power working within this thing. The instant the newcomer begins to believe that, that opens the mind, and they become willing to investigate. And upon investigation we find that simple kit of spiritual tools laid at our feet, the 12 Steps of Alcoholics Anonymous. As we work and apply those steps in our lives we undergo a personality change sufficient to recover from alcoholism. And we find a power greater than human power. When that happens to us, we then have become older members of Alcoholics Anonymous. Now we can go back to the left-hand side of the sheet. And we can help support the next newcomer, help them work their program, so they can have a spiritual experience also. The book plainly states that you can not give something away that you haven't got. Now somewhere down the line when they quit working the program out of the book, then in self-defense they starting measuring success by, how long have you been sober? Rather than by the quality of that sobriety. In the beginning everybody was expected to work the program, have a spiritual experience. If they didn't want to do that they were told you might as well leave here cause we can't help you if you don't to that. So our older membership was based on

quality of sobriety rather than **quantity of sobriety**

Now today you see all kinds of people in AA. You see somebody that has been in here maybe 6 months. They've got a good sponsor. They got immediately into the program. They've worked the steps, they've had a spiritual awakening, and they're always laughing, cutting up, having fun, always helping AA and doing what they can for other alcoholics. They are a delight to beyond and you just love to be around them. Only been sober 6 months. You've got others that have been in the 6-8-10 years. Treated it like a cafeteria. Took some but left what they didn't want. Now they're better than they used to be. But you never know what kind of shape they're going to be in when you run into them. One day they're up, the next day they're down. They're kind of like a yo-yo going back and forth. Then you see some people that have been in here 15-16-18-20 years. Never worked a step, damn proud of it. And they're the ones that say, "By God if you want what we've got and you are willing to go to any damn lengths to get it". Now some of those guys feel so bad you'd like to buy them a drink. You know they would feel better with a drink see.

So we are not talking about quantity of sobriety here. We're talking about quality of sobriety. And only those that have had the spiritual experience can help another have a spiritual experience. You simply can't give away something you don't have.

J & C   I see Bill running this all through his mind. And he probably says to himself, "They're not going to like this idea of a spiritual experience any more than I did." You remember he had an aversion to these things. He and Ebby argued about this for a long time. And I think Bill says **"I need to tell them just exactly what's going to happen to them if they don't have this spiritual experience**." And he writes another chapter and he called it More About Alcoholism. And in this chapter he talks about one thing and one thing only. He talks about **the insanity of alcoholism.**

You know, **Step 2 says "We came to believe that a power greater that ourselves could restore us to sanity."** Well if we've got to be restored to sanity, that indicates we must be insane. And many alcoholics are highly offended when you bring this up. They say "Oh don't tell me I'm insane. Yah I do some pretty crazy stupid things when drinking but when I'm sober I'm much like normal people." Other alcoholics say "Well I don't have any trouble with this insanity because I remember the crazy stupid things I did while drinking." In either case they are referring to **the stupid things we do while drunk. No, that's not insanity**. The stupid things we do while drunk, that's caused by a mind that is filled with alcohol which lowers the inhibitions. And if your mind is filled with something that lowers your inhibitions, look out, you're going to do some pretty crazy stupid things all right. That's why they give all that free booze downstairs (casino). That's not insanity, that's caused by alcohol itself. In order for us to understand this we finally had to go back to the dictionary again and to look up the word sanity or the word sane. And it's defined in the dictionary as

    Sanity - wholeness of mind or completeness of mind

If your mind is whole, if your mind is complete, that means you can see the truth about everything around you. You'll normally make decisions then based on truth and life turns out to be pretty good.

An insane mind is one that is less than whole. A mind that is less than whole cannot always see the truth about everything around it. Sometimes it makes a decision based upon a lie and then life becomes pretty lousy.

To be insane does not mean you're crazy. If you're crazy that means you've lost more than half your marbles. And you've got to be locked up somewhere to protect you and society from you. That's craziness. But insanity is just less than whole.
I think one of the best ways I know to illustrate it is to just…let's take a pie and set it here in front of us. Let's cut that pie into ten pieces. You come along and I give you a piece of pie. My pie is now less than whole but hell I've still got 90% of it. Somebody else comes along and I give them a piece of pie. My pie is now more less than whole but I've still got 80% of it.
Insanity does not mean you're all gone. It just means your not quite all here.

And when it comes to alcohol from time to time is seems as though we're not quite all here, **cause we can't always see the truth about alcohol.**

**We make a decision based upon a lie,
then we run into the truth and
life becomes an absolute living hell**.

So let's look within the mind of we alcoholics just before we take the first drink. Stone cold sober. **Can we or can we not see the truth. If we can see the truth, we're sane. If we can't, we're insane.**
Now Bill is going to show us this by a series of examples. He's going to give us the man of 30. He's going to look at Jim. He's going to look at the jaywalker. And he's going to look at Fred. And each time we're going to look into the mind to see if we can or cannot see the truth about alcohol. Let's look at it just a few minutes.
This chapter is called More About Alcoholism. It could be called More Truth About Alcoholism. I've heard all my life, **if you know the truth, the truth will set you free. And if you're not free it's because you don't know the truth.** And **this chapter here should give me more truth so I can base my life upon truth rather than upon things that are not true.**

Big Book p. 30, par 1   *"Most of us have been unwilling to admit we were real alcoholics. No person likes to think he is bodily and mentally different from his fellows. Therefore, it is not surprising that our drinking careers have been characterized by countless vain attempts to prove we could drink like other people. The idea that somehow, someday he will control and enjoy his drinking is the great obsession of every abnormal drinker. The persistence of this illusion is astonishing. Many pursue it into the gates of insanity or death. We learned that we had to fully concede to our innermost selves that we were alcoholics. This is the first step in recovery. The delusion that we are like other people, or presently may be, has to be smashed."*

J & C   Now be careful. In these two paragraphs that Joe just read, he has used four different words that all mean the same thing. And if you catch him at it, you know what he's doing. If you don't you'll think that he's talking about something else.
He said, "The idea that somehow, someday he will control and enjoy his drinking is the great obsession of every abnormal drinker." Now we know

an obsession is an idea that is so strong it can make you believe something that's not true. It can make you believe a lie.

The persistence of this illusion is astonishing. We know what an illusionist is. An illusionist is a magician. And they can stand in front of you and with slight of hand and a few props they can make you believe something that is not true. So

an illusion also means to believe something that is not true or to believe a lie.

Many pursue it into the gates of insanity or death. Insanity is to believe something that is not true.
In the next paragraph he said, "The delusion that we are like other people, or presently may be, has to be smashed.**"** Delusion means the same thing.

If you've deluded yourself, it means you've come to believe something that is not true.

So you may see him using any one of four terms.

- **Obsession**
- **Illusion**
- **Delusion**
- **Insanity**

All four mean exactly the same thing. **To believe something that is not true, or to believe a lie.**

Let's go over to page 32, second paragraph. Let's look at the lie the man of 30 believed.

Big Book p. 32, par 2   *"A man of thirty was doing a great deal of spree drinking. He was very nervous in the morning after these bouts and quieted himself with more liquor. He was ambitious to succeed in business, but saw that he would get nowhere if he drank at all. Once he started, he had no control whatever. He made up his mind that until he had been successful in business and had retired, he would not touch another drop. An exceptional man, he remained bone dry for twenty-five years and retired at the age of fifty-five, after a successful and happy business career. Then he fell victim to a belief which practically every alcoholic has that his long period of sobriety and self-discipline had qualified him to drink as other men. Out came his carpet slippers and a bottle. In two months he was in a hospital, puzzled and humiliated. He tried to regulate his drinking for a little while, making several trips to the hospital meantime. Then, gathering all his forces, he attempted to stop altogether and found he could not. Every means of solving his problem which money could buy was at his disposal. Every attempt failed. Though a robust man at retirement, he went to pieces quickly and was dead within four years.*
This case contains a powerful lesson. Most of us have believed that if we remained sober for a long stretch, we could thereafter drink normally. But here is a man who at fifty-five years found he was just where he had left off at thirty. We have seen the truth demonstrated again and again: "Once an alcoholic, always an alcoholic." Commencing to drink after a period of sobriety, we are in a short time as bad as ever. If we are planning to stop drinking, there must be no reservation of any kind, nor any lurking notion that someday we will be immune to alcohol."

J & C   Now we know the truth to be this. "Once an alcoholic, always an alcoholic."
We've never seen one single case where one of us was able to go back to successful drinking. Now to believe anything different than that is to believe something that is not true, or to believe a lie.

This guy believed that after 25 years of sobriety he could now drink like normal people. Now based upon that belief he took a drink, triggered the allergy, couldn't stop…four years later he's dead. Now is his real problem though the fact that he has a psychical allergy to alcohol or a form of insanity that tells him it's OK to drink alcohol after 25 years of sobriety?

The real problem centers in our mind telling us we can drink rather than in our body that ensures that we can't drink.

Big Book p. 34, par 2   *"For those who are unable to drink moderately the question is how to stop altogether. We are assuming, of course, that the reader desires to stop. Whether such a person can quit upon a non-spiritual basis depends upon the extent to which he has already lost the power to choose whether he will drink or not. Many of us felt that we had plenty of character. There was a tremendous urge to cease forever. Yet we found it impossible. This is the baffling feature of alcoholism, as we know it this utter inability to leave it alone, no matter how great the necessity or the wish.*
How then shall we help our readers determine, to their own satisfaction, whether they are one of us? The experiment of quitting for a period of time will be helpful, but we think we can render an even greater service to alcoholic sufferers and perhaps to the medical fraternity. So we shall describe some of the mental states that precede a relapse into drinking, for obviously this is the crux of the problem.
What sort of thinking dominates an alcoholic who repeats time after time the desperate experiment of the first drink? Friends who have reasoned with him after a spree which has brought him to the point of divorce or bankruptcy are mystified when he walks directly into a saloon. Why does he? Of what is he thinking?
Our first example is a friend we shall call Jim."

J & C   Now we're going to look in old Jim's mind just before he gets drunk. And we're going to see whether he is sane or insane. Joe loves Jim. Yah I loves old Jim. I identify with Jim.

Big Book p. 35, par 2   *"Our first example is a friend we shall call Jim. This man has a charming wife and family. He inherited a lucrative automobile agency. He had a commendable World War record. He is a good salesman. Everybody likes him.*

J & C   Typical alcoholic isn't he?

Big Book p. 35, par 2 cont. "He is an intelligent man, normal so far as we can see, except for a nervous disposition. He did no drinking until he was thirty-five. In a few years he became so violent when intoxicated that he had to be committed. On leaving the (treatment..) asylum he came into contact with us. We told him what we knew of alcoholism ..."

J & C They told him about **Step 1. The physical allergy, the obsession of the mind, the powerless condition.**

Big Book p. 35, par 3 cont. "... and the answer we had found."

J & C They told him about **Step 2. The power greater than ourselves could restore us to sanity**.

Big Book p. 35, par 3 cont. "He made a beginning."

J & C Step…a little later on the book says, **Step 3 is just a beginning**. So apparently Jim took steps 1,2 and 3 and immediately things started to get better for him.

Big Book p. 35, par 3 cont. "His family was re-assembled, and he began to work as a salesman for the business he had lost through drinking. All went well for a time, but * **he failed to enlarge his spiritual life**." *

J & C The book is going to tell us that **the only way we enlarge on Step 3 is 4-5-6-7-8-9-10-11 and 12** and Jim didn't do any of those. 1,2 and 3. (the A.A. waltz)

Big Book p. 35, par 3 cont. "To his consternation, he found himself drunk half a dozen times in rapid succession. On each of these occasions we worked with him, reviewing carefully what had happened."

J & C Ah these were good AA members. Jim got drunk six times in a row. Each time they went over there and worked with him, carefully reviewing what had happened. *You get drunk six times in a row today and they probably won't have anything to do with you.* These were good solid AA members. "

Big Book p. 35, par 3 cont. "He agreed he was a real alcoholic and in a serious condition. Now he knew he faced another trip to the asylum if he kept on. Moreover, he would lose his family for whom he had a deep affection. Yet he got drunk again. We asked him to tell us exactly how it happened."

J & C They're getting a little tired of Jim now. They said, my God Jim this is seven times in a row. Let's don't go through this any more. You sit down here and you tell us exactly how this has happened. On page 36 we're going to see where Jim was sane and then we are going to see where he went insane.

Big Book p. 36, par 1 cont. "This is his story: "I came to work on Tuesday morning."

J & C We read this book for years before we saw this. "I came to work on Tuesday morning." Where was he all day Monday? We alcoholics are bad about Mondays.

Big Book p. 36, par 1 cont. "I remember I felt irritated that I had to be a salesman for a concern I once owned."

J & C Now I don't think that's insanity, that's probably normal thinking. I think any of us that had to be a salesman for a concern we once owned, we'd probably be a little irritated by that fact too. That's normal sane thinking.

Big Book p. 36, par 1 cont. "I had a few words with the boss, but nothing serious."

J & C The boss probably said "Say Jim, by the way, where were you all day yesterday anyhow?" Nothing serious, just enough to irritate him. A little restless, a little irritable a little discontented.

Big Book p. 36, par 1 cont. "Then I decided to drive to the country and see one of my prospects for a car."

J & C   What's more normal than if you're a car salesman, you want to get away from the shop for a while, drive out in the country, see somebody that we already know that we're trying to sell a car to. That would be normal sane thinking for an alcoholic car salesman.

Big Book p. 36, par 1 cont.   "On the way I felt hungry so I stopped at a roadside place where they have a bar. I had no intention of drinking. I just thought I would get a sandwich."

J & C   What's more normal than if you're hungry, to stop in a roadside place to get a sandwich. The fact that they've got a bar there is beside the point. We have no intention of drinking. We're hungry, we're going to get a sandwich. Normal sane thinking for an alcoholic car salesman.

Big Book p. 36, par 1 cont.   "I also had the notion that I might find a customer for a car at this place, which was familiar for I had been going to it for years. I had eaten there many times during the months I was sober."

J & C   We're not going in there to drink. We've eaten there many times during the months we were sober. We're going to go in there, get a sandwich and maybe sell a car while we're in there. Normal sane thinking for an alcoholic car salesman.

Big Book p. 36, par 1 cont.   "I sat down at a table and ordered a sandwich and a glass of milk. Still no thought of drinking."

J & C   What's more normal than to sit down at a table, order a sandwich and a glass of milk? Normal sane thinking for an alcoholic car salesman.

Big Book p. 36, par 1 cont.   I ordered another sandwich and decided to have another glass of milk.

J & C   Now if you're hungry enough there's nothing wrong with two sandwiches and two glasses of milk. Unless you're a member of Overeaters Anonymous, you'd better look at it. But that would be normal sane thinking for an alcoholic car salesman. Two sandwiches, two glasses of milk. Now comes the squiggly writing. That's italic.

Big Book p. 36, par 2   "Suddenly ,...."

J & C   Suddenly, that means right now

Big Book p. 36, par 2   "Suddenly the thought crossed my mind that if I were to put an ounce of whiskey in my milk it couldn't hurt me on a full stomach."

J & C   Now <u>this is absolute insanity isn't it.</u> For this guy to believe that he can take whisky, mix it with milk and take it on a full stomach and it won't hurt him. Now based on the insane idea, he makes a decision and takes some action.

Big Book p. 36, par 2 cont.   "I ordered a whiskey and poured it into the milk. I vaguely sensed I was not being any too smart, but I felt reassured as I was taking the whiskey on a full stomach".

J & C   Now we've got it inside of ourselves. The physical allergy takes over. Now then we can't stop.

Big Book p. 36, par 2 cont.   "The experiment went so well that I ordered another whiskey and poured it into more milk. That didn't seem to bother me so I tried another."

J & C   Can you imagine how he's going to feel with whiskey and milk back and forth? What a hangover he's going to have.

Big Book p. 36, par 3   "Thus started one more journey to the asylum for Jim. Here was the threat of commitment, the loss of family and position, to say nothing of that intense mental and physical suffering which drinking always caused him. He had much knowledge about himself as an alcoholic. Yet all reasons for not drinking were easily pushed aside in favor of the foolish idea that he could take whiskey if only he mixed it with milk!
Whatever the precise definition of the word may be, we call this plain insanity. How can such a lack of proportion, of the ability to think straight, be called anything else?"

J & C   And if you were looking for a definition of insanity that would be it right there. **The lack of proportion, of the ability to think straight to be called anything else?**

Now is Jim's real problem the fact that he has physical allergy to alcohol?   Or that he has a form of insanity that tells him it's OK to drink alcohol mixed with milk on a full stomach?
The real problem centers in the mind telling us we can drink rather than the body that ensures that we can't.

Big Book p. 37, par. 4   "*Our behavior is as absurd and incomprehensible with respect to the first drink as that of an individual with a passion, say, for jaywalking. He gets a thrill out of skipping in front of fast-moving vehicles.*"

J & C   Now I don't understand this guy at all. But I can see him out here on the interstate, waiting for a truck or bus to come down through there. Jumps out in front of it, spins around two or three times. Sees how close it can come to him without actually hitting him. For some reason he gets a thrill out of it. Don't understand him but I can see him doing it.

Big Book p. 37, par. 4 cont.   "*He enjoys himself a few years in spite of friendly warnings.*"

J & C   People say, "Hey Bill, you better quit doing that. You're going to get yourself hurt."

Big Book p. 37, par. 4 cont.   "*Up to this point you would label him as a foolish chap having queer ideas of fun. Luck then deserts him and he is slightly injured several times in succession.*"

J & C   He's getting a little older now. He can't move as fast. They begin to hit him once in a while. Nothing serious, he just kind of bounces off of them.

Big Book p. 38 cont.   "*You would expect him, if he were normal, to cut it out. Presently he is hit again and this time has a fractured skull.*"

J & C   Now he got hurt bad this time.

Big Book p. 38 cont.   "*Within a week after leaving the hospital a fast-moving trolley car breaks his arm.*"

J & C   He gets hurt bad again. Now he sings our national anthem.

Big Book p. 38 cont.   "*He tells you he has decided to stop jaywalking for good,*"

J & C   He says "Man I'll never do that again as long as I live"

Big Book p. 38 cont.   "*but in a few weeks he breaks both legs.*
On through the years this conduct continues, accompanied by his continual promises to be careful or to keep off the streets altogether. Finally, he can no longer work,"

J & C   He's just so beat up now he can't hold a job.

Big Book p. 38, par 1 cont.   "*his wife gets a divorce,*"

J & C   She's tired of supporting him, the kids and the hospital bills.

Big Book p. 38, par 1 cont.   "*he is held up to ridicule. He tries every known means to get the jaywalking idea out of his head.*"

J & C   Not his body, his head.

Big Book p. 38, par 1 cont.   "*He shuts himself up in a treatment centre (an asylum), hoping to mend his ways. But the day he comes out he races in front of a fire engine, which breaks his back. Such a man would be crazy, wouldn't he?*

You may think our illustration is too ridiculous. But is it? We, who have been through the wringer, have to admit if we substituted alcoholism for jaywalking, the illustration would fit us exactly. However intelligent we may have been in other respects, where alcohol has been involved, we have been strangely insane. It's strong language--but isn't it true?"

J & C   Oh I think that's so appropriate today. You know, once again because of education many, many people are getting to us before they have to lose everything. Occasionally you see somebody come in here that's still married. And once in a while they come in and they've got a job. Believe it or not, I saw one come in about a month ago he still had an automobile. And we start talking to those people about insanity and they say "Man don't tell me I'm crazy. I haven't lost anything. I've got my job, I've got my blah blah". No, uh-uh. We're not talking about that at all. We're talking about one thing and one thing only.

Can we or can we not see the truth about alcohol. If we can we're sane, if we can't then we're insane.

Now the low bottom drunk like Jim, it's probably easier for him to see his insanity because he lost everything that he had period. A high bottom drunk who hasn't lost a lot of stuff, sometimes it's a little more difficult for them to see it. But I'll tell you, **whether you're low bottom or high bottom, if you get drunk, you're going to get drunk the same way. Believing something that is not true**.

Let's go to page, whatever the next one is, 39. My old pages are so tore up I can't read it anymore. Now we're going to look at a guy named Fred. Now Fred is the opposite of Jim. Fred is high bottom. Fred never lost anything. Jim didn't feel too good the day he got drunk. Fred is on top of the world the day he gets drunk, yet he got drunk the same way. He believed a lie. Let's look at Fred's lie.

Big Book p. 39, par 2   *"Fred is partner in a well-known accounting firm. His income is good, he has a fine home, is happily married and the father of promising children of college age. He is so attractive a personality that he makes friends with everyone. If ever there was a successful businessman, it is Fred. To all appearance he is a stable, well-balanced individual. Yet, he is alcoholic. We first saw Fred about a year ago in a hospital where he had gone to recover from a bad case of jitters. It was his first experience of this kind, and he was much ashamed of it. Far from admitting he was an alcoholic, he told himself he came to the hospital to rest his nerves."*

J & C   We see lots of nerve resters in AA today. Just like old Fred is.

Big Book p. 39, par 2 cont.   *"The doctor intimated strongly that he might be worse than he realized. For a few days he was depressed about his condition. He made up his mind to quit drinking altogether. It never occurred to him that perhaps he could not do so, in spite of his character and standing. Fred would not believe himself an alcoholic,"*

J & C   He would not take Step 1.

Big Book p. 39, par 2 cont.   *"much less accept a spiritual remedy for his problem."*

J & C   If you can't take one, you can't take two.

Big Book p. 39, par 2 cont.   *"We told him what we knew about alcoholism."*

J & C   They told him about Step 1 and Step 2.

Big Book p. 40   *"He was interested and conceded that he had some of the symptoms,"*

J & C   He said, "I'm a little bit alcoholic." Borderline case.

Big Book p. 40   *"but he was a long way from admitting that he could do nothing about it himself. He was positive that this humiliating experience, plus the knowledge he had acquired, would keep him sober the rest of his life. Self-knowledge would fix it. We heard no more of Fred for a while. One day we were told that he was back in the hospital. This time he was quite shaky. He soon indicated he was anxious to see us. The story he told is most instructive for here was a chap absolutely convinced he had to stop drinking, who had no excuse for drinking, who exhibited splendid judgement and determination in all his other concerns, yet was flat on his back nevertheless.*

Let him tell you about it: "I was much impressed with what you fellows said about alcoholism, but I frankly did not believe it would be possible for me to drink again. I somewhat appreciated your ideas about the subtle insanity which precedes the first drink, but I was confident it could not happen to me after what I had learned. I reasoned I was not so far advanced as most of you fellows, that I had been usually successful in licking my other personal problems, that I would therefore be successful where you men failed. I felt I had every right to be self-confident, that it would be only a matter of exercising my will power and keeping on guard.
"In this frame of mind, I went about my business and for a time all was well. I had no trouble refusing drinks, and began to wonder if I had not been making too hard work of a simple matter."

J & C   We think Fred began to get drunk right here. He began to say "Ah this staying sober is easy. Nothing to this"

Big Book p. 40, par 3 cont.   "One day I went to Washington to present some accounting evidence to a government bureau. I had been out of town before during this particular dry spell, so there was nothing new about that. Physically, I felt fine. Neither did I have any pressing problems or worries. My business came off well, I was pleased and knew my partners would be too. It was the end of a perfect day, not a cloud on the horizon."

J & C   Everything is on top of the world for old Fred. He's doing great. Making lot's of money. Family's happy. Business associates happy. Everything's good in Fred's life.

Big Book p. 41, par 1   "I went to my hotel and leisurely dressed for dinner. As I crossed the threshold of the dining room, the thought came to mind it would be nice to have couple of cocktails (and go back to the hospital)"

J & C   Now that's the truth isn't it. No way could he drink on the truth. His mind said

Big Book p. 41, par 1 cont.   "it would be nice to have couple of cocktails with dinner. That was all. Nothing more."

J & C   Now based on the insane idea, he makes a decision, takes some action.

Big Book p. 41, par 1 cont.   "I ordered a cocktail and my meal. Then I ordered another cocktail."

J & C   And we've got it inside ourselves now. The allergy takes over.

Big Book p. 41, par 1 cont.   "After dinner I decided to take a walk. When I returned to the hotel it struck me a highball would be fine before going to bed, so I stepped into the bar and had one. I remember having several more that night and plenty next morning. I have a shadowy recollection of being in an airplane bound for New York, of finding a friendly taxicab driver at the landing field instead of my wife. The driver escorted me about for several days. I know little of where I went, or what I said and did. Then came the hospital with unbearable mental and physical suffering.
"As soon as I regained my ability to think, I went carefully over that evening in Washington. Not only had I been off guard, I had made no fight whatever against that first drink. This time I had not thought of the consequences at all. I had commenced to drink as carelessly as though the cocktails were ginger ale."

J & C   Now is Fred's real problem the fact that he has a physical allergy to alcohol or that he has a form of insanity that tells him it's OK to have a couple of cocktails with dinner. **The real problem centres in the mind telling us we can drink, rather than in the body, that ensures we can't.** Page 43, last paragraph.

You know Bill had the idea that self-knowledge would fix it. Rowland had the idea that self-knowledge would fix it. Fred had the idea that self-knowledge would fix it. Bill is trying to show us here, they all had the obsession of the mind. He's trying to show us here through the illustrations, the man of 30, Jim, the jaywalker and Fred, to tell us one thing. The last paragraph says, Once more. You see he just went through all this to say

Big Book p. 43, par 3   "Once more: the alcoholic at certain times has no effective mental defense against the first drink. Except in a few rare cases, neither he nor any other human being can provide such a defense. His defense must come from a Higher Power."

J & C   And that is the solution.
- You can't heal a sick mind with a sick mind.
- Self-knowledge won't get it.

- The more we try to think our way out it, the deeper into it we get.
- It must come from a Higher Power.
- Our defense must come from a Higher Power.

And you notice he didn't say "the practicing alcoholic" or "the drinking alcoholic". He just said the alcoholic. Now what that means to me today is that I have no effective mental defense against the first drink. **Left on my own resources, invariably I'm going to go right back to drinking again, without the aid of a power greater than human power.**

J & C   Now if you're the kind of alcoholic that I am, and if you were raised in the kind of church setting that I was raised in, by the end of Chapter 3 you are now faced with one hell of a dilemma. Because he's convinced me in Chapter 3, without the aid of a power greater than I am, I'm going back to drinking. But I also felt that even though that was true, it would be, it wouldn't be possible for me to get the aid of a power greater than I am.

Because you see, like Joe, I was raised in a good old southern Baptist church. Now I've got nothing against the good old southern Baptist church, it's a great church. But when I was a kid growing up, I'm sure that from time to time they talked about a kind and a loving God. But if they did, the message never got to the pew I sat in. Cause all I ever remember hearing about God when I was growing up in church was hellfire and brimstone and going to hell for lying and cheating and stealing and drinking whiskey and committing adultery. By the time I got to AA I had being doing that for about 20 some odd years. I knew that God had already told St. Peter, "When that little four eyed sucker gets up here send him downstairs. We'll not need his kind." And I knew that if God had anything to do with me it wouldn't be anything good. It would certainly be something bad.

I remember so clearly when I separated from God. In that Baptist church I grew up in, they gave me the rules. They said if you do this, this and this you'll be OK. If you that, that and that you're going to hell just as sure as anything. Now I didn't have any trouble with the rules at all, until I got to be about 12 or 13 years old. And one day it seemed to me that the preacher looked me straight in the eye and he said "Son, to think about doing it is just as bad as doing it". And I said, "Oh shit". I've had it now because I'd been thinking about doing it for a long time. In fact I'd been thinking about doing it long enough I was starting to get brain damage from it. And I said "If you're going to hell for thinking about it then you might as well just go ahead and do it". And I did. And I didn't go to hell immediately. And I said "That sucker has been lying to me all along". I said, he and my parents and my teachers have formed together in a conspiracy to keep me from having any fun. And I said, from this day on I do not intend to pay any attention to what they have to say. I don't have any intention of following God's rules, their rules or anybody else's rules. From this day on I'm going to do it my way. And I'm going to do it whenever I want to and if they don't like it, to hell with them.

Now when I got to AA, I had that attitude of a 12-year-old boy who had defied God, his parents and his teachers. When I first walked into AA I was 38 years old with the spiritual knowledge of God of that 12 year old boy. No wonder we have trouble with this God thing when we get to AA. Anybody else ever have those kinds of feelings about God and people?

And I think Bill recognized that. And I think he said, "Sooner or later I'm going to have to ask these people to make a decision about God". And I think he said in his mind that they're not going to be able to make that decision based upon old ideas. And that's what I had when I got here, old ideas. And I think he said, "I believe I need to give them some new information about God". Where they might be able to discard some old ideas, pick up some new ideas, and then they'll be able to make a decision about this God thing.

And he wrote another Chapter called, **We Agnostics**, which I think is one of the greatest pieces of spiritual information I've ever read in my life. As I read that and studied that I could see where some of my old ideas, old prejudices, about God and religion, were wrong. And when I could see where they were wrong then I could discard them, and then I could accept some new ideas about God and then I could make a decision. Now based on hellfire and brimstone, based on a God of justice, no way could I have ever made the decision about God. Thank God for Chapter 4. Let's look at just a little bit of it just before we go to lunch.

Dr. Jung told Rowland about ideas, emotions and attitudes. That's what we're going to be looking at now. Ideas, emotions and attitudes, which were the guiding force of the lives of these people, are suddenly cast to one side. And certainly the ideas, emotions and attitudes that I had toward God were that of a 7 or 8 year old boy. I couldn't accept it then, I couldn't accept it later, I couldn't accept it when I got here and I can't accept it today because I need new ideas and emotions and attitudes about this. New information is what I'm trying to say.

This chapter We Agnostic, just the word agnostic means something to me.

nostic means knowledge
put the ag in front of it, it means without.
Those of us who are without knowledge.

And that was me. And the knowledge that I did have was not good. And Bill had the same experiences that we did. When Ebby presented him with the solution he was aghast at that solution. Some of us are aghast at that solution also. And Bill said "When they talked of a God personal to me my mind became irritated and my mind snapped shut against such theories." And certainly that's the way that I did. Later on in the book it says to us that when the spiritual malady is overcome we straighten out mentally and physically, the spiritual malady.

The understanding of God of my understanding.

When that is straightened out we will straighten out mentally and physically. And this chapter here, We Agnostic, is an attempt to do that.

And as Father Bill Wilson, some of you know Father Bill said to us many, many times, and I love it, he said that this chapter is not put here to teach me that there is any particular type of religion or type of God. He said this chapter is simply put here so that I might read, question and wonder and get some ideas, emotions and attitudes, some new ones. And open up my mind to the point that God might prove to me there is a God. Now with that understanding of this chapter, it makes more sense to me and becomes extremely valuable in my life.

Big Book p. 44, par. 1   *In the preceding chapters, you have learned something of alcoholism. We hope we have made clear the distinction between the alcoholic and the non-alcoholic. If, when you honestly want to, you find you cannot quit entirely,*

J & C   because of the obsession

Big Book p. 44, par. 1 cont.   *or if, when drinking, you have little control over the amount you take,*

J & C   because of the allergy

Big Book p. 44, par. 1 cont.   *you are probably alcoholic.*

J & C   God isn't that simple? Isn't that simple?

You see how people like to expand on things. They took the 2 questions out of the big book and some years later they made a little pamphlet that had 10 questions in it. And that wasn't enough, they made another one that had 20 questions in it. Hell I think we're up to 44 today aren't we? Thank God that Ebby didn't have the 44 questions with him when he walked into Bill's kitchen. He'd have said "Bill, has alcohol been bothering your reputation?" Hadn't had a reputation in years. Then he would have said, "Bill has alcohol been interfering with your sex life". If he was anything like I was he wouldn't have had any of that in a long time either. There's a statement in the 44 questions says "Do you drink alone?" Well think about it. If I'm buying yes, and if you're buying, no.

We had an old friend that used to live in Tyler, Texas. His name was Wino Joe. I've always felt sorry for everybody in AA that didn't get to meet Wino Joe. He was a real character. He's dead now. But Wino Joe had made up his own list to ask yourself to see if you're alcoholic. And the first question on his list was "Has the roof of your mouth ever been sunburned while drinking?"

He said, "If it has, you're probably alcoholic." I think the second question was "Have you ever been arrested for drunk driving from the back seat of somebody else's car?" The third one I loved was "Have you ever been arrested for public drunk while in jail?" He had a real list of them.

We only need these two. I use them all the time.

End of Tape 3

J & C   People come to me today and say "Charlie do you think I might be alcoholic?" I say, " I have no idea. Let me ask you a couple of questions.**"** Have you been able to quit drinking entirely left on your own resources? If they are a real alcoholic, they've got to so no. And then I say, "Do you have any control over the amount you take after you've once started drinking?" If they are a real alcoholic, they've got to so no. And then I say, "Well you're probably an alcoholic". That's about as simple as you can make it. Now if that be the case, you may be suffering from an illness which only a spiritual experience will conquer.

You know we are very unique people. We number amongst **few people in the world today who suffer from a two-fold illness that can only be overcome by a spiritual experience.** We also number amongst a few people in the world today who have a terminal illness that we can come out of it in better shape then we were when we went into it, if we can have this spiritual experience. We are unique people.

Big Book p. 44, par. 2   *"To one who feels he is an atheist or agnostic such an experience seems impossible, but to continue as he is means disaster, especially if he is an alcoholic of the hopeless variety. To be doomed to an alcoholic death "*

J & C   Step 1

Big Book p. 44, par. 2   *"or to live on a spiritual basis "*

J & C   Step 2

Big Book p. 44, par. 2   *"are not always easy alternatives to face.*
But it isn't so difficult. About half our original fellowship were of exactly that type. At first some of us tried to avoid the issue, hoping against hope we were not true alcoholics. But after a while we had to face the fact that we must find a spiritual basis of life or else. Perhaps it is going to be that way with you. But cheer up, something like half of us thought we were atheists or agnostics. Our experience shows that you need not be disconcerted."

J & C   And I had to stop right here. And see what is my belief as far as this God thing is concerned? And today we find there is only one of three ways that you can believe as far as God is concerned.

One way is to be an atheist. Now an atheist says, "There is no God". Therefore they have no power greater than human power to turn to. The atheist would have to stand on their own two feet, run their own show. And I said "Charlie, are you an atheist?" I said "No". I've always believed in some kind of God, so I'm not an atheist.

I said, "Well then maybe you're an agnostic". So I had to go to the dictionary and look that word up. And like Joe said the word **agnostic means without knowledge**
An agnostic believes that there is a God. But since we've never tried to use Gods power in our life, we've run our own show, stood on our two feet, we've never received God's power so we don't know that God exists. We believe in some kind of God but we don't really know whether that's true or not.

And I think that's what most of us are when we get here. Most of us get here with some belief in a God, but we have never turned to that God and we've been running our own show and standing on our own two feet and doing our own thing. Even though we believed in God, we acted as if we did not believe in Him. An agnostic is one without knowledge of God, just belief.

Now if you're an atheist or an agnostic, then the question becomes **"How do you become a true believer in God?"**
A true believer is one that knows that God exists, don't believe it, knows it.
A true believer is one who has experienced God's power in their life and God has given them whatever they need to have a successful life.

I don't think any of us get here as a true believer. Cause if we knew God and experienced God's power, then we wouldn't have to come to AA to solve our problem. Most of us come here as agnostics.
Now whether we be atheist or agnostic, the question becomes **how do you get from that stage to the stage of one who is a true believer and can receive Gods power in our life.**

Big Book p. 45, par. 1   *"Lack of power, that was our dilemma. "*

J & C   You know if we wasn't powerless we wouldn't be here would we.

Big Book p. 45, par. 1   *"Lack of power, that was our dilemma. We had to find a power by which we could live, and it had to be a Power greater than ourselves. Obviously. But where and how were we to find this Power?*
Well, that's exactly what this book is about. Its main object is to enable you to find a Power greater than yourself which will solve your problem."

J & C   It doesn't say which will enable you to solve it. Or will help you solve it. It says the main object is to enable you to find the Power greater than yourself and then that power will solve the problem. And I find interestingly enough from page 45 on in the big book Alcoholics Anonymous we don't talk about alcohol anymore. We're through with that. We talk about one thing and one thing only. If you are powerless, whether you be atheist or agnostic, if you are powerless,

How do you find the power? And if you can find the power, then the power will solve the problem.

So right after lunch when we come back we're going to start looking at **How do we find that power?**

Ok we're going to go to page 46, in chapter We Agnostics. And the book says

Big Book p. 46, par 1   *"Yes, we of agnostic temperament have had these thoughts and experiences. Let us make haste to reassure you. We found that as soon as we were able to lay aside prejudice and express even a willingness to believe in a Power greater than ourselves, we commenced to get results, even though it was impossible for any of us to fully define or comprehend that Power, which is God.*
Much to our relief, we discovered we did not need to consider another's conception of God. Our own conception, however inadequate, was sufficient to make the approach and to effect a contact with Him."

J & C   You know my sponsor at the time, George, saw that I had a real problem with this idea about God and he asked me about it. And I said I am I'm having a hard time trying to understand. And he said, well I've noticed that. He said why don't you do something that helped him and maybe it would help me. He said why don't you go home tonight and write down on a piece of paper what you would like God to be laying aside all that stuff that you think that you know and just write down on that piece of paper what you would like God to be. And so I went home that night and I wrote down some things and I'm not going to tell you what it is, it's up to you. And I wrote down some things that I wanted God to be and I showed them to George and he looked at them and he said that's good Joe. You can begin with that. See I didn't know you could do that.

Down in the south you go to hell for making up your own God. It's true. You had to believe as they believed. You had to have faith in what they had faith in. If you didn't you was going to go to hell. But George gave me permission and I needed that permission to sit down and to say that I would like God to be these things. And he said that's good. You can start with that and you can begin with that. And that's exactly what I did. Where it says

Big Book p. 46, par 2   *"Much to our relief, we discovered we did not need to consider another's conception of God. Our own conception, however inadequate, was sufficient to make the approach and to effect a contact with Him."*

J & C   Now here is where we can cast aside the first old idea. The old idea that I had was that you had to believe as they believed. And they had me convinced that if you didn't believe as they believed there is no way that you're going to get anything good when it comes to God. So I was real pleased to find out that I can cast aside that old idea and then I can have my own conception of God. And like we said yesterday or last night that I find I have never had any problem with my own conception of anything. And you let me start believing in God the way I want to then I've got an entirely different idea. An old idea cast aside replaced with a new idea begins right here. And the book says

Big Book p. 46, par 2   *"As soon as we admitted the possible existence of a Creative Intelligence, a Spirit of the Universe underlying the totality of things, we began to be possessed of a new sense of power and direction, provided we took other simple steps. We found that God does not make too hard terms with those who seek Him. To us, the Realm of Spirit is broad, roomy, all inclusive; never exclusive or forbidding to those who earnestly seek. It is open, we believe, to all men."*

J & C   See all I had to quit doing was saying no, there is not, no and start seeking saying yes maybe and I started seeking. I said "George you mean I need to find God?" And he said "Joe, God's not lost." Didn't take me long to figure out who was lost. He said it's just like the book says **It's in the seeking it's not in the finding.**

All I had to do was seek. And you know, that's all this book is asking me to do and this chapter is asking me to seek with an open mind and to wonder and to think and eventually God will disclose himself to me. And that's exactly what's happened.

I was taught as a kid growing up that the way to God was a very narrow path, that if you strayed off either side of it you were going to get in to a hell of a shape. I was taught that God was very, very exclusive. That only those that believed, as they believed, would be able to make any contact with God. Those were old ideas. Now my book says

Big Book p. 46, par 2, cont. *"We found that God does not make too hard terms with those who seek Him. To us, the Realm of Spirit is broad, roomy, all inclusive; never exclusive or forbidding to those who earnestly seek. "*

Old ideas cast aside replaced with some new ideas. Beginning to find this power greater than human power by changing of the old ideas to new ideas.

Big Book p. 47, par 1 *"When, therefore, we speak to you of God, we mean your own conception of God. This applies, too, to other spiritual expressions which you find in this book. Do not let any prejudice you may have against spiritual terms deter you from honestly asking yourself what they mean to you. "*

Prejudice is nothing more than old ideas. Do not let any old ideas you may have against spiritual terms deter you from honestly asking yourself what they mean to you.

Big Book p. 47, par 1, cont. *"At the start, this was all we needed to commence spiritual growth, to effect our first conscious relation with God as we understood Him. Afterward, we found ourselves accepting many things which then seemed entirely out of reach. That was growth, but if we wished to grow we had to begin somewhere. So we used our own conception, however limited it was."*

And that was a beginning for me, I needed a beginning place and that's where I started.

Big Book p. 47, par 2 *"We needed to ask ourselves but one short question. --"Do I now believe, "*

J & C   The agnostic has always believed in some kind of God.

Big Book p. 47, par 2, cont. *"or am I even willing to believe, "*

J & C   The atheist can become willing to believe that there is some kind of God

Big Book p. 47, par 2, cont. *"that there is a Power greater than myself?" As soon as a man can say that he does believe, "*

J & C   The agnostic

Big Book p. 47, par 2, cont. *"or is willing to believe, "*

J & C   The atheist

Big Book p. 47, par 2, cont. *"we emphatically assure him that he is on his way. It has been repeatedly proven among us that upon this simple cornerstone a wonderfully effective spiritual structure can be built.*"*

J & C   Again they want to make real sure that we understand what they mean by those terms.
He says **It has been repeatedly proven among us that upon this simple cornerstone a wonderfully effective spiritual structure can be built.*** So the wonderfully effective spiritual structure we're building is the spiritual experience or the spiritual awakening.

And he said the cornerstone of that is to believe or to be willing to believe that there is power greater that human power. We referred to that once before. The foundation of that structure was step one, which is willingness. Now then he tells us the cornerstone of that structure, step two, believing. So we've already put two stones in place if we can say we're willing and yes we believe or we are willing to believe either one of the two. And he said

Big Book p. 47, par. 3   *"That was great news to us, for we had assumed we could not make use of spiritual principles unless we accepted many things on faith which seemed difficult to believe."*

J & C   And there has always been one of my great problems with this God thing. Faith indicates surety. Faith indicates knowledge. Faith indicates after the fact information.

And one of my problems has always been, the minister would say, "Son all you have to do is have faith and everything will be alright". Well I never could have faith because I had no knowledge of God. I didn't know for sure that God would do anything for me. The best I can possibly do is to start with belief. And there is a big difference between belief and faith, believe me there is.

A good example of that…let's say I moved into this area here and 3 or 4 months later I've got a problem with my automobile. I don't know a good mechanic anywhere in this area. But we'll say that you've lived here for a long time. And I assume you will know somebody so I come to you and I say, "Can you recommend a good mechanic for me?" And you say "Why sure. Take your car over there to John, he'll do you a good job and he'll charge you a reasonable price." Well I don't know whether that's true or not. The best I can do with that information is if I believe it strong enough, I'll take my car over there to John. And sure enough he does a good job; he charges me a reasonable price. When I leave there **I know** that he will do that. When I went there **I believed** that he would do that. Now six months from now I have trouble with my car again. I don't ask you or anybody else where to take it. I take it right back to John. This time I took it on faith took it on knowledge. **You can't start with faith; you can only start with belief.** And that's all we have to do. We either have to believe or we become willing to believe that there is a power greater than we are and we're on the road to spiritual recovery. We don't have to know anything. Thank God step two says we came to believe that a power greater than ourselves could restore us to sanity. Didn't say we came to know. Didn't say we had faith in that, we just came to believe. And I came to believe based upon what I'd read in the book and what you told me. That there is a power greater than I am can restore me to sanity. I didn't know that I just believed that. And if I know that the beginning of this thing, the finding of the power is just to believe, or be willing to believe then the next thing I'm going to have know is what procedure am I going to follow in order to find that power. Let's go over to page 51 for just a moment.

Big Book p. 51, par. 1   *"This world of ours has made more material progress in the last century than in all the millenniums which went before. Almost everyone knows the reason. Students of ancient history tell us that the intellect of men in those days was equal to the best of today. Yet in ancient times, material progress was painfully slow. The spirit of modern scientific inquiry, research and invention was almost unknown. In the realm of the material, men's minds were fettered by superstition, tradition, and all sort of fixed ideas."*

J & C   And I used to wonder why it is that we today have cellular phones and TVs and automobiles and airplanes. Why those people a hundred years ago or two hundred years ago or five hundred years ago didn't have or invent those things. I thought we were just smarter than they were. But I've come to find out that they had the same intellect as we do. Intellect means the capacity to learn. They had the capacity to learn as we do. But the one thing that kept them in those dark ages so to speak it was **superstition, tradition and all sorts of fixed ideas**

That's why I say I need an open mind more today than I've ever needed an open mind and I think we as a society have done that. Right here in the Northeast corner of the United States some 225 years ago or so people came over her for religious freedom. They wanted to practice a religion as they saw as they understood it. And as long as you agreed basically with their religion and you practiced your religion somewhat like they did you were OK. But if you had any thoughts or ideas that were different and you expressed those thoughts and ideas openly and it didn't agree with what they had and what they agreed with they would burn you at the stake as a witch. Right here in America they did that. So if you had any ideas like that you certainly didn't express them, you kept them to yourself.

So superstition, tradition and all sorts of fixed ideas kept people from growing.
And I think we as a country have gotten over that today. Our minds are open to many, many things.

Big Book p. 51, par 1   *"Some of the contemporaries of Columbus thought a round earth preposterous."*

J & C   Now I think Columbus is one of the greatest examples of what you can do based upon belief, if you're willing to change your belief. Some 500 years ago most of what they call the civilized world was situated around the shores of the Mediterranean Sea, the western shores of Europe. They had found a place called the East Indies. And in the East Indies you could get gold, silk, and spices. Lots of goody goodies. But it took literally years to get to the East Indies so they were trying to find a new trade route to the East

Indies. And somebody said. "Is there any possibility that we can sail a ship there?" And they said, "Well, no dummy, don't you know you can only sail to the northeast end of the Mediterranean Sea, and then you have to go by land". Camelback, horseback, footback, however they traveled, and that trip took literally years to do. And they said, "Well what would happen if we sailed in the other direction?" And they said, "Well idiot, don't you know if you sail out there you're going to sail off the edge of this sucker."

You see everybody in those days thought the world was flat and they assumed if you sailed out there you would sail off the edge of it. Well I don't know why they believed that. I assume some people sailed out there, didn't come back, and they thought they had sailed off the edge of it. And Joe said the other day wouldn't it be great if the world was flat. We could take all this environmental junk, just take it out there and go pff, push er overboard and be done with it.

Now here comes Columbus, and we believe that Columbus had to be an alcoholic.
Cause if you're going to believe differently than the world and everybody in it, and you're going to stand there and express that belief, you're going to have to be tougher than hell to do it. Because many times if you express a belief different than what everybody else believes they would burn you at the stake or hang you from a tree, or cut your head off or something. And Columbus was tough enough and bullheaded enough to be able to stand there and he said, "I believe that the world is round, I do not believe it's flat". Then he made one of the most drunk statements the world has ever heard. He said, "I believe we can get east by sailing west". Now if that isn't drunk thinking I don't know what is. Many of his mannerisms indicated he was alcoholic.

When he left he didn't know where he was going.
When he got there he didn't know where he was.
When he got back he didn't even know where he had been.
But what really made him an alcoholic was a woman financed the whole trip for him. She did that twice.

Columbus followed a little formula. You'll want to write down these key words in the formula. He followed a little formula that the world has always known. **That if you want to change anything at all there are certain things that have to take place.**

And the first thing you have to do in order to change anything is to be willing to do so. Circumstances are what make us willing. Trying to find the new trade route to the East Indies is what made him willing to change.

The second thing you have to do to change anything is to believe you can do so. When he said, "I believe that the world is round it is not flat, I believe you can get East by sailing West." But his belief didn't do him any good either, cause he's still standing on the shore of the ocean the day he expressed that belief.

Some days, weeks, months, years later he did **the third thing, he made a decision**. He said by golly I'm going to go find out whether this thing is round or flat, can you really get east by sailing west. But his decision didn't do him any good either, cause he's still standing on the shore of the ocean the day he expressed that decision.

Some days, weeks, months, years later he did **the next thing you have to do, he started taking action**.
And the first thing he did he went to the King of Portugal to get the money. But the King of Portugal being a very astute businessman said, " There's no way I'm going to let you have this money cause you'll sail out there and sail right off the edge of this sucker and I'll lose it all". That's why he ended up with the Queen of Spain. Sweet-talked her out of the money on the promise that he would bring back gold, silk, spices and the goody goodies of life. She gave him the money. He bought three ships. He put provisions in those three ships, he put crewmembers in those three ships, and they began to go east by sailing west. Sailing west, day, after day, after day. Now we don't know for sure, but we have a suspicion that on that first trip he hired a special sailor, put him on the bow of the lead ship at night with a lantern. Whispered in his ear, "I believe this thing is round, but if you see the edge of this damn thing you holler so we can get turned around in time."

Now after having sailed straight west for several days they got results. They found land on the other side, which was the result of the action that they had taken. Now we know that he thought it was the East Indies, it wasn't, it was the West Indies. But he had proven himself the world is not flat, it is round, you will not sail off the edge of it. Turned right around came right back to Europe, went right back to the Queen of Spain. And she said "Columbus, where's the gold, silk and spices you promised you would bring me?" And he said, "Sweetheart I'm sorry but I didn't find any". But he said, "Tell you what I'll do; if you'll refinance me I'll go back. Trust me honey please. And this time I'll find it". And she re-financed him and he got some more ships, more provisions, more crew members and began to go east by sailing west with one big difference. The second trip he didn't hire the special sailor, put him on the bow of the lead ship at night. **This time he went back on faith; he went back on knowledge. The first time he went back on belief.**

You can't start with faith
The only thing you can do is
start with belief   (Step 2)
make the decision (Step 3)
take the action   (Steps 4-11)
get the results and then you'll have faith

I would love to sit here and tell you today that the Twelve Steps of Alcoholics Anonymous are brand new; the world has never seen anything like them before. But if I did I'd tell you a lie. Because they are based on the same identical formula that Columbus and any other human being has ever used to change anything.

The first thing you and I have to do in order to recover from alcoholism is to be willing to change.
And that's what **Step 1** gives us is the willingness.
Whenever we can see that what we're doing is no longer going to work, then we become willing to change.

The second thing we have to do is to **belief we can do so,** and that's **Step 2.**

But that belief will do us no good unless we **make a decision about it.** And that's **Step 3**.

And the decision will do us no good unless we **take the action**. And that's **(Steps) 4, 5, 6, 7, 8, 9, 10 and 11.**

As the result of the action **then we will get results** too.
(1st part of Step 12)
Having had a spiritual awakening **as the result of these steps…**
We now have faith. We now have knowledge. We no longer believe.

You see I don't believe today that God will restore me to sanity, I know that he will, because he has done so.
(2nd part of Step 12)
Now those of us who have been restored to sanity and we have the faith, then we can go back and help

the next newcomer come to **believe**. (Step 2)
they can make a **decision**, (Step 3)
and we can take them by the hand and walk with them through the **action steps**, (Steps 4-11)
then they will get **results**, they will have a spiritual awakening, and then they will know, (1st part Step 12)
and then they can go help the next newcomer come to believe (2nd part Step 12)

Now there's only one thing you and I can't do for the newcomer, **we cannot make them willing**. (Step 1)
That's a job they have to work on themselves.

How does an alcoholic become willing to change?

Very simple, drinking lots of whiskey. I hear people come to AA and they say I've been working on Step 1 for three years in AA and I say no you haven't

You don't work on Step 1 (willingness) in AA   You work on Step 1 out there.
And when you drunk enough of that whiskey, you just can't stand it any longer, then you become willing to change.

Then we can begin to help you by helping you come to believe, decide, act and have a spiritual awakening; same formula that the world has always used to change the status of anything. Now if

I know I need the power, and if
I know the beginning of the finding of the power is just to believe, if
I know the procedure (formula) to follow to find the power, then
I only need to know one more thing,
where am I going to find that power?

And I think we get here just as confused about where God is, as we were ever confused about anything else. As a kid growing up, somewhere I got a picture in my mind. Now I don't know whether I dreamed it or saw it, but in my mind when I was thinking about God, he was a tall elderly gentleman. Stood on a cloud up in the sky. Long flowing white robes on, long white hair, golden halo around his head, and sunrays shooting out of that halo, and a big stick in his right hand. And I don't know whether I saw that or whether I dreamed it, but one of the reasons I thought God was there is because every time the minister talked about God he always pointed up there so I knew he had to be up there somewhere. But then what really confused me, I noticed every time the minister wanted to talk to God, he always looked down here. He points up, hell no wonder we get confused as kids about where God is**.**

And I looked and I looked and I looked and I looked, and I never could find God because I never did know where he was.

And it took the Big Book Alcoholics Anonymous to tell me just exactly where I'm going to find him.
Page 55

Many years ago I was working, not working but involved in a half way house in Tulsa and I was heavily involved and there was this young man there who asked me to be his sponsor and he said well what do you think I ought to do? And I said well it would probably be a good idea if you had a job you know, start somewhere here, and he said easy for you to say I don't have any car and I can't get back and forth with no money, can't even ride the bus. And I said well I'll take you around and help you find a job, and if you find a job I'll take you back and forth till you can get a couple of pay cheques and then you can buy a car or do whatever you need to do. He said fine, so I'm taking him back and forth to work, and one morning he told me a story that really helped me a lot. And this is the way the story goes.

He said there was the three Wiseman of the east, he said and they took from man the crown of life, the thing that would make us the happiest and took it away from them. And they said, "Now we took it away from them, what are we going to do with it?" One of them guys said I'll tell you what we'll do, we'll take it to the highest, highest crevice on the face of the earth in the highest, highest mountain and we'll hide it up there, and they'll never be able to find it. And the other two said yeah, but you know how they are, they'll hunt and they'll search and they'll eventually find it. The third one said I'll tell you what, we'll take it to the deepest, deepest crevice of the deepest ocean and hide it there and they'll never think about looking for it there. He said yeah, but you know how they are, they'll hunt and they'll search and they'll eventually find it. The third one said, I'll tell you what we'll do, we'll hide it within himself, and he'll never think about looking for it there. Page 55, first paragraph

Big Book, p.55, par. 2   *"Actually we were fooling ourselves, for deep down in every man, woman, and child, is the fundamental idea of God. It may be obscured by calamity, by pomp, by worship of other things, but in some form or other it is there. For faith in a power greater than ourselves, and miraculous demonstrations of that power in human lives, are facts as old as man himself.*
We finally saw that faith in some kind of a God was a part of our make-up, just as much as the feeling we have for a friend. Sometimes we had to search fearlessly, but He was there. He was as much a fact as we were. We found the Great Reality deep down within us. In the last analysis it is only there that He may be found. It was so with us.
We can only clear the ground a bit. If our testimony helps sweep away prejudice (closed mind, old ideas), enables you to think honestly, encourages you to search diligently within yourself, then if you wish, you can join us on the Broad Highway. With this attitude you cannot fail. The consciousness of your belief is sure to come to you."

J & C   A God of your own understanding is sure to come to you with an open mind

It seems as though all human beings are born with some basic knowledge, deep down inside themselves, probably lying at a subconscious level. And that basic knowledge seems to be able to tell us what we should do and what we shouldn't do. It seems to be able to tell us how we should live and how we shouldn't live. And I'm sure a lot of people would like to refer to that as just plain old common sense. I think others might want to call it innate intelligence. Some might want to call it the conscious. And others might want to call it the soul. I don't think it makes any difference what we call it, as long as we **recognize the fact that it's there**. If you're anything like I am, as far back as I can remember, I've always been aware of that knowledge. There used to be times that I would be getting ready to do something, and some voice somewhere from within side me would say Charlie, "I don't believe you ought to be doing this. And I wouldn't pay a bit of attention to it, and I'd go right ahead and do it and I'd get in one hell of a mess. And that same little voice would say see, "I told you not to do it in the first place". Now if that's true, and if that's God, then what that means to me today is

if God dwells within me, then I've got my own personal God.

I don't worry anymore about whether he's the God of the Baptist Church or not, I don't worry whether he's the God of the Catholic Church, the Hebrew religion or anybody else's God.

If he dwells within me, then he's my own personal God and
He and I can come together in very simple, in very understandable terms.

This is one of the greatest pieces of information that I have ever learned is

I can have my own God, and he dwells within me, and
my knowledge comes from him and through him I'll be able to find that power.

J & C   Now then am I ready to make a decision? You betcha. When he was the God of justice, when he was hellfire and brimstone, I wasn't ready to make that decision. But throughout this chapter my concept of God has changed entirely and I'm beginning to believe he just might be a kind and loving God. And just maybe he'll start doing some good things for me, not hellfire and brimstone, and now I'm ready to make a decision. And I don't think it's by accident that the very next chapter is entitled How It Works.

You know back on page 45 it said the main object of this book was to enable me to find a power greater than myself which would solve my problem. And Bill's going to sit down here now and he's going to right some of the best spiritual information the worlds every seen a little formula, or proposals he called them, the Twelve Steps of Alcoholics Anonymous. And I can just see Bill with the problem that he has. You know we've got Protestants in AA and we've got Catholics in AA, we've got Jewish people in AA, we got a sprinkling of Muslims in AA, we got some Buddhists come into AA at that time and how are you going to write a set of steps or proposals that's not going to offend these people, quite a chore for a guy like Bill or anybody, to tell you the truth. The Oxford Groups were coming from 1st Century Christianity, they had those 4 absolutes and they were really, really strong. They wouldn't give you any slack at all. They were more interested in the letter of the law rather than the spirit of the law. Bill was interested in the spirit of these things rather than in the letter of them, that's why it's a spiritual program. So Bill had one gigantic problem here try to write these steps in order to in such a manner they wouldn't offend anybody. And he accomplished that through the Twelve Steps of Alcoholics Anonymous

These 4 absolutes that the Oxford Group had said you were to practice absolute love, absolute purity, absolute honesty, absolute unselfishness. And these alcoholics were having a hell of a time being absolute anything except drunks you know. And they said Bill we need to get rid of that kind of stuff. Also they had made their own little steps, six of them which came from the Oxford Group tenets. And Bill could see loopholes in these steps that the alcoholic mind was slipping through and he knew they were going to have to have more strength, and he knew they were going to have to be expanded, but he didn't know how far. And in trying to satisfy that bunch, in trying to satisfy the people from all different religions, and trying to satisfy those that didn't want God in here, Bill had a terrible time with it. By that time AA had really divided into you might say three factions.

In Akron where Dr. Bob was they didn't have any problem with God. Dr. Bob was a highly religious man, he used the bible and he insisted that everybody he worked with use it too. God was no problem there.

But the New York City people were an entirely different breed of cat. They really didn't want anything to do with God if they could avoid it. They would have preferred a book dealing with the mind rather than spirituality period. There was finally a third faction that said, let's talk about God, but let's not talk about him too much, let's come down somewhere in the middle of this thing. So Bill's trying to satisfy them all, and he said he tried, and he tried, and he tried and he tried to get started on Chapter 5. This is going to be the **directions** on how to recover. And he said I simply could not do it. He said one night while in bed leaning with a pillow behind his back leaning against the headboard, pad and pencil in hand trying to start Chapter 5 he said I finally just gave up. He said I put down the pad and the pencil and said I prayed and asked God for help and direction and said I meditated for maybe 10 or 15 minutes and he said after a while I reached over and picked up the pad and the pencil and he said it felt as if the pencil had a mind of its own as it raced across the pages. In less than 30 minutes he had written How It Works. On of the greatest pieces of spiritual information the world has ever seen. After he had written it he went back and numbered these proposals and he found out there was 12. He didn't set out to write 12. He went back and numbered them and there was 12 of them there. Now almost immediately after having done that somebody knocked on the door. One of the guys in the New York City group had one of his sponsees with him, they knew that Bill stayed up late working on the book anyhow so they had come by to see Bill on the way home. Bill could hardly wait to show this to this old older member. Look, look, look, at the new 12 steps, and the older member said what in the hell is this. He said we only had Ten Commandments and now you got twelve. Six has been sufficient until everything up till now. And he said, I don't like it at all, and the fight was on. And they fought and they fought and Lois finally came in and gave them a cup of coffee and settled them down. Then Bill presented this How It Works to the other members and that's when the crap really hit the fan. Cause they began to say to Bill, this sounds too much like the Oxford Group absolutes. You're going to have to get some of that stuff out of there. And they said, Bill you're trying to give directions to people and you don't have the right to tell anybody what they have to do. And Bill this, and Bill that, and Bill this and Bill that. And they almost destroyed, not only the book project, but the little fellowship in its entirety. Now Joe is going to read How It Works from the original manuscript which most of you have probably heard before, and if he reads through there I think you'll be able to see the differences between what Bill wrote that night and what the fellowship forced him to change in order to have what we have today. Let's go through it for just a moment and see the differences.

Can you imagine what kind of fight you would have if you left here today went back to your group and you had 12 steps when you left but now you had 24? They're be a little fightin' going on wouldn't it? That's what Bill was up to. And here's how it works

Chapter 5 - Original Manuscript

"Rarely have we seen a person fail who has thoroughly followed our **DIRECTIONS** (path). Those who do not recover are people who cannot or will not completely give themselves to this simple program, usually men and women who are constitutionally incapable of being honest with themselves. There are such unfortunates. They are not at fault; they seem to have been born that way. They are naturally incapable of grasping and developing a **WAY OF LIFE** (manner of living), which demands rigorous honestly. Their chances are less than average. There are those, too, who suffer from grave emotional and mental disorders, but many of them do recover if they have the capacity to be honest.

Our stories disclose in a general way what we used to be like, what happened, and what we are like now. If you have decided you want what we have and are willing to go to any length to get it--then you are ready to **FOLLOW DIRECTIONS** (take certain steps). At some of these **YOU MAY BALK** (we balked). **YOU MAY THINK YOU CAN** (we thought we could) find an easier, softer way. But **WE DOUBT IF YOU CAN** (we could not). With all the earnestness at our command, we beg of you to be fearless and thorough from the very start. Some of us have tried to hold on to our old ideas and the result was nil until we let go absolutely.

Remember that **YOU ARE DEALING** (we deal) with alcohol--cunning, baffling, powerful! Without help it is too much for **YOU** (us). But there is One who has all power--that One is God. **YOU MUST** (may you) find Him now.

Half measures **WILL AVAIL YOU** (availed us) nothing. **YOU STAND** (we stood) at the turning point. **THROW YOURSELF UNDER** (We asked) his protection and care with complete abandon. **NOW WE THINK YOU CAN TAKE IT.**

Here are the steps we took, which are suggested as **YOUR** (a) program of recovery:

1. We admitted we were powerless over alcohol--that our lives had become unmanageable
2. Came to believe that a Power greater than ourselves could restore us to sanity.
3. Made a decision to turn our will and our lives over to the care **AND DIRECTION** of God, as we understood Him.
4. Made a searching and fearless moral inventory of ourselves.
5. Admitted to God, to ourselves, and to another human being the exact nature of our wrongs.
6. Were entirely **WILLING THAT** (ready to have) God remove all these defects of character.
7. Humbly **ON OUR KNEES** asked Him to remove our shortcomings- **HOLDING NOTHING BACK.**
8. Made a list of all persons we had harmed, and became willing to make **COMPLETE** amends to them all.
9. Made direct amends to such people wherever possible, except when to do so would injure them or others.
10. Continued to take personal inventory and when we were wrong promptly admitted it.
11. Sought though prayer and meditation to improve our (conscious) contact with God (as we understood him), praying only for knowledge of His will for us and the power to carry that out.
12. Having had a spiritual **EXPERIENCE** (awakening) as the result of this **COURSE OF ACTION** (these steps), we tried to carry this message to **OTHERS, ESPECIALLY** alcoholics, and to practice these principles in all our affairs

NOW YOU MAY EXCLAIM (many of us exclaimed) "What an order! I can't go through with it." Do not be discouraged. No one among us has been able to maintain anything like perfect adherence to these principles. We are not saints. The point is, that we are willing to grow along spiritual lines. The principles we have set down are guides to progress. We claim spiritual progress rather than spiritual perfection.

Our description of the alcoholic ....that's The Doctor's Opinion, Bill's Story, Ch. 2,3
the chapter to the agnostic ....……Chapter Four.
and our personal adventures before and after ....Bill's Story, and those in the back of the book.
HAVE BEEN DESIGNED TO SELL YOU (make clear) three pertinent ideas:
(a) That **YOU ARE** (we were) alcoholic and **CAN NOT** (could not) manage **YOUR** (our) own **LIFE** (lives) .... Step One.
(b) That probably no human power **CAN RELIEVE YOUR** (could have relieved our) alcoholism. .... Step Two.
(c) That God **CAN AND WILL** (could and would if He were sought)............................. The rest of Step Two.
IF YOU ARE NOT CONVINCED ON THESE VITAL ISSUES, YOU OUGHT TO RE-READ THE BOOK TO THIS POINT, OR ELSE THROW IT AWAY.

You could see that Bill, his intention was not suggestions, he was going to give us **real directions on how to work the steps and when to work the steps**. And he's going to give us **precise, specific, clear-cut directions** on how to do that and he was very adamant about that. But the crap hit the fan and they asked him and they made it through the argument to make some changes in this original "How It Works" and so today's How It Works that we have in the book and the changes that were forced upon Bill. And Bill said he would compromise with them in this area, but he made a deal with them and I can imagine through all the arguments that they had up to this point back and forth in this program the kind of arguments that they had and were almost ready to disband and run the little fellowship of Alcoholics Anonymous at that time. So Bill made a little compromise. He said I will make these changes but from now on I will complete the rest of this book or else you can do. Well they didn't want to complete the rest of the book; they wanted Bill to continue to do that, so they agreed to continue to let Bill write the rest of the book without much interference on their part

I can just see old Bill when he wrote this and gave it to them and they begin to fight and argue over it and they begin to tell him he's going to have to change it. Remember Bill's stubborn and bullheaded just like the rest of us. And he said no, I'm not going to change this and they said, well Bill you are, don't you remember it's not your book it's our book. That's the deal we made to begin with. He said that doesn't make any difference, I'm not going to change this part of the book. And they said, well you are going to change it. And he said what you guys don't realize is **these aren't my words anyhow, these are Gods words. They came after prayer and meditation.** And they said, we don't give a damn whose words they are, it's our book, and you're going to change it.

And finally, finally Bill realized that if he didn't compromise, they would destroy this project and maybe the whole fellowship. And there was a non-alcoholic psychologist around in those days and he made some suggestions. He said, why don't you change it from directions to suggestions, you'll still get your meaning across and probably more people would accept it. And he said, where you're saying you, you, you, he said don't do that; don't tell them what they have to do, change that to we. Say this is what we had to do. You'll get your message across and more people will probably accept it. And he said, where you're saying must, must, change that to ought, ought and it will be more acceptable. Now Bill very, very reluctantly made those changes. Now today we don't know if they hadn't made the changes, if they'd left it like it was originally maybe instead of two million world wide (1988), we'd have 10 million. But also if they hadn't made the changes instead of 2 million world wide we might only have ten thousand. Who knows? Nobody knows, we just know this is the history behind this particular part of the book.

Bill was cunning, baffling and powerful also. Cause he said okay, I'm going to compromise with you, but you're going to have to compromise with me. And they said what do you want? He says, I'm tired. I've fought with you all I'm going to fight. He said, If you want me to finish the book, give me the authority to do so. If you don't want to give me the authority, then you finish the book. Well they didn't want to give him that authority, but they didn't want to finish the book either. So they very reluctantly agreed to that.

What Bill knew that they didn't know, is two pages later he's going to put **DIRECTIONS**, and **YOU**, and **MUST** right back in the book. He's had it in the book all the way up to How It Works, they jerked it out, then he puts it back, and that ruins some of the continuity of the book. But know that we see what happened it makes more sense.

The other thing that is so apparent is when he says back here about the three pertinent ideas

> "Our description of the alcoholic, the chapter to the agnostic, and our personal adventures before and after have been designed to sell you (make clear) three pertinent ideas."

He's talking about the <u>Doctor's Opinion and the first four chapters and the stories in the back of the book</u>

Now if we've been sold on those three pertinent ideas

(a) That we were alcoholic and could not manage our own lives."
Then we're through with Step 1

If we've come to believe that no human power could relieve our alcoholism and that God can and will.
Then we're through with Step 2

Now the very next statement says if you are convinced then you are now at Step 3.

You see the fallacy of trying to start somebody in Chapter 5 is that it starts at Step 3. And it's hard to start with Step 3 unless you've got 1 and 2 behind you.

People come to us today and they say, well how do you work **Steps 1 & 2**

You don't, they are not working steps. There is **no action involved** here. **These are conclusions of the mind** that we draw based upon information presented to us in the Doctors Opinion and the first four chapters.

I've always been powerless over alcohol and my life has been unmanageable because of that. I just did not know that, nor did I know why until I read the Doctor's Opinion and the first four chapters.

There's always been a power greater than I am could restore me to sanity, I just did not believe that he would nor did I understand the insanity until I read the Doctor's Opinion and the first four chapters.

Now if I can say to myself today, you betcha, I'm powerless over alcohol, my life is unmanageable I'm through with Step 1
If I can say to myself today, I have come to believe there's a power greater than I am can restore me to sanity I'm through with Step 2
Now then I'm ready to look at Step 3. Now I might make a decision.

Big Book p. 60, par 3   "Being convinced, we were at Step 3"

we haven't took Step 3 yet we were just there

Big Book p. 60, par , cont.   "which is that we decided to turn our will and our life over to God as we understood Him. Just what do we mean by that, and just what do we do?"

Well that's a very good question now isn't it? What does Step 3 mean? Well, **we're going to make a decision**, that's part of it. To do what? To turn our will, and what is our will? Our will is our thinking, and our life is our actions. We're going to make a decision to turn our will and our life over to the care and direction, is what the Step used to say, to God, as we understand him.

Our will is our thinking
Our life is our actions

We're going to make a decision to let God direct our thinking and direct our life in Step 3. We haven't done that yet, but we're getting willing to do that.

I've always heard a lot of people say one of the most misunderstood steps in the Big Book is Step 4, and I'll agree with that. But I don't think Step 4 is any more misunderstood that Step 3 is. I hear people today say, I've been in AA about 5 years, my life's still all screwed up and I don't understand why cause I turned it over to God three years ago when I took Step 3. Now

We don't turn anything over to God in Step 3.
We make a decision to do something in Step 3,
and the decision itself implies we're going to take some further action to carry it out.

Now one of the greatest examples I can think of is probably 4,5,6 years ago now Barbara and I made a decision to come to Los Angeles, California to visit some of our relatives. But we didn't do anything to carry that decision out, and sure enough we didn't get to Los Angeles that year either. Second year in a row we made a decision to come to Los Angeles and visit our relatives. Again we didn't do anything to carry that out and we didn't get to California either. Third year in a row we made that decision. Only this time it was a little different. This time I took the car down and had it serviced. Barbara packed the clothes and a little food, and we got in our car and we drove from our home to Tulsa, Oklahoma. Then we drove to Oklahoma City. Then we drove to Amarillo, Texas. Then we drove to Albuquerque, New Mexico. Then we drove to Flagstaff, Arizona. Then we drove to Barstow, California. Then we drove to San Bernardino, and then we drove to Los Angeles. And by golly one day we ended up visiting our relatives in Los Angeles. Not because we made a decision, but because we took the action necessary to carry out that decision.

Now what is it we're **deciding** to do?

Well, we are making a decision to turn **our will** over to the care and direction of God as we understood him.

What is our will? Well, our will is nothing more than our thinking apparatus. Our will is nothing more than our mind. Our will is nothing more than this thing up here that tells us what to do, and what not to do.

A good example of the word will, tying it together with mind. Let's say that some of us are beginning to approach the end of our lives, which a few of us in here are. And we've gathered up a few material things and we've become concerned about what's going to happen to them when we pass on. We'll go down and sit down with an attorney and we'll tell that attorney what we want done with those things. I want this to be my spouse's, this to go to my daughter, I want this to be my sons, and etc. Now that attorney will take my thinking coming from my mind that day, write it down in legal terms on a piece of paper. I'll sign it, the attorney will sign it and we'll put it in a safe. Now a year or two or three later, sure enough I kick the bucket. If my family's like most of them they're going to call the undertaker and say come and get him, get him ready and let's get him out to that cemetery about as soon as we can. A couple of days later they all gather out at the cemetery, they have me suspended over a hole in the ground, they're all standing around that hole. Somebody says a few words and gives a little prayer. And I hope it's somebody from AA that does it. And when the ceremony's over they start dropping me down in that hole. If my families like the rest of them they're not going to wait until I get to the bottom of the hole. As soon as I start down they jump in the car and they head for that attorney's office. And that attorney gets out that piece of paper and reads to them what my thinking was two or threes years prior to that time when I was sitting there in that office. We know they call that piece of paper a will. It's not by accident.

Will, thinking, mind are all synonymous.

I'm making a decision to turn my **thinking apparatus** over to the care and direction of God as I understand him. What else am I deciding to turn over? Well I'm deciding to turn my **life** over to the care and direction of God as I understand him. And what is my life?   My life is nothing more than my actions. What I am right now as of this moment is a sum accumulated total of all the actions that I've taken throughout my entire lifetime has made me what I am today.

All action is born in thought

You can say that again please. All action is born in thought. Sometimes we react to a situation so fast we think that we do it automatically but we don't. I can't even reach out and pick up this cup of water unless my mind tells my body to do so. So if all action is born in thought then it stands to reason my **life is going to be determined by how I think.**

If my thinking is okay, chances are my actions will be okay, chances are my life's going to be okay too.

If my thinking is lousy, chances are my actions I take will be lousy and chances are I'm going to have a fouled up life too.

When I got to this stage of the program I went to my sponsor and I said I don't think I'm going to be able to take Step 3. And he said Why? And I said because if I turn my will and my life over to the care of God as I understand him, I have no idea what he would have me be. And he may want me to be a missionary, and he may send me to China, and I sure as hell don't want to go there. And he just laughed and he said let's look at it this way, at least it wouldn't be in the hands of an idiot would it? He said let's look back through your lifetime. He said you've always been a selfish, self-centered, self-willed human being. You've always done what you wanted to do whenever you wanted to do it and to hell with the rest of them. Is that right? We'll you know it is. He said the end result of that is that you almost destroyed your life and just as importantly, you've almost destroyed the lives of those around you that care for you. He said just think,

If God could direct your thinking it might become better.
If you're thinking becomes better, then your actions and your life's going to become better.

And just as importantly, the lives of those around you that care for would probably become better too.

Left on your own resources, you're always going to do the same things you've always done.
You're going to remain restless, irritable and discontented.
You're going to stay filled with shame, fear, guilt and remorse.
Sooner or later under those conditions, you're going to go back to drinking again.

If you don't find someway to be sober and have a little piece of mind, serenity and happiness,
you'll never have any long lasting sobriety and
you can't do that on self will.

And he made if clear to me in such a manner that I was able to make the decision to turn my will, which is my thinking apparatus, and my life, which is my actions, over to the care of God as I understood him. Absolutely amazing what has taken place since that time. Joe?

Remember last night in the area of the Foreword to the First Edition they said that "precisely, specifically, with clear-cut directions". You know Bill wrote down those precise, specific, clear-cut directions in the original "How It Works", but they forced some changes on him. And when these changes came out, what we see in the book now, those are the changes that we're make so a little continuity of the book kinda got mixed up here. Bill's precise, specific, clear-cut directions were altered a little bit but later on he puts them back in the book.

By the way, as far as we know, we're the only species on earth that's ever faced with this decision. It seems as though all the other species on earth don't have self-will. Whatever they do, at any given time, is always done on God's time at God's direction. It seems as though we human beings are the only species that God gave this thing called self-will to. Therefore you see very few of the other species here on earth in trouble. I've never seen a tree hit a car yet.

The one thing wrong with self-will is everybody's got one, that's one of the things wrong with it.

So our book says and he gives us these little instructions now and there going to come short and sweet and we have to be prepared to see them. And he says,

Big Book, p. 62, par 3   *"The first"*

he's going to tell us what to do first.

Big Book, p. 62, par 3   *"The first requirement is that we be convinced that any life run on self-well can hardly be a success. On that basis we are almost always in collision with something or somebody, even though our motives are good. Most people try to live by self-propulsion. Each person is like an actor who wants to run the whole show; is forever trying to arrange the lights, the ballet, the scenery and the rest of the players in his own way. If his arrangements would only stay put, if only people would do as he wished, the show would be great. Everybody, including himself, would be pleased. Life would be wonderful."*

Wouldn't that be nice if everybody would mind? They won't mind me they just won't do it, because they have self-will. My will for my wife and my children is one thing. Their will and their life is another. They have self-will and their thoughts are different from mine. Sometimes and most of the times they are in conflict. They just won't mind me. I know they'd be a lot better off if they would, but they won't. Now some twelve or thirteen years after Bill wrote the Big Book, and after many, many years experience with some of the great teachers and minds in the world, and after many, many years of experience with us alcoholics, Bill was forced to write the Twelve and Twelve. And he was really trying to push the Traditions on the fellowship. He was hard selling the Traditions to the fellowship and they weren't buying a lot of it, but they needed the Traditions and he knew that. So he decided to write the Traditions and he thought well I'll put some short stories or short essays about the Steps in with the Traditions and maybe if they will read the Steps they will eventually read the Traditions. So he wrote the Twelve and Twelve for us. The Twelve and Twelve again is just the short essays, short stories about the Steps. It doesn't tell you how to work the Steps it is the short stories about the Steps

The only piece of literature in A.A. that tells you how to work the Steps, is the Big Book of Alcoholics Anonymous

But in the area of the 4th Step, in the Twelve and Twelve there is some of the best information the world's ever seen on self-will and what makes people tick. It's called, "The Basic Instincts of Life". And I always suggest to people that I sponsor that they go to the Twelve and Twelve, read the first three or four pages about the Basic Instincts of Life, get a working knowledge about the words that you see in there, and then look them up in the dictionary because they're very important words, and then we're going to use them a little later on in the third column when we get ready to do the 4th Step inventory. So I needed a working knowledge of that information, and Bill in his usual manner wrote some of the best information about the basic instincts of life. Very, very important information

J & C   I think we have to face the fact that in 1937/38/39, when Bill was writing the Big Book he was not a spiritual giant. He was not a great student of human nature. Bill was a night school lawyer and New York City stock speculator yet he was able to write one of the most spiritual books the world has ever seen dealing with human nature. Surely, surely God took a hand in the writing of the Big Book and used Bill's hand to write the book.

But by 1950/51/52 Bill knew a lot more about spirituality, a lot more about human nature, a lot more about we alcoholics than he did back in the 30's. He'd studied with some of the greatest minds in the world for a period of years. And I think he felt that he had some new information that he could give us that would make it easier for us to work the steps according the Big Book Alcoholics Anonymous.

Basically that's what he says in the 12 and 12, that the Big Book has always been the basic text and always will be. You simply can not work the program out of the 12 and 12. I see lots of people try it. But they can't do it because there are no directions on how to work the steps. And I think that's why a lot of people love it. They can get in it and dance around and philosophies and they never have to do anything except talk. But there is some information in there that is absolutely invaluable, that if we can see it and understand it and accept it, it makes the working of the steps out of the Big Book so much simpler and so much easier.
And these three basic instincts of life that Joe's talking about, he taught me in step 4 in the 12 and 12 more about what makes me tick and what makes me do the things I do and act the way I act. He taught me there more in 2 or 3 pages than I had learned in some 40 years of living at that time. Let's look at them for just a moment. I think it will make it a lot easier to be able to see why we need to make our decision in three plus it sets us up really with information for step 4. Now in your handout sheets you've got a little picture in here about the middle in there somewhere I think it's page 7 and 8 in your handout material, which says the basic instincts of life which create self.

GLOSSARY OF WORDS USED IN STEPS FOUR AND FIVE

EXACT	- Very accurate, methodical, correct
NATURE	- The essential characteristic of a thing
WRONG	- Acting, judging, or believing incorrectly
FAULT	- Something done wrongly, an error or mistake
MISTAKE	- To understand or perceive wrongly
DEFECT	- Lack of something necessary for completeness -- Same as shortcoming
SHORTCOMING	- Falling short of what is expected or required -- Same as defect
SELF-CENTERED	- Occupied or concerned only with one's own affairs -- Same as selfish
SELFISH	- Too much concern with one's own welfare or interests and having little or no concern for others -- Same as self-centered
SELF-SEEKER	- A person who seeks only or mainly to further his own interests
DISHONEST	- The act or practice of telling a lie, or of cheating, deceiving, stealing, etc.
FEAR	- A feeling of anxiety, agitation, uneasiness, apprehension, etc.
FRIGHTENED	- A temporary or continual state of fear
INCONSIDERATE	- Without though or consideration of others

BASIC INSTINCTS OF LIFE WHICH CREATE SELF

SOCIAL INSTINCT	SECURITY INSTINCT	SEX INSTINCT
COMPANIONSHIP—Wanting to belong or to be accepted **PRESTIGE**—Wanting to be recognized, or to be accepted as a leader. **SELF-ESTEEM**—What we think of ourselves, high or low. **PRIDE**—An excessive and unjustified opinion of oneself, either positive (self-love) or negative (self-hate). **PERSONAL RELATIONSHIPS**—Our relations with other human beings and the world around us. **AMBITIONS**—Our plans to gain acceptance, power, recognition, prestige, etc.	**MATERIAL**—Wanting money, buildings, property, clothing, etc. in order to be secure in the future. **EMOTIONAL**—Based upon our needs for another person or persons. Some tend to dominate, some are overly dependent on others. **AMBITIONS**—Our plans to gain material wealth, or to dominate, or to depend upon others.	**ACCEPTABLE**—Our sex lives as accepted by Society, God's principles or our own principles **HIDDEN**—Our sex lives that are contrary to either Society, God's principles or our own principles. **AMBITION**—Our plans regarding our sex lives either acceptable or hidden.

(SELF) — (WRONGS)

RESENTMENTS	FEAR	HARM OR HURTS
Feelings of bitter hurt or indignation which comes from rightly or wrongly held feelings of being injured or offended.	Feelings of anxiety, agitation, uneasiness, apprehension, etc.	Wrong acts which result in pain, hurt feelings, worry, financial loss, etc... for others and also self.

And he said that

**All human beings are born with three basic instincts of life.
They are God given,
They are absolutely necessary for survival of the human race
Therefore they are a good thing.**

The first thing he talked about is the **social instinct**. And he said all human beings are born with the desire to be liked, to be accepted, to be respected by other people. He said all human beings ware born with the desire to come together in groups with other people. He said if we didn't have those desires and cared nothing for each other that the world would go into complete anarchy, dog eat dog situation would reign, and eventually under those conditions the human race would fail to survive.
Now he used several terms under the social instinct. He uses the term
        companionship…that's nothing more than wanting to belong or to be accepted.

So many of us grew up on the outside of the crowd looking in, wanting to be and knew we could not be.
He uses the term
        prestige…that's wanting to be recognized or to be accepted as the leader of the group.

And the world needs leaders. I guess somebody back in the old caveman days had to say "John, get behind that tree with your spear. Jack you get over there with your club. And Mary-Jo and I will run this sucker through here and we'll have something".
Somebody's got to do that. Most people will take one of two directions. Either let me be a part of or let me be the leader of. And in either case it's based upon what other people think of us.
        self-esteem…is what we think of ourselves.

And that's usually high or low based upon what other people think of us or what we think other people think of us. If they seem to like us and accept us we feel pretty good towards ourselves. If it feels like they reject us and they don't want us then we feel pretty lousy towards ourselves.
Pride. And I'm glad I got into the habit of going to the dictionary. I always thought pride was something you ought to have. All I ever wanted to be as a young boy growing up, I wanted to grow up to be a man who walked tall with pride and just a little bit sideways like John Wayne does. Until I looked it up in the dictionary and it says
        pride… is an excessive and unjustified opinion of oneself.

We either think too well of ourselves or too little of ourselves. In either case it's not the truth.
        personal relationships… is our relations with other human beings and the world around us.
        ambitions… are the plans for the future.

To be liked, to be accepted, so on and so forth.
All human beings have these things. Now if I want to be liked and accepted and respected by the world and the people in it the first thing I've got to do is decide, well what do they want from me?

Society teaches us those things as we grow up. It'll vary in different parts of the world. One part of the world perhaps it's a good education. Another part of the world it's to be large landowner. Another part of the world it's to have a large family. Any number of things based upon where we live in the world. And as we grow up and they teach us these things and we ourselves set goals for ourselves as to what we want to become in the future. And if we're going to reach the goals that we set for ourselves we're going to have to work at it. You can't just be a bum and sit on your duff and be successful and people like you and accept you. If it's a good education you're going to have to work at, whatever it might be.

By the same token we're going to have to make some sacrifices. There are some things that I would really like to do as a human being that are very pleasurable and very exciting that if you catch me at it you're not going to like me at all. And I don't think you and I would do the work necessary to reach the goal nor make the sacrifices necessary unless we get a reward for doing so. And the great reward, Bill said it in his story when he said **I had arrived**.

God how many of us have done it. We set that goal and we just literally worked our tails off for years and the day we reach the goal and they pat us on the back and they say "Ah Joe you're a fine fellow, you're a good man, you're doing great". There's a feeling that comes over us which is one of those indescribably wonderful feelings. Great, great feeling. The only thing wrong with it, it seems to be just a temporary feeling. No sooner do we reach the goal, we get the praise, we get the recognition, we get the prestige from it and we look around we say "Is this all there is to it?" And we set another goal. And we work and we work and we strive and we strive and we sacrifice and we reach the new goal and we get the praise and recognition, feels great, doesn't last long and we set another goal.

It seems to create within we human beings an insatiable desire for more and more power, more and more recognition and we're not getting it fast enough or they're not giving it to us the way we think they ought to, so what do we do about it? Well we start taking shortcuts. We start doing a little lying, a little conning, a little manipulating, a little stepping on other peoples toes and climbing on their backs and the instant we do so we create pain and suffering for others. They in turn retaliate against us and create pain and suffering for us.

Plain that a life run on self-will could hardly ever be a success.
Under those conditions we will always be in collision with people, places and things.

Second basic instinct he talked about is the **security instinct**. Now, I know that in AA we try to live one day at a time. But I also know that just about everybody in this room has got an insurance policy. The purpose of the insurance policy is to protect ourselves in the future. Bill said all human beings are born with the desire to be secure in the future. He said if we didn't have that desire we wouldn't provide the food, the clothing, the shelter, the things that we need to survive. And next winter we would just simply freeze to death or the next drought season we would starve to death. So this desire that we have to be secure in the future is a God given thing and it is necessary for our survival. Now once again if you're going to be secure in the future you have to decide well what is it that I need in order to be secure?

Society usually teaches us those things as we grow up and it varies in different parts of the world. In one part of the world you only need $4. In another part of the world you need $4,000. In another part of the world maybe you need $4,000,000. In another part of the world you 198 coconuts. Whatever it is that they use to measure, trade and barter with. Based up what we're taught, we set goals for ourselves and we begin to work at it. Now if you're going to be secure in the future you can't just sit on your duff and be a bum. You're going to have to work, you're going to have to make some money, you're going to have to invest it.

At the same time you've got to sacrifice. Hell we can't blow it all today and be secure tomorrow. And I don't think you and I would do the work necessary to reach the goal or make the sacrifices necessary if we didn't get a reward for it.

Once again the great reward is that great feeling that comes at the moment of successful completion of the goal. How many of us have done it? We set the goal for the new dress, for the new shoes, for the new suit, for the new drapes, for the new couch, for the new home, for the new car, for the new piece of property, for the new business and we work and we work and we strive and we strive and the day that sucker is paid for and nobody can take it away from us. What a great, great feeling that is. Hell back when I was a kid hardly anybody owned their own homes. Once in a great while somebody would buy a home and they would sacrifice everything they had to pay that sucker off and the day they paid it off the feeling was so great they would call in the neighbors and we would have a great party and celebrate it by burning the mortgage. How great that was. The only thing wrong with it is that it's just a temporary feeling. No sooner got the sucker paid off that I looked around and his house is bigger than mine. Yah and he's got a Cadillac and I'm driving a Chevrolet. And he's got a Brooks Brothers suit and I bought mine at Kmart. And that causes us to set another goal. And we work and we work and we strive and we strive and we reach the new goal, feels good, doesn't last long, we set another….seems to create an insatiable desire for more and more and more and more. And we're not getting it fast enough. They're not giving it to us like we think they should. So what do we do? We take shortcuts. We lie, we cheat, we con, we manipulate, and the instant we do we hurt other people. They retaliate against us, creating pain and suffering for us.
Plain that a life run on self will can hardly ever be a success.

Third basic instinct he talks about is the **sex instinct**. He said all human beings are born with the desire to have sex. Now, it may get turned off by bad teachings or bad happenings but he said all human beings are born with the desire to have sex because if we don't have sex we can't reproduce ourselves. And if we don't reproduce ourselves, sooner or later the human race is going to fail to survive.

So just like the other two, if you're going to reproduce yourself through the sexual act you're going to have to work at it. Hell you can do more work in three minutes of sex, if you can last that long, than you'll do all day digging a ditch. Don't you older fellows remember how it used to be when we got through with it? My God you'd just fall over sideways, the sweat is just pouring off of you, and you can hardly get your breath. You feel like you've died, gone to heaven and come back two or three times. Gets excited doesn't he? And I don't think you and I would do that kind of work if we didn't get a reward for doing so. And the great reward is that great feeling we get both physically and emotionally at the moment of the successful completion of the sex act. One of the greatest rewards that a human being can experience. But also just like the other two it seems to be just a temporary feeling. Hell you no sooner get through doing it that you get to thinking about doing it again. And it's such a pleasurable and exciting thing that the next thing you know you get to thinking about doing it in different ways. Then you get to thinking about doing it in different positions. Then you get to thinking about doing it with different people. And the next thing you know we're doing it at the wrong time in the wrong way with the wrong people and the instant we do so we create pain and suffering for others. They in turn retaliate against us, which creates pain and suffering for us.

It's plain that a life run on self will can hardly ever be a success.
The fulfillment of these things are so pleasurable
that all human beings from time to time will overdo in one or more of these areas
and create pain and suffering for others.

You'll notice on that little chart there's a circle called Self. That's where self-will comes from, from these three basic instincts of life. You'll also notice coming out of the self circle there is one called wrongs which is another word we need to look at. Somewhere we got the idea that wrongs meant a list of dirty filthy nasty items. But if you go to the dictionary and look it up you'll find several definitions of it.

wrong - incorrect judgement of other people = resentment
wrong - incorrect believing = fear
wrong - are the harms and hurts that we do to other people

Now it's easy to spot a selfish, self-centered human being. One who is running on self-will, not running on God's will. A selfish, self-centered human being is always madder than hell. Damn him. Damn her. By God I'll show them. They're not going to treat me that way. Blahdy blahdy blah blah blah. . A selfish, self-centered human being is always scared to death. Can't depend on God. Can't depend on other people. And if we're an alcoholic reaching the end of the road we can't depend on ourselves any longer and we're running absolutely scared to death all the time. . A selfish, self-centered human being, in order to fulfill the basic instincts of life are always overdoing and creating harms and hurts for others. Then we've got to be scared to death of what they're going to do when they catch us. And even if they don't catch us, if God dwells within each of us, we know the difference between right and wrong and guilt and remorse associated with those things begin to eat us up.

A person who's mind is filled with resentment. A person who's mind is filled with fear. A person whose mind is filled with guilt and remorse **does not feel good**.

And eventually searching for a way to feel better we begin to think about the sense of ease and comfort that comes at once by taking a couple of drinks. Next thing you know we believe we can drink and we end up drunk all over again. So at the very least we're going to have to do something about this selfish self-centered human being and it seems the only way you can do anything about that is through God's help because God made self-will. And only God has the power to overcome that. And at the very least we're going to have to do something about these resentments and these fears and this guilt and remorse in order to find the peace of mind, serenity and happiness for good long term sobriety.

J & C   You know if every human being in the world today could fulfill these three basic instincts at the level that God intends there would be no conflict on earth today. But all human beings have self-will.

All human beings from time to time will overdo in one or more areas creating conflict for others and for themselves. I never knew that. I just knew I was always in trouble. I just knew I was always madder than hell. I just knew I was always scared to death. I knew guilt and remorse was eating me up but I didn't know where it came from. See they gave me the rules but they never taught me how to play the game. AA has taught me how to play the game. And now that I know how to play the game I don't break the rules anymore and I don't hurt other people and I'm not scared to death and I'm not filled with guilt and remorse. This is the greatest information I have ever seen about what makes me tick and what causes me to do the things that I do. Joe.

Big Book p. 62, par. 1, line 3   "Whatever our protestations, are not most of us concerned with ourselves, our resentments, or our self-pity?"

J & C   It's not that I thought too well of myself, or that I thought too little of myself. It's that I thought of myself only. That was my problem.

Big Book p. 62, par 2., line 1   "Selfishness, self-centeredness! That, we think, is the root of our troubles. Driven by a hundred forms of fear, self-delusion, self-seeking, and self-pity, we step on the toes of our fellows and they retaliate. Sometimes they hurt us, seemingly without provocation, but we invariably find that at some time in the past we have made decisions based on self which later placed us in a position to be hurt."

J & C   You know alcoholism: I, self and me. You see if you don't have a God in your life, and I didn't, there's only one thing left to live by and that's the satisfaction of these basic instincts of life. And I tried to live my life based upon the satisfaction of those basic instincts. And I overdid in many, many of those areas.

Big Book p. 62, par 3, line 1   "So our troubles, we think, are basically of our own making. They arise out of ourselves, and the alcoholic is an extreme example of self-will run riot, though he usually doesn't think so.
Above everything, we alcoholics must be rid of this selfishness. We must, or it kills us! God makes that possible."

J & C   Can't heal a sick mind with a sick mind. Only God makes that possible.

Big Book p. 62, par. 3, line 19   "And there often seems no way of entirely getting rid of self without His aid. Many of us had moral and philosophical convictions galore, but we could not live up to them even though we would have liked to. Neither could we reduce our self-centeredness much by wishing or trying on our own power. We had to have God's help."

Big Book p. 62, par 4, line 1   "This is the how and the why of it."

J & C   You see he told how it works. Then he told us why it won't work because of selfishness and self-centeredness. And now he's going to tell us how it really works.

Big Book p. 62, par 4, line 1   "This is the how and the why of it. First of all, we had to quit playing God. It didn't work."

J & C   Everything I read leads me to believe that this is a God directed world. Now if it is a God directed world then those of us who have been self directed and those of us that have tried to direct everything and everybody around us …we've been trying to do God's job for him. We're not God, we've just been playing at being God. And the book says we're going to have to quit doing that if we want any peace of mind, serenity and happiness in the future. I think

One of the great mistakes I see today in AA is people <u>trying to force themselves to be better.</u>
And self-will cannot overcome self-will.
Only God can overcome self-will.
So if we want any peace of mind, serenity and happiness it looks like we're going to have to turn to God and let him be the Director. Let him do his job, which is direction.

Next direction.

Big Book p 62, par 4, line 28   "Next, we decided that hereafter in this drama of life, God was going to be our Director."

J & C   Not our suggestor, our Director. He's got his word back now. From here on it'll be directions.

Big Book p. 62, par 4, line 30   "He is the Principal; we are His agents. He is the Father, and we are His children. Most Good ideas are simple, and this concept was the keystone of the new and triumphant arch through which we passed to freedom.

J & C   And what is that idea of this concept. That he is the principle and we are his agents, He is the Father, and we are His children, **he is the boss, I work for him**. Now when I first got into this area of the 3rd Step I used God like you would an errand boy. I said, God please help me to stay sober, and by the way, while you're at it, help me get my wife back. Which one? The second one, I don't want that first one back. That first one didn't drink, she was mean and ugly. I like the one that drank.
God get me a job by the way pick up a little extra money for me, I need some money. I used God like you would an errand boy, send him out like that. And after I got sober I got to reading in that other book, that big, big book and in the front of that book

There's a story about this fellow he worked for six days and rested. Now to my knowledge he didn't have to go back to work anymore. So it looks as though if there's any work being done around here it's going to be me doing the work. He's the principle, we're the agents, He's the Father, we're the children,
He's the boss, I'm the employee.
Most good ideas are simple, and this concept was the **keystone** of the new and triumphant arch through which we passed to freedom. Now he's referring once again to that wonderfully effective spiritual structure.

Step 1   Willingness   Foundation
Step 2   Believing   Cornerstone

Now he tells us what we're building. A triumphant arch through which we're going to pass to freedom.
He said the keystone to that arch is a simple little idea that we're going to let God be the Director

You know in the old, old days when they built arches, the stones were all stacked loosely without mortar, and they began to lean together and there was a center stone up here called the keystone.

If it was cut right, it would support the entire arch, but if it wasn't, it would slip out and the arch would collapse.

Well the keystone of the new and triumphant arch through which we're going to pass to freedom, is this simple little idea - that we're going to let God be the Director. For most of us that's the first time we ever had that idea. If we once had it as children we lost it somewhere. Instead of letting God be the Director, we we're the director, cause we told God what we wanted. God do this, God do that, God give me this, God give me that, God if you do this for me, I'll do that for you. And now only did we direct God we directed everybody around us. Now we can quit doing that. We're going to let God be the Boss from this day on. Now that is a radical idea for people like us. This is the decision that we're making

Big Book p. 63, par. 1, line 1   *"When we sincerely took such a position, all sorts of remarkable things followed. We had a new Employer. Being all powerful, He provided what we needed, if we kept close to Him and performed His work well. Established on such a footing we became less and less interested in ourselves, our own little plans and designs. More and more we became interested in seeing what we could contribute to life. "*

J & C   You see I was always a taker. And takers are losers in life. Contributors are those that win I've noticed.

Big Book p. 63, par. 1, cont.   *"As we felt new power flow in, as we enjoyed peace of mind, as we discovered we could face life successfully, as we became conscious of His presence, we began to lose our fear of today, tomorrow or the hereafter. We were reborn. "*

J & C   You know they used to come over to my house on Monday night from that little church about two blocks from my house, and these guys wanted to talk to me about being reborn. And you know what I did for them, I'm drinking and man it's Monday night football, and they'll be talking about reborn about 8 o'clock they'd be knocking, and I'd run them off, I'd say you guys get out of here, it's Monday night football, I don't want to talk to you, get. And that's the way I did with those guys, and I didn't understand this reborn then at all. And I got to reading in that other book when I got sober and there's this story in there and this guy's name was Nicademus. And Nicademus was about like me, just dumber than a stump. And he asked that guy, what do you mean by being reborn. Do you mean I've got to go back into my mother's womb. See how dumb he was? And he looked at him and shook his head and said Nicademus don't you know you can't do that? Didn't you go to the University? Aren't you educated? You can't do that.

When I'm talking about being reborn
I'm talking about the renewing of your mind.
Old ideas cast aside, new ones accepted.
Reborn in my mind

I understood that then. And now I'm ready to do business, I'm ready to do the third Step.

And I knew what they did on Sunday morning at that little church up there about 11o'clock, and I couldn't wait till I got there. And they basically asked people to come down and do the third Step prayer. So I waited till next Sunday, got there about 3 or 4 minutes till 11:00, I didn't want to get there too early I might hear something that would help me. I got there about 3 or 4 minutes till 11:00 and sure enough they asked people to do that and I came down there and I did, just as the book says,

Big Book p. 63, par 2, line 1   "We were now at Step Three. Many of us said to our Maker, as we understood Him: **God, I offer myself to Thee -- to build with me and to do with me as Thou wilt. Relieve me of the bondage of self, that I may better do Thy will. Take away my difficulties, that victory over them may bear witness to those I would help of Thy Power, Thy Love, and Thy Way of life. May I do Thy will always!** We thought well before taking this step making sure we were ready; that we could at last abandon ourselves utterly to Him." *[Step 3 Prayer]*

J & C   And I don't know what exactly happened that particular morning, but I do know this. From that Sunday morning till this moment, my life hasn't been the same. It's as if I been walking on the dark side of the street all those years and all of a sudden I'm on the sunny side of the street. And I don't know what happened except I do know that my life has changed. Thank God.

Big Book p. 63, par. 2, line 20   "We thought well before taking this step making sure we were ready; that we could at last abandon ourselves utterly to Him."

J & C   I think the word utterly means completely, whole hardedly, all the way, the entire ball of wax. I hope you don't make the mistake I did. The first time I took Step 3 I got on my knees, which I very seldom did in those days. I said God, I offer myself to Thee -- to build with me and to do with me as Thou wilt. Relieve me of the bondage of self, that I may better do Thy will. Take away my difficulties..... so on and so on and so forth. And as I finish it up I said now this applies to my alcohol, don't fool with my sex life. Stay out of my money. I can handle that too.   God probably said, What an order, I can't go through with it. I said you take the alcohol and I'll take care of the rest. Today I realize the fallacy in that is as far as I know God doesn't even drink, he don't want the alcohol, He's wants me, and He wants all of me.

Just think. If God could direct my thinking in all areas, it might even become better in my sex life, if might even become better in my money areas. If might even become better in all areas. When my thinking becomes better in all areas then surely my life will become better in all areas too. I think we need to realize this is really ....

End of Tape 4

To do it again later on. I think there's a valid reason behind this. I am told that we alcoholics are born to live in three dimensions. We are born to live with God, with ourselves, and with our fellow human beings.

And if we are praying with other human beings for the first time, we are beginning to get ourselves back together in all three dimensions the way God intended in the first place.

We alcoholics are the funniest people in the world. We'll let our families see us on our knees in the bathroom hugging the porcelain bowl, puking our guts up, morning after morning, after morning. We come to AA and try to straighten out our lives, and we're ashamed and embarrassed to let people see us prayer. Isn't that something. Praying in the company of other human beings is always better. Anybody I work with that I sponsor I require that they take Step 3 with me for two reasons. Number one, if they take it with me I know they have taken it. That's the only way I know for sure. But the real reason is that every time we do it together it means more to me. And it has more strength and more power for myself. I think it's a great idea.

J & C   We've made our decision, we've uttered our prayers, and the book says

Big Book p. 63, par. 4, line 1   "Next we launched out on a curse of vigorous action, the first step of which is a personal housecleaning, which many of us had never attempted. Though our decision (Step 3) was a vital and crucial step, it could have little permanent effect unless at once followed by a strenuous effort to face, and to be rid of the things in ourselves which had been blocking us (Step 4). Our liquor was but a symptom. So we had to get down to causes and conditions."

J & C   We always like to stop here for just a moment and look at the time element between Step 3 and Step 4. We always hear people asking the question, How long should you wait after you do Step 3 until you start on Step 4?" And we hear all kinds of answers.   Sometimes they'll say 30 days, maybe 90 days, or maybe 6 months. We heard a professional in the field one time counseling people to wait a minimum of two years. And our question back to that person was, "How many people have you killed with that statement?"

We're trying to find a way to live where we not only can be sober, but we can have a little peace of mind, serenity and happiness. And everyday that we put off and procrastinate Step 4, is the day that we're still filled with resentments, a day that we're still filled with shame and fear and guilt and remorse. Another day that we don't feel good. And we really don't know how many days we can go without our mind beginning to think about taking a drink. And the next thing you know we've convinced our self that it's okay to drink, and we end up drunk all over again.

I don't know how many days I could go under those conditions, and frankly I'm not very interested in finding out. Our book tells us when we should take Step 4

**Step 3 will have little permanent effect unless at once followed by
this strenuous effort which is Step 4**

and you know that does make sense doesn't it. Far back as I can remember, 4 has always followed immediately after three.

Now knowing that, and knowing we might get drunk if we don't get on with Step 4, why would we still tend to procrastinate?

I think one two or three reasons behind it. Number one is fear. Some of we older members tend to play King off of the Mountain with this Step. We tell the newcomer how tough it is. By God, just wait till you get to Step 4. Blah, blah, blah. We literally scare them to death. Let us be the first to say today that if we take Step 4 according to the Big Book of Alcoholics Anonymous there is nothing whatsoever to be afraid of. And I think we're all going to see that in just a little bit.

Knowing there's nothing to be afraid of, why would we still tend to procrastinate?
I think one of the greatest reasons is simply confusion. For years we could not see how to do Step 4 according to the Big Book. The reason we couldn't see it is the instructions are there but they are so simple that we alcoholics with our keen, intellectual, alcoholic minds looking for something more complicated, overlooked the simplicity of Step 4. So in our desperation, we read over in Step 5 something about sharing your entire life story, and we say that's what they want us to do in Step 4. Is write our life story so we can share it in Step 5. That's what I did in the beginning. My life story might not have been important to others but it must have been to me, there was 92 pages in it. I took it to another poor, suffering human being and asked him to read and he did. He said it's not very pretty is it? I said no it isn't. He said you'll never have to be that way again and he threw it in the waste paper basket. And I learned nothing from my life story to contribute to my alcoholism, certainly nothing new. Everything I wrote down I already knew it, so nothing knew came out of it. Today I realize that 95% of my life story really doesn't have anything to do with my alcoholism anyhow. The fact that I was born in 1929, I don't think it's got a thing to do with my alcoholism. It may have had something to do with some else's alcoholism but not mine. The fact that I graduated from High School at age 17, went immediately into the service, I don't think it has a thing to do with my alcoholism. The fact that I was married at age 21. I don't think that has anything to do with it. But I'll tell you what it did do, the 95% that had nothing to do with it, very effectively covered up the 5% that did. I learned nothing from my life story to contribute to my alcoholism. So in our desperation again, somebody in Minneapolis, Minnesota wrote a 4th Step Inventory guide. We took the Minneapolis guide and combined it with the Big Book and got more confused yet. Somebody in Dallas, Texas wrote a 4th Step Inventory guide. We took the Dallas guide, combined it with the Minneapolis guide, combined it with the Big Book and got more confused yet. Have no idea how many are floating around today. We saw one that had 20 pages in it. I guarantee if you wasn't crazy as hell as you took it, you would be when you were through with it. It was one of those. All the time the instructions have been here. We just never could see them before because we didn't understand how Bill writes.

I think today, if we can just sit back and relax, look at a few simple ideas; we're going to see how easy this thing really is. There are two things we've got to remember. First he loves to use comparisons, talking about one thing that we already know to teach us something knew. Also he did not like to repeat himself using the same words over and over. So he would tell us something and then turn around and tell us again using different words the second time. And bearing those two thoughts in mind I think we can see how simple this thing really is. He starts out by saying

Big Book p. 64, par. 2, line 1   "Therefore, we started upon a personal inventory. This was Step 4."

J & C   Immediately <u>he jumps into business</u>

Big Book p. 64, par. 2, line 2   "A business that takes no regular inventory usually goes broke."

J & C   I think his first comparison is this, if you had a business, I don't care what it is, selling ladies purses, watches, bicycles or whatever. if you did an inventory once in a while. And by the way, inventory is defined as a written list of items. If you didn't go in there and make a list of the things that are in there, you wouldn't know what was stolen that you didn't get paid for. If you didn't inventory once in a while, you wouldn't know what's been sold and you need to re-order to put new stock in its place. If you didn't inventory once in a while you wouldn't know what's become damaged.   Nobody wants to buy it, it's sitting there taking up valuable floor space day after day after day.   You're probably paying interest on borrowed money to put it in there in the first place. If you didn't inventory once in a while you wouldn't know what's become out of style.   You need to put it on sale so you can get it out of the store to put something new in its place.
If you had a business and didn't inventory once in a while you probably would go broke, and I think we can all see that.

In our personal lives we have a business too. Greatest business in the world for us. It's the business of find a way to live where we can have a little peace of mind, serenity and happiness so we don't have to go back to drinking. If we don't inventory in our personal business, chances are we're not going to find what's damaged and unsalable in our heads that's going to cause us to go broke too. And going broke for us is simply going back to drink.

So whether we're dealing with a personal business or a business business, in either case, we would probably go broke without the inventory. Now then he's going to tell us how to take a business inventory

Big Book p. 64, par. 2, line 10   "Taking a commercial"

J & C   He could have said "business again" couldn't he? But he'll use the word commercial which means the same thing.

Big Book p. 64, par. 2, line 10   "Taking a commercial inventory"

J & C   Now Joe up here on the screen, and you also have it in your handout materials, we're going to have a little picture up here that's going to be called Inventory Comparison, I think it's Step 5 in your hand out sheet. On one side it says business, the other side says personal. We're going to take a few key worlds out of the Big Book and put it under business.

STEP 4
INVENTORY COMPARISON

BUSINESS		PERSONAL
FACT-FINDING	<->	SEARCHING
FACT-FACING	<->	FEARLESS
TRUTH	<->	MORAL
STOCK-IN-TRADE	<->	OURSELVES

OBJECT:

DISCLOSE DAMAGED OR UNSALABLE GOODS	<->	FIND FLAWED THINKING PROCESSES
GET RID OF THEM PROMPTLY WITHOUT REGRET!	<->	GET RID OF THEM PROMPTLY WITHOUT REGRET!
STOCK IN TRADE THAT IS DAMAGED	<->	1. RESENTMENT 2. FEAR 3. HARMS DONE TO OTHERS

Big Book p. 64, par. 2, line 10   "Taking a commercial inventory is a fact finding. (put under Business) and a fact facing process (put under Business). It is an effort to discover the truth (put under Business) about the stock in trade (put under Business)."

J & C   The stock in trade is what's in there to sell. The ladies purses, the men's watches, the bicycles, or whatever.

Big Book p. 64 par. 2, line 13   "One object is to disclose damaged or unsalable goods, (put under business) to get rid of them promptly and without regret. (put under Business)."

J & C   In other words, we're going to go in there and we're going to find the facts. When we find them, we're going to face the facts. We're looking for the truth about the stock in trade. We're trying to find the damaged and unsalable goods. The good items will not cause us to go broke. They resale everyday and we're making money off of them. The damaged and unsalable goods, they're the ones that's blocking the floor space and the shelf space and costing us money. When we finally find them, we're going to try to get rid of them promptly and without regret. We can't put anything new in their in their place until they're gone. We're trying to find the stock in trade that's damaged and get it out of there

Big Book p. 64, par. 2, line 15   "If the owner of the business is to be successful, he cannot fool himself about values."

J & C   He's got to be honest. Once in a while he'll try to fool himself. He'll say the reason these ladies aren't buying these purses is they just don't understand what's good for them. He made the decision to buy them; he hates to admit he made a mistake. He may keep them in there longer than he should, and if it does it's going to cost him money every day.

Is there anybody in here that would have any problems with what he's told us about the business inventory? That we're going to try to find the facts. That when we find them we're going to try to face them. We're looking for the truth about the stock in trade. We're looking for the damaged and unsalable goods. When we find them we're going to get rid of them promptly and without regret, always looking for the stock in trade that's damage. Anybody's got any problems there? Ok now watch it. He used a series of words that tells us how to take our personal inventory, it means basically the same thing.

Big Book p. 64, par. 3, line 1   "We did exactly the same thing with our lives. We took stock honestly"

J & C   So now we go to Step 4   (Step 4 says that now we're under Personal on the right side of the sheet)

Step 4   Made a <u>searching</u> and <u>fearless</u> <u>moral</u> <u>inventory</u> of <u>ourselves</u>

"Made a <u>searching</u> ..."
We're putting **searching across from fact-finding they mean the same thing.** To find the facts, to search out the facts.

"Made a searching and <u>fearless</u> ....."
We're putting **fearless across from fact-finding, they mean the same thing. To face the facts, to fearlessly look at them.**

"Made a searching and fearless <u>moral</u>..."
And that's where we got in trouble. We said oh damn, there's that list of dirty, filthy, nasty items. We don't want to look at them and we sure as hell don't want to show them to anyone else. Now I'm not sure what Bill Wilson knew, but I know one thing, this guy understood the English language. And I really believe that **if he wanted you and I to make a list of dirty, filth, nasty items, he would have said**

We made a searching and fearless <u>amoral</u> or <u>immoral</u> inventory

He didn't say that, he said **moral**. Bugged the hell out of us, until eventually we went back to the dictionary. Do you know what the word moral is defined as

Truth. Things as they really are. The right and wrong of any given situation. The truth about things.

Truth and moral mean exactly the same thing

"Made a <u>searching</u> and <u>fearless</u> <u>mor</u>al <u>inventory</u> of what..."

Of ourselves. We're the only stock in trade that we have in the business of staying sober. Nobody else can make us sober, and nobody else can make us drink.

Oh I'll agree they can make us thirty as hell once in a while, but they can't make us drink. **We decide whether we drink or not.** What part of us decides whether we drink or not? Is it our body or is it our mind?

The real problem of the alcoholic centers in the mind.

We're going to look inside our selves, in our minds, and we're going to **find those flawed thinking processes**, which is the damaged and unsalable goods, **that block us off from God**.

We made a decision to turn our will over to God, and **as long as our mind is filled with damaged unsalable goods then God can't direct our thinking**

We're going to have to find them. And after we once find them, we're going to have to get rid of them promptly and without regret.

When those flawed thinking processes leave our minds, then our mind is opened up for God's thinking to enter.

But it's only after they are gone that God can enter

J & C   Now there are three common manifestations of a life run on self-will, and we've already talked about them.

The flawed thinking processes in our mind that blocks God out are our resentments fear, guilt and remorse associated with the harms done to other people. And as long as our mind is occupied with those thoughts then God's thoughts can't come in.

It's just that simple. Now I like to look at my head up here as a little bitty store, not much, a little bitty Quick Trip or Seven11, not a hell of a lot in it, never has been. Over here in this part of my store I've got some display cases and they are filled with resentments. Damn him, damn her, my God I'll show them, bladdy, blah blah. Those display cases are already full. God simply can not get in there because he is blocked out by the damaged and unsalable goods called resentments. Over here in this part of my store I got a little file cabinet and it's filled with fear: Oh my god, what's she going to do when she finds out about this one. Oh my God what's the banker going to say when that cheque hits there this time, he already told me he's going to file on me next time. Oh my God, is that my car sitting there out front, front end torn up, don't know how, oh my God, and on and on and on. God can't get in there. He's very effectively blocked out by those fears. Back here in the back of my store I got a little file ready and it's filled with guilt and remorse.

God dwells in each of us and we know the difference between right and wrong.

We do these things that hurt other people, we're scared to death that there going to do when they find out, and the guilt and remorse begin to eat us up. God can't get in that store room, he's already blocked out of there.

If I want God to direct my thinking then I'm going to have to do something about these resentments, fear, guilt and remorse. If I can remove them then God's thinking can enter into my mind and direct those portions of my mind where he was effectively blocked out.

Now my book is getting ready to show me just exactly how to look at these things truthfully. It's getting ready to show me how to remove them. Then the greatest thing it's going to show me is how to keep them from coming back in the future.

And if I do my part, then God can direct my thinking. But until I've done my part, God can't, it's **just that simple.**

Big Book p. 64, par. 3, line 17   "We did exactly the same thing with our lives. We took stock honestly."

J & C   Truthfully, morally.

Big Book p. 64, par. 3, line 18   "First, we searched out the flaws in our make-up which caused our failure. Being convinced that self, manifested in various ways, was what had defeated us, we considered its common manifestations.*

Resentment is the "number one" offender. It destroys more alcoholics than anything else. From it stem all forms of spiritual disease, for we have been not only mentally and physically ill, we have been spiritually sick. When the spiritual malady is overcome, we straighten out mentally and physically. In dealing with resentments, we set them on paper"

J & C   So the first thing we're going to do is look at these resentments. Now I think we need to look at that words and make sure we understand what it means. The word resentment is made from two old old words. First are the letters RE.

When you see RE in front of another words it always means "to do again", like repaint, replay, redo. It always means to do again. The last part of this word, "SENTMENT" comes from an old word called "sentire", which means to feel.

Resentment means to re-feel.

Let's say we're going through life which we do on a daily basis, remembering always that everybody has got self-will. That's one of the problems; it's standard equipment. Everybody's got self-will. From time to time other people get sick in self; maybe their social instinct is out of kilter. Maybe their security instinct or their sex instinct is fouled up.

And they do something to me that **threatens one of my basic instincts of life.** Maybe they put me down in the eyes of other people, and it threatens my <u>self-esteem.</u> Maybe they do something to threaten one of my <u>personal relationships.</u> Maybe they rip me off and steal my <u>money</u> from me. Maybe they do something to interfere with my <u>sex life</u>. Maybe they do something that threatens one of my <u>ambitions for the future.</u>

Now when they do that, that's a wrong on their part for doing so, that's not a resentment.
It doesn't become a resentment until I go over in the next room, or I go home that evening, and
I replay that thing in my mind, and I feel the pain the second time.
The first time they did it to me hurt me, but **when I go over it and replay it, and feel the pain the second time then I'm doing it to myself now.** They did it to me the first time, but I'm doing it to me the second time. And after a while **I'll replay it again and I'll feel the pain the third time.**

And what I've found in my life is that I'm not always completely honest with me.
Because it seems as though **when I replay this thing, each time I tend to change it just a little bit.**
I tend to make what they did to me just a little bit worse.
> **I tend to make what I did just a little bit less.**
> **I tend to make the pain just a little bit deeper.**

And if you let me play it over in my head enough times after a while I can say to myself I was just standing there doing nothing, and they came along and did it to me.

I love to watch football games, and in a football game you'll see a guy called a quarterback, and sometimes he'll throw a pass. And the guy that's supposed to receive it, many times it's thrown up high on purpose so the other guys can't catch it. And the guy that's going to receive it, so many times has to jump way up in the air to catch it. Now the members of the opposing team, they have learned that if you can hit this guy while he's still up in the air before he really gets good control of that ball, you can knock it loose from him. So they wait until he jumps up in the air, and when that ball touches his fingers they knock the hell out of him. Now he's completely defenseless now and they'll hit him and sometimes it'll just turn him upside-down. He'll fall on his head, his neck bends sideways, his legs spread apart, one arm bends completely behind his back, and it just hurts the hell out of him. You can see that he's hurt. Now the football game though, is like the game of life. It's going to go on, they're not going to stop it very long. One of two things will happen with his guy. They'll run out there and check him over and if he isn't hurt too bad they'll pump a little air in him and get him up and get him going again. If he's hurt too bad, they'll drag him off to the side, put somebody in his place, and the game starts again. The football game is going to continue, I don't care what's happened.

Now the announcer up in the booth though, he's got a resentment machine. Cause after a while he'll say let's look at that again. And this time it is in slow motion and living color. My God it looks twice as bad as it did the first time. You can see how back his neck really did bend, how far his legs spread apart and how badly that arm was bent and it looks twice as bad as it did the first time.

After a while the announcer will say, let's look at that again. The games been going on now for fifteen minutes, the announcers still bouncing this guy up and down, up and down, up and down off the ground.

Now we alcoholics have up here in our heads a little resentment replay machine

And we get up in the morning, and we tune it up in living color, we clean the lens on it cause we don't want to miss nothing, and we shine it on the world on day long, and we record everything they do to us that's bad, and we go home at night and sit down and play it over in our head, make ourselves sick and blame it on them.

Now once in a while we have a bad day. Once in a while they won't do anything to us. We got our machine cleaned up, the lens is clean, tuned up we shine it on the world, and nobody will do anything to us.
We don't have anything bad to record. You know what we record those days? By God **we record what they're thinking.**, that's what we do we go home at night and play it over in our head, make ourselves sick

Now there's a bad thing about a resentment, each time you play it over in your head, each time you throw it out there, after a while it turns around and comes back at you

When it comes back at you it comes back as <u>self-resentment</u>

and we begin to resent ourselves for being in a position to have those things happen to us. After a while

self resentment turns to self-pity

and that's the sickest, sickest that a human being can be up in their head, is too be filled with self-pity. And we alcoholics love self-pity.

We like to get up early in the morning, put self-pity on as a cloak of dignity, and as we go out the door we say here we come mean old world, just do it to mean. I know you're going to get me cause you always do. It is a sick, sick way to build our self-esteem. Cause after all if the whole world is picking on us we must really be somebody, and my God we love that self-pity. If you want an alcoholic mad, if you want to make them mad you try to feel sorry for one of us. We'll tell you in a hurry, don't you feel sorry for me, that's my damn job.

Is there any way God can enter a mind filled with that kind of crap? No way, our thinking is controlled and dominated by these resentments and all the things that go along with it.

God is absolutely, completely blocked out of our mind through these resentments.

At the very least, we're going to have to do something about them. Now the instructions on how to do them are here in the Big Book of Alcoholics Anonymous are just so simple that we never could see them before. We've given you a sheet in your handout material called "A Review of Resentments".

REVIEW OF RESENTMENTS

INSTRUCTIONS FOR COMPLETION

Instruction 1 In dealing with resentments we set them on paper. We listed people, institutions or principles with whom we were angry. (Complete Column 1 from top to bottom. Do nothing on Columns 2, 3 or 4 until Column 1 is complete.)

Instruction 2 We asked ourselves why we were angry. (Complete Column 2 from top to bottom. Do nothing on Columns 3 or 4 until Column 2 is complete.)

Instruction 3 On our grudge list we set opposite each name our injuries. Was it our self-esteem, our security, our ambitions, our personal or sex relations which had been interfered with? (Complete each column within Column 3 going from top to bottom. Starting with the Self-Esteem Column and finishing with the Sexual Ambitions Column. Do nothing on Column 4 until Column 3 is complete.)

Instruction 4 Referring to our list again. Putting out of our minds the wrongs others had done, we resolutely looked for our own mistakes. Where had we been selfish, dishonest, self-seeking and frightened and inconsiderate? (Asking ourselves the above questions we complete each column within Column 4.)

Instruction 5 Reading from left to right we now see the resentment (Column 1), the cause (Column 2), the part of self that had been affected (Column 3), and the exact nature of the defect within us that allowed the resentment to surface and block us off from God's will (Column 4).

COLUMN 1	COLUMN 2	COLUMN 3 "SELF" AFFECTS MY (Which part of self is affected?)									COLUMN 4 What is the exact nature of my wrongs, faults, mistakes, defects, shortcomings:			
		Social Instinct		Security Instinct		Sex Instinct		Ambitions						
I'm resentful at:	The cause:	Self-Esteem	Personal Relationships	Material	Emotional	Acceptable Sex Relations	Hidden Sex Relations	Social	Security	Sexual	Selfish	Dishonest	Self-Seeking & Frightened	Inconsiderate
1														
2														
3														
4														
5														
6														
7														
8														

And what I would ask you to do know, is to take those last 2 columns, try to fold them over to where you can't even see them, where all you're looking at is column 1, 2 and 3. The example on page 65 has already been filled out, and we didn't know the procedure Bill used to fill it out. That's where a lot of our confusion is. So what we've given to you in the first three columns is page 65 in a blank form. We want to emphasize we're not trying to bring another inventory to AA, we've already got enough of those. Page 65, the resentment sheet that you have, is 65 in a blank form.

Column 1	Column 2	Column 3
I'm resentful at:	*The Cause*	*Affects my:*

Now let's see if we can't find the instructions on how to fill it out.

Big Book p. 64, par. 4, line 28   "*In dealing with resentments, we set them on paper.*"

J & C   Okay, you got the paper now, we're going to start setting them down. You know we're always taught to read from left to right, and if you read from left to right in trying to figure out the inventory on page 65 you would start with Mr. Brown. You would write down the resentment, change your mind and go to the second column and write down the cause, change your mind again and go to what part of self was affected. You have to use those basic instincts of life, and write down what part of self was affected. Then you'd go back to the first column, mentally, and write down Mrs. Jones, and then you'd change your mind again and go to the second column. You get the idea, if you do that long enough, if you have a mind like mine it says, tilt, just too much information. And I say, what the hell, all they wanted was a life story anyhow. So I just disregarded this. But we didn't know how to fill out this column. It seems to us you fill this out one column at a time from top to bottom, leaving a little space in between the names in column one. You'll fill that in column two a little bit later. Our book says,

Big Book p. 64, par. 4, line 29   "*We listed people, institutions or principles with whom we were angry.*"

J & C   Period. From top to bottom in column one. We would simply write down all the people, principals and institutions with whom we were angry from top to bottom leaving a little space between each one of them all the way down.

People	That's self-explanatory
Institutions	Those things such as the Police Department, Internal Revenue Service, Federal Government, Church
Principals	old, old guiding "laws", natural laws that's interfered with our style of living

Ten Commandments, that's a set of principals. When I was out there drinking I didn't want to here nothing about the Ten Commandments. I'm breaking all of them but one, and maybe I broke it in a black out too, I don't know. Another old principal I always hated was, "What goes up must come down". I never cared for that one. Another one said, "What you give out is what you get back". Another one said, "There are no free rides you pay for whatever you get". And my Dad used to say, "When you lay down with dogs, you'll get fleas on you every time". Those old, old principals that interfered with our style of living. Now you don't need to be sober very long to do this. All we've got to do is take these things out of our head and put them down on paper. You don't have to have a high education to do this. If you can't write, you feed the names to somebody else and let them write them down. **And while <u>our mind is on one thing, and one thing only</u>, let's fill out the first column from top to bottom**. I've never seen an alcoholic yet that did not know just who and what by God we're mad at. We spend thousands of hours sitting around in bars talking about it. All we've got to do is take it out of our head and put it down on a piece of paper, and we would have completed the first instruction.

And hopefully the same thing will happen to you that happened to me when I did this. They came to me and they said, list your resentments, and I said, I don't have any. And they said, surely you have one or two, maybe you don't understand what a resentment is. And they explained to me that it was to **re-feel old pains and old hurts**. And I said yeah I got a couple of those. They said put them on paper, leave a little space in between each one. So I got a sheet of paper and leaving a space between like the book does, first thing I know I got about 8 names on that sheet of paper. I reached over and got another sheet of paper, and after a while I had eight more listed. I got another sheet of paper and the next thing you know I had eight more listed and I got another sheet of paper. I got up to about 152, and I said man, you're madder than hell at everything. I did not know that. **You can only see one resentment at a time in your head.**

I don't think any of us will ever see how many resentments we really do have, and how much they control and dominate our thinking until we get them down on a sheet on paper and see them in their entirety for the first time.

Now we made a decision (Step 3) to let God direct our thinking, and

**if we've got that many resentments then
resentments direct our thinking**

and God can't

And it's just by the listing of the names, we learn something very valuable about ourselves - just how resentful we really are. You just can't see this stuff in your head, it has to go on paper.

So we filled out the first column. Now Bill said, Mr. Brown, Mrs. Jones, My employer and My wife. He probably had more than that. I think he just didn't want to use anymore space in the Big Book. Mine was that long, long list of about 152 names. Joe.

Big Book p. 64, par. 4, line 31   "We asked ourselves why we were angry."

J & C   Period. Stop right there and go to the second column *The Cause*
In the illustration he uses here **very short and sweet, just four or five little words, not too many words to describe the cause. Simplicity is the key here in the second column.**

I'm resentful at: *The Cause*

Mr. Brown	His attentions to my wife.
	Told my wife of my mistress.
	Brown may get my job at the office.
Mrs. Jones	She's a nut - she snubbed me.
	She committed her husband for drinking. He's my friend.
	She's a gossip.
My Employer	Unreasonable - Unjust - Overbearing. (refers to p. 36)
	Threatens to fire me for drinking and padding my expense account.
My Wife	Misunderstands and nags.
	Likes Brown.
	Wants house put in her name.

So simply in the second column we just write down, we ask ourselves why we were angry. Beside each name one at a time, using four or five little words to describe the cause. There may be one cause, or there may be two or three causes, but we simply write them down in the second column.

We're not going to write any long essays, just a few simple words by each name. It may be one cause, or it may be multiple causes as we have here. Whatever it is we put it down.

I filled out the second column and I began to realize something that's become very valuable to me.

**I began to realize that it's not the People and the Institutions that I'm upset with.
It's what they've done to me that's got me upset.**

I can take Mr. Brown out of here and put Mr. Green in. I'll be just as upset with Green as I am with Brown if he does the same thing to me. I could take Mrs. Jones out of here and put Mrs. Smith in. If Smith does the same thing I'm going to be just as upset with her as I am with Jones. I can take my wife out of here and put my mistress in, and if she does the same thing I'll be just as upset with her. I begin to realize it's not them that's got me upset, it's what they've done to me that's got me upset.

Now the reason that's valuable is because of this. I'm getting ready to start out on a lifetime changing process to develop the best possible relationship I can with the world and everybody in it so I can have maximum peace of mind and serenity. A part of that relationship is a little later on in my program I'm going to have to go to a bunch of people and ask them to forgive me for what I've done to them. By the same token, I'm going to have to forgive others for what they've done to me.

**And a part of that forgiving process can start right here when I begin to realize it's not them,
it's what they've done that's got me upset.**

That starts getting names out of the way. And it's going to make it a lot easier to handle this in the future. So I've filled out two columns now.

1. I learned how resentful I really am, how much that blocks me from God.
2. I learned it's not them I resent; it's what they've done to me that I actually resent.

Two valuable things. Now let's look at the third column.

Big Book p. 64, par. 4, line 33   *"In most cases it was found that our self-esteem, our pocketbooks, our ambitions, our personal relationships (including sex) were hurt or threatened. So we were sore. We were burned up. On our grudge list we set opposite each name our injuries. Was it our self-esteem, our security, our ambitions, our personal, or sex relations, which had been interfered with? We were usually as definite as this example:"*

J & C   And again using that information that we got from **the basic instincts of life**, we set to fill out the third column, what <u>part of self was affected</u> by that, <u>what basic instinct was threatened</u> by the action those people did.

I can't be upset with you unless you've done something to threaten one of these basic instincts of life.
If you threaten my <u>social instinct</u> in any way, my <u>self-esteem</u>, my <u>personal relations</u>, you're going to upset me, make me angry.
If you threaten my <u>security, either material or emotional</u>, you're going to upset me and make me angry. If you threaten my <u>sex life</u> in anyway, you're going to upset me and make me angry.

And as I begin to <u>fill out the third column and put down the part of self that is affected</u>, in most cases I begin to see a pattern develop.
Maybe beside each name I'm putting down self-esteem. Maybe I begin to see my main problem is self-esteem.
Maybe I'm putting down security. Maybe I begin to see my main problem deals with security.
Maybe I'm putting something under sex each time and I begin to realize the sex thing is my main problem.

I begin to <u>see what part of self really does stand out.</u>

Probably going to be a combination of all three, but I can certainly see what part of self really does predominate and stand out when I keep seeing it appear over and over and over and over again.

When I filled out the third column here's where I learned something that I think is the most valuable thing I ever learned about me. As I filled out the third column, for the first time in my life I could see where anger comes from. I've always had a problem with anger; I've always acted and re-acted with anger. I would do something to hurt other people I'd be ashamed of it, I'd say I'd never to it again, I'd turn right around and get angry and do it all over again.

You can't do anything about a problem until you understand the problem. I never did understand where anger comes from. I always thought it was just one of those feelings that flitted into your mind, you could do nothing about it. Today I realize that **anger comes from a threat to one of these basic instincts of life.**

If my basic instincts are under control at the level that God intended, if my relationship with God is okay, you can do anything you want to me and I'm not going to experience anger over it.

I'll guarantee you if my instincts are out of control, if my relationship with God is not right, about anything you do to me that threatens a basic instinct, creates anger.

And I romp and stomp and raise hell with you and everybody around you. Now this lady that I'm married to today, hopefully I can introduce you to her tomorrow, she's her with us this weekend, a beautiful lady name Barbara. If there's any such thing as a black belt Al-Anon, she's one of them. She's got now about 31 or 32 years in the Al-Anon fellowship, great, great program. But Barbara is like all human beings. She has self-will too. Now once is a great while, she'll get <u>sick in self</u>. Al-Anons do that once is a while, not too often but once is a while. She'll do something that threatens one of my basic instincts of life. And when she does it, it hurts. I've found that if my relationship with God is right, my instincts are at the level God intended, I'm able to say, the poor old thing. They're sick just like we are and they cant' help it anymore than we can, and that thing will just slide off of my back and just won't bother me at all and I'll just go on about my business. Now thirty days later though, the same lady does the same thing, only this time my instincts are not under control and my relationship with God is not right today. And I react to what she did with anger, and I romp and I stomp and I raise hell with Barbara and everybody around me all day long. The same lady did the same thing but I choose to react to it in an entirely different manner based upon my relationship with God and where my instincts are that day. Thank God I've learned that, cause you see I can't do anything about Barbara, and

**I can't do anything about any other human begin on earth,
but I can do something about my relationship with God
and keeping my instincts under control where I don't have to get angry.
And if I don't have to get angry, <u>I'm in much less chance of drinking</u>
than I am if I just continue that anger over and over and over.**

Thank God I learned that. One of the best pieces of information I ever found. Now we have filled out three columns.

Column 1
We listed the people we're angry with, resentful at.
And we realize how resentful we really are, and how much that blocks us off from the sunlight of the spirit.

Column 2
We learned it's not them we're resentful at; it's what they've done to us.

Column 3
We learned it's not even what they've done to us. It's how we choose to react to it based on our relationship with God and whether our instincts are under control or not.

Now we're going to fill out a couple names here from our inventory. We're not going to do the whole thing, but just two or three names as an example. The first name on my sheet was this lady named Barbara. Thirty some odd years ago I hated this lady with a purple passion. If I could have done away with her and not got caught I believe I would have done it. I used to lay awake at night fantasizing about this thing. Tomorrow morning while she's on the way to work and by the way she always worked. I believed in her being self supporting through her own contributions. Always thinking of others. Tomorrow morning while she's on the way to work she's going to get run over by a big semi truck. And it's not just going to be any trucking company, it's going to be a very affluent trucking company. And they're going to run over her and kill her and I'm going to sue them. And I'm going to come out of this deal getting rid of her with two or three million dollars in hand. You Al-Anon's are not the only ones that fantasize, we alkis did it too, believe me we did. The second name on my sheet was the Internal Revenue Service. God, I hated those people with a purple passion. Just mention their name and I began to froth at the mouth immediately. Joe, what was the first name on your inventory sheet? Rose, wife number one, Rose. Now it's just that simple, that's how you fill out the first column.

We go to the second column. Why am I so upset with Barbara? The last year before she went to Al-Anon she had the audacity to file for divorce three times. She's spending more money on lawyers and divorces than I'm spending on booze and everything that goes with it. And my God I hated her for that. Why am I so upset with the Internal Revenue Service? Well they're trying to put me in jail, that's why. Joe, how come you're so upset with Rose? Had an affair with another man, after all I done to her, I mean after all I done for her. Had an affair with another man, really upset with her.

Now we go to the third column.

Barbara filing for divorce three times, is that a threat to my self-esteem?
You betcha. What are other people going to think about me now, taking this lady back after she's filed for divorce three times?

Barbara filing for divorce three times, is that a threat to my personal relationships?
Sure it is. She's going to take the kids and she's going to leave or they're going to kick me out, one of the two. No personal relationships.

Her filing for divorce three times, is that a threat to my security?
By the time she's through, she'll have it all don't worry about that.

Is it a threat to my sex life?
She probably wont let me have any sex if we get a divorce.

The Internal Revenue Service trying to put me in jail, is that a threat to my self-esteem?
What are people going to think about me after this deals over with?

Is it a threat to my personal relationships?
They're not going to let me have any relationship with my wife and children if I'm in jail

Is it a threat to my security?
They're going to take every penny I've got by the time it's over with.

Is it a threat to my sex life?
The kind I'd like to have, you betcha it's a threat to it.

Rose had an affair with another man, is that a threat to Joe's self-esteem?
Is it a threat to his personal relationships?
Is it a threat to his security?
Yeah he'll have to go to work now, she's been supporting him for the last ten years.

A threat to his sex life?

All these things are a threat to those things. OK. When we have finished up these three sheets/columns, and we've been able to see

column 1 - how many resentments we have
column 2 - the cause of the resentment
column 3 - the part of self that was affected

and we've learned valuable information about ourselves, just by filling out those three sheets.

J & C   Now then let's see what we do with those three sheets after they're filled out. Joe.

Big Book p.65, par. 4   "We went back through our lives. Nothing counted but thoroughness and honesty. When we were finished we considered it carefully. The first thing apparent was that this world and its people were often quite wrong. To conclude that others were wrong was as far as most of us ever got. The usual outcome was that people continued to wrong us and we stayed sore. Sometimes it was remorse and then we were sore at ourselves. But the more we fought and tried to have our own way, the worse matters got. As in war, the victor only seemed to win. Our moments of triumph were short-lived. It is plain that a life which includes deep resentment leads only to futility and unhappiness. To the precise extent that we permit these, do we squander the hours that might have been worth while. "

J & C   And I read that last statement and I stopped. And I tried to look back in my life and see how much time I've squandered in resentments. Now I don't know about you guys, but I know about me. When I've got a good resentment churning around here in my head I'm pretty well paralyzed from doing anything worthwhile. And one of my favorite things that I was doing back when I was drinking was to get up early in the morning, have a drink of whiskey and a cup of coffee and turn on my resentment reply machine. And replay what she did to me yesterday and replay what that guy did to me a month ago and replay what the person said to me six months ago and replay what that damn boss did to me about a year ago. And replay what that damn policeman did to me about 5 years ago. And replay what my uncle did to me 10 years ago. And replay what my mother did to me 15 years ago. And replay what my father did to me 20 years ago. And it took me just about an hour to run through that tape. And I loved every moment of it. When that tape would run out I'd have another drink of whiskey and another cup of coffee and I would turn on my get even machine. Now by God the next time she does that I'll do this and she'll do that and socko I'll put it on here. They're not going to treat me that way. . And it took me just about an hour to run through that tape. And I loved every moment of it. When I came into AA I found out the only difference was I wasn't taking the drink of whiskey. I was having the cup of coffee turned on the resentment replay machine run it for an hour another cup of coffee turn on the get even machine run it for an hour. I have spent literally thousands and thousands and thousands of hours in resentments. And as far as I can tell they've never done me any good whatsoever. They certainly never made me any money. They never made me feel better. They only made me feel worse. They never straightened up a relationship with another human being, they only made then worse and worse and worse. And as far as I can tell that was absolute complete wasted time. Now as a human being, I really believe today that I'm allotted just so much time to be here on earth. And I'm beginning to approach the end of mine. And for the first time in my life not only am I sober but I am peaceful, happy and free. For the first time in my life I'm sober and I feel great. I didn't know that you could be sober and feel as good as I feel today. What little time that I have left I want to enjoy every moment of it. I don't want to waste any more time in resentment or anything else that blocks me off from God. I want to enjoy every moment of every day that I've got left. I simply do not intend to waste any more time in resentments. They block you off from God they block you off from your fellow man. They just make you sicker and sicker and sicker. And what time we spend in them is an absolute waste of time. That's one of the worst things about a resentment wasting what time we have left in resentments. But that's not the worst thing. Here's the worst thing about a resentment.

Big Book p.66, par. 1, line 4   *"But with the alcoholic, whose hope is the maintenance and growth of a spiritual experience, this business of resentment is infinitely grave. We found that it is fatal. For when harboring such feeling we shut ourselves off from the sunlight of the Spirit. The insanity of alcohol returns and we drink again. And with us, to drink is to die."*

J & C   That's the worst thing about a resentment. When we've got a good resentment churning around in our head we don't feel good. We're blocked off from God. And after awhile the mind wanting to feel better begins to think about the sense of ease and comfort that comes at once with taking a couple of drinks. Next thing you know we become insane. We convince ourselves it's OK to drink. And we end up taking a drink and we trigger the allergy and we end up drunk all over again. That's the worst part about a resentment. The book says

Big Book p. 66, par. 2   *"If we were to live, we had to be free of anger. The grouch and the brainstorm were not for us. They may be the dubious luxury of normal men, but for alcoholics these things are poison. We turned back to the list,"*

J & C   And you see this is why you've got to have a written inventory. If you had it in your head you would have lost it already.

Big Book p. 66, par. 3   *"We turned back to the list, for it held the key to the future. We were prepared to look for it from an entirely different angle."*

J & C   Always before I looked at it to see what those suckers had done to me. Today I would look at it to see what that resentment is doing to me. And if it's blocking me off from God and maybe causing me to get drunk then I'm looking at it from an entirely different angle.

Big Book p. 66, par. 3, line 3   *"We began to see that the world and its people really dominated us. In that state, the wrong-doing of others, fancied or real, had power to actually kill."*

J & C   And I stopped and I said Charlie how dumb can you be? All my life I've been proud of the fact that I stand on my own two feet, nobody tells me what to do. I don't need your advice thank you. And I suddenly realized that other people through my resentment toward them have controlled and dominated my thinking as far back as I can remember. And if they've controlled and dominated my thinking, they've controlled and dominated my actions they have absolutely completely controlled and dominated my entire life for me. I always thought I was in charge, but I suddenly realized other people had been in charge as far back as I can remember through my resentment towards them. And then I said Man you really are stupid aren't you. Cause some of these people have been dead and buried in the graveyard for years. And they've been reaching out from the grave and they've had me by the yang yang for as far back as I can remember. And when I saw that I said to hell with them. I'm not going to let those people alive or dead, live in my head rent-free any longer. I've made a decision to let God direct my thinking and if others direct it, alive or dead justified or unjustified, then God can't. And it's just that simple. And an amazing thing happened to me right here. We alcoholics fancy ourselves as reasonable intelligent people. And I don't know that we're smarter than anybody else but I think we're reasonably intelligent people. And we don't like to look stupid. And when I saw the stupidity of letting those people control me and dominate me it looked so dumb that about 95% of these resentments begin to disappear automatically. When I saw how stupid that really was. But I found that I had 4 or 5 or 6 that were so deeply embedded in my mind for so long that they didn't automatically disappear when I saw the stupidity behind them. And for those I had to have some additional help. We now come to the first prayer in the Big Book in step 4. We always here about the step 3 prayer , the step 7 prayer but we never here about the step 4 prayer. Let's see how we can use prayer to remove those deep, deep seeded resentments.

Big Book p. 66, par. 3, line 6   "How could we escape? We saw that these resentments must be mastered, but how? We could not wish them away any more than alcohol."

J & C   You see you can't heal a sick mind with a sick mind. You can't wish your way out of it.

Big Book p. 66, par. 4   "This was our course: We realized that the people who wronged us were perhaps spiritually sick. Though we did not like their symptoms and the way these disturbed us, they, like ourselves, were sick too. We asked God to help us show them the same tolerance, pity, and patience that we would cheerfully grant a sick friend. When a person offended we said to ourselves, "This is a sick man. How can I be helpful to him? God save me from being angry. Thy will be done."

J & C   And I'm like Charlie. I spent many, many years in my life, many hours of life thinking and my mind was racing uncontrollably, and figuring out some way I could get even with those people. And I finally figured out a way to get even with them. Well the way you get even with people is you pray for them. And when you pray for them then you're even. You see I didn't know that. And after I got sober, id been sober about 3 or 4 months, o went to a little conference in Apache, Oklahoma. And I met a lady there, some of you know, her name was Alabam Carruthers. Some of you all knew Alabam. See become a big influence on my life. And she said a couple of things that night that really struck me. She said she had a soul sickness. And I could identify with that. Cause my last night of drinking I was sitting on a barstool and I had a real sick feeling in my stomach and it wasn't the throwing up type sick it was sick feeling. And she said it was a soul sickness and that's what I had. A soul sickness. And then she said another thing that night. She said I have peace of mind today. And boy I mean that really struck me. Cause that's all I've ever wanted was peace of mind. And I loved Alabam. She was always excited about life and what was going to happen next. And after that meeting was over with we were sitting around the lobby of this hotel and it was about 3:00 in the morning and I was sitting there watching Alabam operate and I wasn't saying anything. Finally it was just Alabam and myself and my little sponsor George, a little black guy laying in her lap. And I began to talk to Alabam. And I said Alabam you said you had peace of mind tonight how did you get peace of mind? I want peace of mind. And she said well Joe tell me what's going on in your mind. And I told her how I was going to meetings and going to meetings and going to meetings. But then at night I'd go home and lay down and my mind would fly open and I'd begin to think about all those situations that we talked about. And she said well Joe you're just full of resentments. And I said what is a resentment? See I didn't know. She said a resentment was old angers and old hurts that were refelt over and over and over again. And all that anger that you intended to use up on them you're turning it in on yourself and making yourself sick and blaming it on them. She explained that to me and it took a while for me to understand. Finally I did. And I said well is there any solutions for these? And she said well yes there is. There just happens to be. and she referred to page 67 and she showed me this information here. And she said some of those deep seeded resentments like you have you'll need some additional help. And she said on page 551 of this book is the story of a lady who had those deep seeded resentments. And if you would turn to that page in the book she said we will see what it had to say. Well Alabam had purse that was about hit big and it was about that deep and she began to look in that purse. You know how they are, digging around. And she finally found one of these books. I didn't think she was ever going to ding it. She pulled it out of there and she said well let's look at page 551 and see what this says. So I turned over to page 551 in her book and in the third paragraph this book says

Big Book, p. 551, par. 3   "I've had many spiritual experiences since I've been in the program, may that I didn't recognize tight away, for I'm slow to learn and they take many guises. But one was so outstanding that I like to pass it on whenever I can in hope that it will help someone else as it has me. As I said earlier, self-pity and resentment were my constant companions and my inventory began to look like a thirty-three year diary, for I seemed to have a resentment against everybody I had ever know. All but one "responded to the treatment" suggested in the Steps immediately"

J & C   All but one automatically began to disappear when she saw how dumb they really were.

Big Book, p. 551, par. 3, line 11   "but this on posed a problem.

It was against my mother and it was twenty-five years old. I had fed it, fanned it and nurtured it as one might a delicate child, and it had become as much a part of me as my breathing. It had provided me with excuses for my lack of education, my marital failures, personal failures, inadequacy, and of course my alcoholism and, though I really thought I had been willing to part with it, now I knew I was reluctant to let it go.

One morning, however, I realized I had to get rid of it, for my reprieve was running out, and if I didn't get rid of it I was going to get dunk -- and I didn't want to get drunk any more. In my prayers that morning I asked God to point out to me some way to be free of this resentment. During the day a friend of mine brought me some magazines to take to a hospital group I was interested in , and I looked through them and a :banner" across the front of one featured an article by a prominent clergyman in which I caught the word "resentment".

He said, in effect: "If you have a resentment you wasn't to be free of, if you will pray for the person or the thing that you resent, you will be free. If you will ask in prayer for everything you want for yourself to be given to them, you will be free. Ask for their health, their prosperity, their happiness, and you will be free. even when you don't really want it for them, and your prayers are only words and you don't mean it, go ahead and do it anyway. Do it every day for tow weeks and you will find you have come to man it and to want it for them, and you will realize that where you used to fell bitterness and resentment and hatred, you now feel compassionate understanding and love"

J & C   Well I went home after that meeting and I got in my bed that Sunday night, laid down and my old mind flipped over again and started racing, uncontrollably. And I said now I think I'll pray for those people. So I started praying for those people that night. And my list got longer. The next day I prayed for those people again. And that afternoon I prayed for those people. And that night I prayed for those people. I don't know how long it went on it was 2 or 3 weeks or more I don't' know. But it seems like I was in constant prayer for them, day and night, praying for those people. I don't know exactly what happened but I do know that one morning it was one of the beautiful spring mornings we have in Oklahoma and I got stuck at this stop light. Just the length of a stoplight is what happened. I looked over at that beautiful house sitting over there and the grass was so green just beautiful. Greenest green I'd ever seen. The tulips were in full bloom, red and yellow. The little squirrels were in the trees and the birds were in the trees whistling and I got…it was just a beautiful morning. And I thought to myself, my God how long has it been since I've seen that. You know I could not remember, I could not remember. And when this book talks about being cut off from the sunlight of the spirit I really do know what that means. I really do. Cause that morning it was so vivid. Now what happened was that those people did not change. But my thoughts and feeling towards them did change. You see. And has never returned again. Thank God for this program called alcoholics anonymous. I've been there and I don't want ever to return again.

J & C   I think the reason this works so well is prayer for another human being, prayer for their welfare and their happiness is probably one of the greatest expressions of love that one human being can have for another. And love and hate can't exist on the same plane. And as we pray for that human being, asking that God give them in their lives the same things we want in ours, peace of mind, serenity, happiness, etc, over a period of time that resentment will begin to disappear. Sometimes it just takes 2 or 3 prayers. Sometimes it takes everyday for 2 weeks. Sometimes it might take everyday for 2 months. But if we will consistently do it, we will find sooner or later that that resentment is replaced with love and the resentment disappears.

Now if you've got a resentment that you don't want to get rid of, for God's sake don't pray about them. Cause if you do, you're going to lose it. I know I speak form experience.

You know I had a guy that I really, really, really resented. And again I think I would gladly have put him away if I could have gotten by with it without getting caught. And when I got to this part of the inventory I went to my sponsor. Now this is going to be one of those "take it to the grave" resentments. I had no desire to remove it at all. And I had worked on all of the others but this one just stuck in there. And I went to my sponsor and I told him about it. And he said "Charlie, you've got to get rid of that resentment. " And I said, "I don't want to get rid of this resentment." And he said, "Well that's beside the point." He said, " If you don't get rid of it sooner or later it's going to get you drunk". And in my smart mouth way I said, "Well how in the hell do I do it?"

And he said, "Let me show you". And he took me to this prayer too. And he said "Now read that and go home and do what it says and you'll get rid of that resentment". And I went home and got down on my knees, which again I very seldom did in those days, and I said "God, I want you to give that son of a bitch everything he deserves" and that's the only prayer I had for him that day. And I prayed again and again and again and 3 or 4 or 5 days later, I don't know when, I found myself saying something I didn't really mean to say. I found myself saying "God give him in his life what I want in mine. The same peace of mind, serenity and happiness that I seek for myself." And 4 or 5 or 6 or 7 days later, I don't know when, I woke up one morning and that resentment was gone, completely gone. And it's never returned since that date. And I think the irony in the whole situation is that it wasn't 30 days later this guy moved in as my next door neighbor. This thing really does work.

See what I learned from this experience is that

Love is forgiving and love is for giving

Now just think, this old head up here, these display case over here were filled with resentments has now been emptied out. The resentments, the damaged and unsalable goods called resentment has now been removed from my mind. Now when that happens to me there's another natural law that applies. That says nature abhors a vacuum. No such thing as a vacuum or void. There is always something trying to rush in and fill it up. If those resentments disappear God's not going to leave another hole in my head. I've got enough of those already. They will have to be replaced with something else. And the only thing that can replace them will be the opposite of them. Where my mind used to be filled with resentments, that portion of it is now filled with love, patience, tolerance, compassion, and goodwill toward my fellow man.

> **That's God's thinking. My thinking was the resentment.**
> **God's thinking is love, patience, tolerance, compassion, and goodwill**
> **and that part of my mind is now filled with God's thinking.**

You see there's nothing negative here at all. This is a positive happening. In part of my mind I've now got peace of mind, serenity and happiness. Much less chance of my drinking no than when I started the inventory process. And what really blew my mind is this. I didn't have to go to any other fellowships, and I didn't have to read any other books to find love, patience, tolerance, compassion, and goodwill.

> **If God dwells within me and my book says he does and that's always been a part of my makeup I just never could use it before.**
> **In my chase for money, power, prestige, sex and what I thought were the good things of life those thoughts had to be repressed to let me to operate on the level that I wanted to operate on.**
> **But now that resentments are gone they automatically come to the surface.**

I've never seen anything like this before. I don't really understand how this works. I simply know that if I do the simple things the book tells me to do this happens automatically and resentments are replaced with love, patience, tolerance, compassion, and goodwill toward my fellow man.

But it will do me no good to get rid of resentments if I didn't know how to keep them from coming back. Cause the world is full of sick people and their going to do it to me again tomorrow. And if I'm not careful I'll resent. And it seems as though I don't get just one. When I get one, let me play with it just a little bit and then I've got two. And let me play with those two and then I've got ten. And the next thing you know I'm a basket case and I'm sick all over again. I've got to do one more thing. Let's unfold those last two columns on your inventory sheet, and let's go to page 67, and well see if we can't find the information to fill out the last two columns. In the second paragraph on page 67 it says

Big Book p. 67, par. 2   *"Referring to our list again."*

J & C   You see you've got to have written inventory. This is the second time we've had to go back to it now.

Big Book p. 67, par. 2   *"Referring to our list again. Putting out of our minds the wrongs others had done, we resolutely looked for our own mistakes. "*

J & C   Uh-oh. We've never done this have we? We've always looked to see what they did. We've never looked to see what we did.

Big Book p. 67, par. 2   *"Where had we been selfish, dishonest, self-seeking and frightened? Though a situation had not been entirely our fault, we tried to disregard the other person involved entirely. Where were we to blame? The inventory was ours, not the other man's. When we saw our faults we listed them. We placed them before us in black and white. We admitted our wrongs honestly and were willing to set these matters straight."*

J & C   So we go to the fourth column. And if you'll notice the heading on the fourth column says, "What did I do?" Putting out of mind the wrongs others had done, I resolutely looked for my own mistakes. What did I do, if anything, to set in motion trains and circumstances which in turn caused people or institutions to hurt me and eventually led to my resentment of them for doing so?

So I went to column 4, and I looked at this lady named Barbara and I said " Now Charlie you forget what she did. You forget her filing for 3 divorces. What did you do, if anything, to set that in motion?" And it took me just about 5 seconds to realize that if I hadn't been out there screwing around she probably wouldn't have caught me. And she probably wouldn't have filed for divorce in the first place. Took me another 2 or 3 seconds to say to myself well if I hadn't been sneaking around behind her back lying to her all the time, completely dishonest with her, she probably wouldn't have filed for divorce in the first place. Another 3 or 4 seconds and I was able to say to myself well if I hadn't been blowing all of her money on booze and what I think was important she probably wouldn't have filed for divorce in the first place. And I begin to realize why I love that resentment. Cause you see when I could concentrate on her filing for divorce and play that over and over and over and over in my head, gradually distorting the picture every time I played it over making what she did a little bit worse and what I did a little bit less. And let me play it long enough I could gradually transfer all blame to her and make myself as pure as the driven snow. And it was all her damn fault in the first place. I thought my God Charlie, have you done that with any other resentments here?

I looked at the IRS. I said "Now forget what they're doing to you, trying to put you in jail. What did you do, if anything, to set in motion the fact that they are trying to put you in jail?" Well that didn't take 2 seconds to be able to say that if I hadn't been cheating on my income tax they wouldn't have been trying to put me in jail anyhow. And rather than look at what I had done to them. I had played it over and over and over and over, distorted the picture and transferred all blame to them. Made myself as pure as the driven snow. That way I could continue through life doing what I wanted to do and never have to look at me. Because after all it's all their fault in the first place.

Joe in this resentment against Rose, what did you do, if anything, to set that in motion.

Charlie was out there screwing around but I was committing adultery.

OK. Sneaking around behind her back and lying to her all the time. And Rose finally got enough of it. She said, "I'll show him". And she went out and had her own affair. And Joe had, over a period of time, played that resentment over and over, gradually transferred all blame to her, made himself as pure as the driven snow. I went down through my list of resentments. I never found a name on there that I hadn't done something to them to set this thing in motion and I had resented it and played it over and over and distorted the picture. Transferred all blame to them and made myself as pure as the driven snow. If you're a practicing alcoholic you've got to develop these kinds of skills. You know we have a conscience. We're not drunken bums. We know the difference between right and wrong. And I don't think we could live with ourselves if we had to honestly see what was going on whenever we're out there doing our thing. But you see, we never have to see it because we've got this convenient thing called resentments, that we play them over and over, distort the picture and transfer all blame to others. And we men go from woman to woman to woman, and you ladies go from man to man to man and we go from job to job to job and we go from city to city to city and we go from country to country to country and it's always their damn fault. That's the only way we could live the kind of life we were living. By being able to transfer blame to others. And none of us realize how much we've been doing that until we take an honest look at these resentments and see the part that we played.

Now in the fifth column you see the major character defects talked about in the big book.

Where had I been selfish, dishonest, self-seeking, frightened or inconsiderate?
All other character defects stem from these.

In the fifth column I asked myself this question. Which of the above character defects caused me to do what I did. Or caused me to want to hold on to the old resentment even though I may have done nothing to cause it. Now going back to Barbara again, if I hadn't have been so selfish I wouldn't have been out there doing those things that hurt my wife and children. If I hadn't have been so dishonest I wouldn't have been sneaking around behind her back lying to her all the time. If I hadn't have been so self-seeking and frightened, saying to myself "Man you're getting close to 40 years old if you're ever going to do some of that you'd better go do it before it's too late".

Fear drives us to things like that.

If I hadn't have been so inconsiderate of my wife and children I wouldn't have been taking the chance of hurting them in the first place. I begin to see in the fifth column the type of character I had become through my years of living my life based on self will. And when I saw it I didn't like it. It made me sick. You see I always fancied myself as a reasonably good person until I saw how I had become so selfish and so dishonest and so inconsiderate of other people. That I was continually doing things that hurt others. And they retaliated and I resented for it. I begin to see that if I don't change those things in the fifth column, if I stay selfish, dishonest, self-seeking, frightened and inconsiderate that I'm going to keep right on doing the same old things I've always done. Drunk or sober. I'm going to keep right on hurting people and they're going to retaliate and I'm going to resent and eventually it's going to block me off from God and I'm going to get drunk over it. But just think, if I could become a little less selfish, oh I don't have to get perfect I never will. But if I could become a little less selfish, if I could become a little less dishonest, if I could become less frightened and self-seeking, if I could become a little more considerate of other people, and their needs and their wants maybe I wouldn't have to do some of that kind of stuff. Maybe I wouldn't hurt people and maybe they wouldn't retaliate and I wouldn't have to resent. And just maybe I wouldn't have to get drunk over it. You see what we're really doing here is step 4. This is the resentment part of it. And out in the fifth column I now see the exact nature of the wrongs that I'm going to talk to another human being about when I take step 5. The resentment is the wrong that's what blocks me off from God but what's the exact nature of it. That means what's the truth of it. What's at the core of it, what's the inherent characteristic of it. That's what we'll talk about in step 5.

You know when a guy comes to me and he's committed adultery 44 times, I don't care about that. All I want to know is what is within him that caused him to do it in the first place. If he's stolen 364 times, I don't care about that. What I want to know is what is within him that caused him to do that. That's what we'll talk about in step 5. In that fifth column I now see the character defects that I am going to become willing to turn loose of in step 6. Out there in that fifth column I see the shortcomings now I'm going to ask God to take away in step 7. And in my case all the names from column 1 came off of this sheet to be added to the sheet later to be used for steps 8 and 9. Cause you see when I get to step 8 it says I've got the list. I made it when I took step 4. In my case every one of those. In your case probably some of them. In my case, all of them. Now what I have really done if I have done this the way the big book says is I have prepared myself with all the information I need for steps 4,5,6,7,8 and 9 resentment-wise. Not only have I gathered all the information I need for 4,5,6,7,8 and 9. Well I've had a positive result here. Resentments have disappeared. And they've been replaced with love, patience, tolerance, compassion and goodwill.

> **Did we do anything to be afraid of? No.**
> **Did we make a list of dirty filthy nasty items? No.**
> **Did we do anything that was too complicated? No.**

I've never seen anything like this inventory according to the big book.

J & C   Now I hear some of you saying, and I hear awful good, I've got good hearing. Charlie hears good. I hear some of you saying "Well Charlie that's probably right on those that we did something to them. But how about those that did it to us? And we didn't have anything to do with that. How about those that hurt us as kids growing up? How about those that hurt us in our marriages that we didn't do anything to cause it? Aren't we justified in having that kind of resentment? " Well I guess we are if we want to get drunk over it.

But you see a justified resentment blocks you off from God just like an unjustified resentment does.

When you've got a justified resentment churning around in your head, then whoever or whatever you're resenting is controlling your thinking. If they're controlling your thinking, they're controlling your decisions. They're controlling your life for you. And you have given them power to actually kill you. Cause you've given them power to cause you to get drunk again. Now if you've got one of those resentments and I don't care what it is, I don't care whether it's physical abuse, mental abuse, sexual abuse or whatever. And I keep hearing in AA all the time this sexual abuse thing. If usually centers on young women. Now let me tell you something, men know about that too. I don't know how many 5th steps I've taken with men, and nearly every one of them, somewhere in the background we've had that kind of stuff too, it's not just women it's men. If you've got one of those kind of resentments and you don't want to get rid of it knowing full well it might get you drunk then we'd better get it on this sheet of paper and take a look at it. And see what we're doing with it. We're probably using it for rationalization and justification. To rationalize not doing things we ought to go do or just as importantly to rationalize and justify things doing things we shouldn't be doing in the first place. Oh the greatest excuse in the world is

"If they hadn't have done that to me then I wouldn't have to be the way I am today".
They call that victimization.

I don't really think we have any place for that in AA. We're all adults. It's time for us to realize that whatever **has happened to us in the past does not have to control what we do today.** Now the only reason for that is to justify, rationalize and etc.

The woman in the book...
She used her resentment against her mother to justify her lack of education. Bull. She could have gotten an education if she wanted to bad enough.
She used it to justify her marital failure. Bull. Mama didn't have anything to do with her marital failure.
She even used it to justify her alcoholism. Mama had nothing to do with her alcoholism. She became alcoholic because she drank whiskey. And she drank enough of it she became alcoholic.

Now I think it's time for us to realize we are responsible for what we think and how we feel. We are responsible for what we do today. Mother and daddy and other people are no longer responsible for that. Maybe they were when we were little kids but we're not little kids any longer. And if really doesn't make any sense to let somebody hurt me 5, 10, 15, 20 years ago and then let them hurt everyday for the rest of my life. If I'm resenting them they've got me. And they're going to kill me. I need to put them on this sheet. Put down their name. What did they do to me? What part of self is affected? What did I do, if anything, to set it in motion, in this case nothing? But then let's look in the fourth column. Are we so dishonest with ourselves we refuse to see the truth?

If you've got a resentment in your head today it's not true. I'm going to say that again. If you've got a resentment in your head today it's not true.

Oh it was based on truth and it's partially true. But if you've played it over and over and over you've distorted it and it's no longer true. Can we honestly look at it and see the truth behind it?

Let's look in the fifth column and see if maybe are so frightened of facing life without it we've refused to turn it loose. Cause you know after all if we turn it loose then we've got to take responsibility for our own behaviour. It's a hell of a lot easier to blame it on others. Are we so afraid of facing life without it we won't turn it loose? Are we so inconsiderate of another human being? Have we failed to recognize that people that do those things to us, they're not necessarily bad people. They're sick people. They didn't necessarily do it to us. They would have done it to anybody in that position. If we could even begin to consider that, maybe we can start a forgiving process. Maybe we could straighten up a relationship with another human being before it's too late. After they're dead it's too late I'll guarantee you it is. Maybe we can do it while we're all still alive.

If we will do those things I think we can get rid of that resentment too when we really see the truth behind it and what we're doing with it. If we can't get rid of it that way then we can use the ultimate tool. By golly we can pray for them. And if we pray for one of those people we resent that doesn't mean that we approve of what they did. That doesn't mean we're going to take them by the hand and walk hand in hand with them for the rest of our life. What it means is that we are tired of letting them control us, dominate us and rule us everyday for the rest of our life. We can get rid of those kind of resentments too. And if we don't want to do that then chances are we are using it for some reason and we need to take a look at it very, very carefully. Joe?

Takes 2 people to make a prison...the prisoner and the jailer. Have to turn them loose and let them out and turn them loose. All those people that I hated I had to turn them loose. Charlie said "I don't want to be a victim anymore" and I don't think...Alcoholics Anonymous may be the only association left on the face of the earth that won't allow us to be victims. There's victims going on all out there. Everybody wants to be a victim of something. You know. But we in AA won't let each other do that cause we have a way out. When everything else fails we can pray for them. They need the prayers and we need the practice.

You know I see in many AA meetings where we've gone into this group therapy stuff and we sit around the table and we discuss what those people did to us. And we try to figure out why they did it. We'll never understand why they did it. The thing is they did it. Then we start trying to discuss and figure out why it made us the way we are? We'll never understand that. The fact is that's the way we are. The real question is "What are we going to do about it?" Are we going to continue to let them kill us? Or are we going to get rid of that jazz? That's what AA is about. It's not to sit around and talk about problems. It's to sit around and talk about how do you solve the problems. And resentment is the number one problem for every alcoholic. And if we can get rid of them then we're peaceful, happy and free. Until we do we'll never be free of it.

Now the next part of our inventory is fear and sex and Joe leaned over to me a while ago before when he walked behind and he said " Charlie, I've got a headache and I don't feel like sex today." He said "Let's get a good nights rest and have sex on Sunday morning." Is that OK with you guys?

Wherever you're going tonight you're going to work on your resentments. When we see you tomorrow morning you're going to be the most beautiful people in the world. You're going to be 100% resentment free. It's going to be great. Thank you all for being here today. We'll see you in the morning.

Good morning everyone. My name is Joe and I'm an alcoholic. And it's truly by God's grace and the fellowship of Alcoholics Anonymous and the program of Alcoholics Anonymous that I found in the book call Alcoholics Anonymous I'm sober today and for that I'm very, very thankful. And I've been sober ever since I quit drinking. And that was on November 3, 1973 and for that I'm truly thankful. And it's good to be here this morning isn't it? You guys have really been great this weekend. We really appreciate all the friendship and the friendliness that we've found her this weekend. It's been great. Made us feel real good and welcome. And I want to thank the committee again for all the hard work that they've done in putting this thing on and thank each and every one of you for being here. It's been a great weekend. Thank you.

Good morning everyone. My name is Charlie Parmley…lack of power was his dilemma…and I'm a very grateful recovering alcoholic this morning….because I'm a member of the fellowship of Alcoholics Anonymous and by the grace and the power that I found in the 12 step program of Alcoholics Anonymous I haven't found it necessary to take a drink in 10518 days today one day at a time and for this I am very grateful.
You guys look great this morning. Golly, not a resentment left in the whole bunch. Isn't that something? How many of you went back to where you were staying last night and worked on at least one resentment? Can I see your hands? Oh yah a bunch of you did. How many of you got rid of at least one resentment? Can I see your hands? Great. How many of you did we give a new resentment to yesterday afternoon? Can we see your hands? Pray for us. We need the prayers and you need the practice.

Oh I think I'll start out this morning with a little spiritual story, a little spiritual joke. Since it is Sunday morning.

This is a story about a new young priest. And he was so nervous at his first mass that he could barely speak. And before his second week in the pulpit he asked the Monsignor what he could do to relax himself. And the Monsignor said "Well next week before you do the mass" he said " why don't you put a little vodka in your water pitcher and after a few sips everything would probably be OK". Well sure enough the new young priest, before the next mass he put the vodka in the water pitcher and everything turned out just great. No embarrassment, could talk freely, no problems whatsoever. Well when he returned back to the rectory, he found a note from the Monsignor which said
#1 – Next time I suggest you sip at the water pitcher rather than gulp at it
#2 – There are 10 commandments not 12
#3 – There are 12 disciples not 10
#4 – David slew Goliath he didn't kick the shit of him
#5 – We do not refer to our Savior Jesus Christ and his apostles as J.C. and the boys
#6 – Next week there's a taffy pulling contest at St Peters not a peter pulling contest at St Taffys
#7 – We do not refer to the cross as The Big T
#8 – Last but not least, the Father, Son and Holy Ghost are not referred to as Big Daddy, Junior and the Spook

That's probably about as spiritual as we'll get this morning too. We went through a process yesterday afternoon, the first part of the inventory process. There we learn how to look at our resentments. To take an honest, truthful, moral inventory. And as we listed those resentments we begin to see the truth about them really. Now the first thing we saw in column 1 is how many resentments we really did have. How much that blocked us off from the sunlight of the spirit. The second thing we saw in column 2 is it's not those people or institutions we resent, it's what they've done to us that we actually resent. The third thing we found out in column 3, it's really not even what they've done to us, it's how we choose to react to a threat to one of our basic instincts of life which is going to determine whether we are resentful or not.

So just in filling out those three columns we've learned some very valuable information. Also we're able to see in the big book that resentments was an absolute waste of time. That whenever they're churning around in our heads we're pretty well paralyzed from doing anything worthwhile, and we find that if we honestly look at them, most of us have spent literally thousands and thousands of hours in resentments and as we look back at that time in our lives we can see where they never did do us any good. They never did straighten up a relationship with another human being. Never made us feel better, only made us feel worse. Never made us any money for sure. And as far as we can tell it's absolute wasted time. Now we also said that's not the worst thing about a resentment. The worst thing is it very effectively blocks us off from God. Blocked off from God we don't feel good. We begin to become insane. We begin to think about taking a drink. The next thing you know we end up drunk all over again. And when we truthfully and honestly looked at those resentments we could really begin to see how other people have controlled and dominated us throughout our entire lifetime through those resentments.

Now we always thought that we had it under control. That we determined what we said and what we did. But we suddenly realized that we really have done nothing but react to others through our resentment toward them. That looked so stupid to us that about 95% of those resentments disappeared. The other 5% that were so deeply embedded we found through prayer that we could remove them also so we could be resentment free if we follow the procedure outlined in the big book. The real revealing thing is though, the amazing thing is that after we became resentment free God wouldn't allow another hole in our head it had to be replaced with something else. The only thing that could replace it was the opposite of the resentment. And where we used to feel resentment we now feel serenity, a little peace of mind, a little happiness, compassion, goodwill, love. Those are all God's thinking rather than our individual thinking. And we found that that came to us automatically. Those things had always been a part of us, we just never could use them before.

Now the resentments are gone and God's thinking automatically begins to replace the resentment and we're much less chance of getting drunk now than we were when we started the process. We went back to the resentment sheet and we looked at it from an entirely different angle now. We begin to look at it to see what had we done to set that thing in motion or what did we do, we had never looked at before. And in our fourth column we found that in almost all cases whatever the resentment was we ourselves did something to set it in motion. And we hurt other people, the retaliated, we resented, we played the resentment over and over and over, distorted the picture, finally transferred all blame to other people. A good practicing alcoholic has to be able to do that. We just couldn't live if we didn't have that ability. So we really in the fourth column really did begin to look at the truth of the resentment to see the part that we had played. And in most cases we ourselves set the ball rolling. We looked in the fifth column to see the exact nature of that resentment. The resentment was the wrong, but what was the actual core of it or at the center of it? And in the fifth column we found the type personality that we had developed through the years of living on self-will and living as a practicing alcoholic. And we found that just about every time that we had hurt anybody in the past it was either through selfishness or through dishonesty or because we were self-seeking frightened or through inconsideration of other people. And we begin to see in the fifth column that if we don't change those things were going to keep right on doing the same things in sobriety that we use to do when drinking. We're going to continue to hurt people, they're going to retaliate, and we're going to resent and eventually get drunk over it. And we begin to see in the fifth column the things that we will need to change in our personality if we want to live with peace of mind, serenity and happiness in the future.

We summed it up by saying we're in the process of doing the resentment part of step 4. In the fifth column we now had all the information we needed for steps 5,6 and 7. And then the names in the first column, those that we had harmed, they come off of there to be added to the list to be used for 8 and 9 at a later date. So we really ended up in this simple little inventory with all the information we needed for 4,5,6,7,8 and 9 resentment wise. Very positive thing took place. Resentments disappeared and they were replaced with patience, tolerance, compassion and goodwill. So there was nothing to be afraid of. There was nothing too complicated. There was not a list of dirt, filthy, nasty items, just a simple inventory.

Now we don't want to give you the impression that you can always be 100% free of resentments. You know God never gave us anything bad. It depends on what we do with things on whether they become bad or not. A resentment used right can be used for a worthwhile purpose. If somebody does something to me that threatens my self esteem, if it would cause me to look at me and see some things that I need to change and I go ahead and make those changes then that resentment can be used for a worthwhile purpose. For instance if we are living in a neighborhood. All the old houses are run down. Mines no worse that anybody else. They all need painting, they've got broken window screens and panes. And I sit on my front porch every evening after work and I rock and I rock and I'm very complacent about that situation. One day I look up though and some idiot has moved in across the street. He's put there painting his house, fixing his window screens and windowpanes. Makes my house look bad. I resent the hell out him for doing that. I say, "Who in the hell is he moving in here and screwing up this whole neighborhood? "Now if I use that resentment right it will cause me to look at my house and become a little bit ashamed of it. Next thing you know I paint my house, fix my window screens and windowpanes. My next door neighbor resents me for doing so. Next thing you know he fixes his house up and his neighbor resents him and after a while God's got the whole neighborhood cleaned up like it should have been in the first place. That's the proper use of a resentment. But we alcoholics won't use it that way. We'll sit on the front porch and we'll rock and we'll rock and we'll resent and we'll resent. Thirty days later we'll go over there at midnight and we'll burn his damn house down. We'll show him. So it really depends on what we do with resentments that determines whether they are going to be for bad or good. And if we use one rightly it's going to disappear anyhow.

The ones that kill us are those that we just leave in our head and they just fester and fester and fester and we get sicker and sicker until eventually it creates a real problem for us. Joe?

J & C   This morning we're going to talk about fears a bit, we're not going to psychoanalyze ourselves in any matter, we're simply going to do like the book suggested yesterday. We're going to find the facts, we're going to face the facts eventually through this process, and we're going to accept the facts as they really are truthfully. And it says also that when the spiritual malady is overcome we straighten out mentally and physically. The spiritual malady is not only my relationship with God, but my relationship with me, my mental attitudes and my relationship with other people. So that's another form of spiritual malady that I had. And Dr. Jung said we're going to have to look at our ideas, emotions and attitudes and that's what we're doing through this inventory process. Looking at ideas, emotions and attitudes and see where they came from. And if we will we'll go back now to page 18 and I'm going to read this little paragraph it tells my whole story in one little paragraph

Big Book p. 18, par.1   "*An illness of this sort, and we have come to believe it an illness, involves those about us in a way no other human sickness can. If a person has cancer all are sorry for him and no one is angry or hurt. But not so with the alcoholic illness, for with it there goes annihilation of all the things worthwhile in life. It engulfs all whose lives touch the sufferer's. It brings misunderstanding, fierce resentment, financial insecurity, disgusted friends and employers, warped lives of blameless children, sad wives and parents anyone can increase the list.*"

J & C   In other words it's a family illness; it affects everybody in the family to some extent. And if you live with one of us very long you'll be affected by it in some manner for sure. And as I look back in my life to see where these ideas, emotions and attitudes that would become the guiding force of my life started way, way back.

My dad was an alcoholic I know that today. He had an obsession to drink and my mother had an obsession to see that he didn't drink and I grew up in that. My dad was a farmer there in Oklahoma and he couldn't make it there real well there during the Depression and they came to California and eventually we didn't fit in real good out here in that time. Later on we fit in real good. But we moved back to Oklahoma, back to West Tulsa, Oklahoma that's we're all the poor people lived and the menial labor people lived and that's where we lived. My dad got a job as an iceman. Worked six days a week carrying ice to the people's homes, backbreaking work. Saturday he would come home after work and he would stop by the bootlegger and pick up a half-pint or pint of that rotgut whiskey and had a little drink. And he needed a drink for sure. My mother saw that fifty cents or a dollar going for whiskey that could have gone for these five kids that she had and she was fearful too and she raised hell with him and he raised hell with her and I grew up in this, that's the way I grew up. And we know it's a progressive illness this alcoholism and my family got progressively worse. My dad got to be physically and verbally abusive to my mother and us children and as time went by he would put out a gun once in a while or a knife and wave it around the house and threaten my mother with it. And from time to time when I was a young fellow and he would take my mother out and would tell us before he left, boys I'm going to kill your mom this weekend, and they'd be gone. And I'm sitting at home, seven or eight years old and I'm growing up in this and it affected me emotionally in lots of manners. Later on his drinking got to be so bad my mother had to have him committed to the Eastern St. Hospital of Bonita, which is our local nut house and they didn't have any treatment centers for alcoholics at that time so they put him in the criminally insane ward. And that's what they did with alcoholics of our type in those days 1949, 50, 51. He was committed there till he got well, think about that. My dad was there for three years and seven months and thirteen days and he was an alcoholic in the criminally insane ward. And my brother and I used to hitchhike up there about seventy miles and take a couple of dollars and a carton of cigarettes to see him and we'd go into the criminally insane ward and I'd see things in there that I can't describe that you're not ever supposed to see what they did with people in those days. And some of the ideas, emotions and attitudes began to form in my life right around there and on the way home sometimes I would think this, If God, you got to blame it on somebody, if God is going to do this to me then to hell with God. And I'll never be calling on him any more thank you. And that's the way I lived my life. Another thought came to my was this. If it hurts this much to love people I'm not going to love anybody anymore either, quit loving people, it hurts too much. So I began to push people out of my life. And another thought came to me was this, if anything good is going to happen in my life it's going to happen because I alone without any help made it that way. A totally selfish and self-centered attitude, but I didn't know that**.** I thought those were very brave attitudes on my part, and I thought that way for a long time. And I'm trying to say it's not very good coping skills we have here. They put you in jail for some of these ideas that you have, and they divorce you for those kinds of things. I see people today who are very loud and profane, verbally abusive, cussing, raising cane everywhere, and I know exactly what's wrong with them, they're scared to death. Cause that's exactly the way I was and if you threatened me in any manner I would jump right in your face. I did that; I did that over here across the river in Arizona one time. They gave me seven to fifteen for that, told me never to come over there again, but I didn't... I went back one time, well anyhow, just briefly. We went to Flagstaff and did a Big Book Study and he was looking behind him all the time. They told me never to come back and I meant it, when I left there I meant never to come back.

What I am trying to tell you is that I didn't need God, I didn't need other people, I just needed me, and that's the way I lived my life way after I got into Alcoholics Anonymous. So now let's go back to p. 67. There again we're not trying to psychoanalyze ourselves. I found the facts, I accepted the facts and I looked at the facts and I could see where I'd come from

Big Book p. 67, last par. "Notice that the word 'fear' is bracketed alongside the difficulties with Mr. Brown, Mrs. Jones, the employer, and the wife."

J & C Six times along that column (3rd column, example on p. 65)

Big Book p. 67, last par., line 3 "This short word somehow touches about every aspect of our lives. It was an evil and corroding thread; the fabric of our existence was shot through with it. It set in motion trains of circumstances which brought us misfortune we felt we didn't deserve."

J & C You know you do the crime, you do the time. That's the way that is.

Big Book p. 67, last par., line 7 "But did not we, ourselves, set the ball rolling?"

J & C You see I did that myself, to me cause I didn't know any better.

Big Book p. 67, last par., line 8 "Sometimes we think fear ought to be classed with stealing. It seems to cause more trouble. We reviewed our fears thoroughly. We put them on paper, even though we had no resentment in connection with them. We asked ourselves why we had them.
Wasn't it because self-reliance failed us? Self-reliance was good as far as it went, but it didn't go far enough. Some of us once had great self-confidence, but it didn't fully solve the fear problem, or any other. When it made us cocky, it was worse."

J & C So what we're going to do here his morning is basically about what we did with resentment. We have a little list here; it's a review of our fears. And we're simply going to
(a) look at our fears,
(b) where they come from - the ideas, emotions and attitudes behind them and
(c) what we're fearful of.

REVIEW OF FEARS

INSTRUCTIONS FOR COMPLETION

Instruction 1 In dealing with fears we put them on paper. We listed people, institutions or principles with whom we were fearful. (Complete Column 1 from top to bottom. Do nothing on Columns 2, 3 or 4 until Column 1 is complete.)

Instruction 2 We asked ourselves why do I have the fear. (Complete Column 2 from top to bottom. Do nothing on Columns 3, or 4 until Column 2 is complete.)

Instruction 3 Which part of self caused the fear. Was it our self-esteem, our security, our ambitions, our personal or sex relations which had been interfered with? (Complete each column within Column 3 going from top to bottom. Starting with the Self-Esteem Column and finishing with the Sexual Ambitions Column. Do nothing on Column 4 until Column 3 is complete.)

Instruction 4 Referring to our 1st again. Putting out of our minds the wrongs others had done, we resolutely looked for our own mistakes. Where had we been selfish, dishonest, self-seeking and frightened and inconsiderate? (Asking ourselves the above questions we complete each column within Column 4.)

Instruction 5 Reading from left to right we now see the fear (Column 1), why do I have the fear (Column 2), the part of self that caused the fear (Column 3), and the exact nature of the defect within us that allowed the fear to surface and block us off from God's will (Column 4).

COLUMN 1	COLUMN 2	COLUMN 3 "SELF" AFFECTS MY (Which part of self caused the Fear?)									COLUMN 4 What is the exact nature of my wrongs, faults, mistakes, defects, shortcomings:			
		Social Instinct		Security Instinct		Sex Instinct		Ambitions						
I'm fearful of:	Why do I have the fear?	Self-Esteem	Personal Relationships	Material	Emotional	Acceptable Sex Relations	Hidden Sex Relations	Social	Security	Sexual	Selfish	Dishonest	Self-Seeking & Frightened	Inconsiderate
1														
2														
3														
4														
5														
6														
7														
8														

And we're going to write them down in these columns just like we did with resentments and it won't take very long to do this. The first column it says

Column One
Who or what do I fear?
I list People, Principles and Institutions whom I fear

And again in Column One I **simply** write down the people, institutions and principles that I fear, leaving a little space from top to bottom one column at a time, we list those.

Now we men tend to say we don't have much fear, we're tough, we're macho. We're not talking about physical fear anyhow, we're talking about all these fears that run through the mind from time to time. I think if we carefully look at them we'll find we all have fears connected with
- our marriages
- our children
- our jobs
- (Revenue Canada)
- Police Department
- Federal Government
- Church

We could just go on and on and on and name literally thousands of fears that people have. Now I am not going to attempt to psychoanalyze myself. I not going to say that these fears are things that come from things way back in my early childhood like mother setting me sideways on the potty when I'm two years old or something. Some fears we're supposed to have anyhow. It's just like resentments; fear can be used for a worthwhile purpose, if they're used right.

Mainly what we're looking at are these fears in our head that just continuously
- control us and
- rule us and
- dominate us

We've made a decision to let God direct our thinking (Step 3)
and if we have that many fears than God can't,
the fears do

And I found out the same thing here with these fears as I did with resentments.

I didn't think I had very many fears until I started putting them on a piece of paper.
You can only see one at a time in your head

And as I began to fill our sheet after sheet after sheet I began to realize how much fear really does control me, rule me and dominate me. So I did the same thing I did with resentments

Column 1
started top to bottom, list each fear, leave a little space between each one of them

And it's amazing when we see how much fear we really do have we'll never see it until we put it on a piece of paper

For many years I didn't think that I had any fears at all. I thought I had a very brave attitude. After I filled out this column I could see the fears was throughout my whole attitude and outlook on life was permeated every part of my life. I was fearful of everything and everyone and I did not know that. I did not know that.

So I **simply** go to the second column and I write down beside each of these People, Principals and Institutions of whom I am fearful, what am I afraid of in conjunction with those people?

Am I afraid that one of them is going to do something to me?
Am I perhaps going to go to jail for some of the things that I did?
Am I going to lose something of value?

Am I going to lose face?
Will it result in divorce?
Will it destroy a personal relationship?
Might I lose my job?

Those kinds of questions I asked myself beside each of those people and institutions and principles that I listed in Column 1.

Column 1	Column 2
Who or What do I Fear	What Am I Afraid of

- Marriage
- Children
- Job
- (Revenue Canada)
- Police Department
- Federal Government
- Church

Once again as we fill out that second column, when we begin to look at these fears we're going to find that nearly all of them are going to revolve around about one, two or three things anyhow.

Nearly every fear I've ever had revolves around the fact that
(1) I'm not going to get something that I really want, or
(2) I'm going to lose something that I've already got, or
(3) I've done something to another human being I shouldn't have done, and
(4) I'm worried to death about what they're going to do whenever they catch me.

Nearly all of them will center somewhere around those things, so we **simply** just put down the cause of the fear.
Then again I'm not going to say I'm afraid of the dark cause Mother set me one the potty sideways. Some fear I'm supposed to have. You betcha. I'm a little bit afraid of the dark. Why? Well I don't have headlights and I can't see at night. That keeps me from getting hurt; it brings caution. I'm a little bit afraid of heights. Why? Well I don't have wings and I can't fly. Keeps me from getting hurt.
But if those kinds of fears should keep me from going outside after dark, if they should keep me from riding in an elevator or an airplane, then I better look at them closely. They're beginning to really, really rule me and dominate me.

Most of my fears though, center around just basically two or three things. I'm afraid

(1) I'm going to lose what I got
(2) I'm not going to get what I want
(3) I've done something I shouldn't have
(4) What are they going to do when they catch me?

Very simple process.

Column 3 - What part of self was affected?

Column 1	Column 2	Column 3
Who or What do I Fear	What Am I Afraid of	What part of self was affected?
- Marriage		
- Children		
- Job		
- (Revenue Canada)		
- Police Department		
- Federal Government		
- Church		

Again that's why I need that information of the basic instincts of life and the working knowledge of some of those words and ideas that enable us to do the third column. If you don't have a God in your life and you're living without God and you don't need other people and you're living on your own will then there's only one thing you can do and that's try to satisfy your basic instincts of life and that's what I was doing I was operating on my own.

So what part of myself was affected? Was it
my self-esteem?
my security?
my ambitions?
personal or sex relations?

Which had been interfered with. Those are the things that had happened and I looked down on the third column and beside each name I'd write down one of those basic instincts of life, the part of me that was affected by these things.

You know I can't experience fear unless there's a threat to one of the basic instincts of life. And I found out as I filled out the third column, just like I did with resentments I found out where fear comes from. You know I didn't know where resentments came from, I didn't know where anger came from, I didn't know where fear comes from.

Today I realize (fear) it comes from the threat to one of the basic instincts of life. And just like with a resentment, if my basic instincts are at the level that God intends for them to be, if my relationship (with God) is right, then you can do about anything you want to to me and I'm not going to experience fear because of it.

> But I'll guarantee you if my instincts are not under control,
> my relationship with God is not right
> then about anything you do or say to me is going to create fear.

Absolutely amazing what we learn about ourselves, just by filling out these simple little columns.

J & C   Now let's go the fourth column.

We go to the fourth column and we try to put out of our minds all these things that happened so far and we write down "What did I do?" What did I do to set the ball rolling? Did I do the crime to do the time? Yes I did that. When my wife was going to divorce me and I was fearful of it, what did I do? What were some of the things that I did? Well I was uncaring for her, I didn't care about her. Didn't consider her in any manner, in any way. And therefore I was afraid and I didn't know that. See I really did know that I was afraid of those things.

It told us way back in step 3 that we invariably find that we've made decisions based on self, which later placed us in a position to be hurt. And we made decisions trying to satisfy our basic instincts of life and running on self-will those basic instincts become insatiable things, we never get enough to satisfy them, and we are continually doing things that end up hurting and harming and creating other people. Then we've got to be scared to death of what they're going to do whenever they catch us. And even if they don't catch us, the guilt and the remorse eats us up here just like with resentments. So we begin to look at the part we played and we find that we did the same thing with fears that we did with resentments. As we play them over and over and over in our head, we actually distorted the picture and the fears that we have in our head today are not true. Oh they started on truth but they are no longer true. You see that's one of the definitions of one of those wrongs

fear is incorrect believing

And if we carefully look at each one of these fears we're going to find that they are absolutely wrong. They started with truth, we distorted the picture, and once again we've used them to transfer blame to others so we don't ever have to look at ourselves. Same identical thing as with resentments.

Now let's look into the fifth column. In the fifth column I simply looked down in these instances.
Was I selfish in those instances, in those particular items? Yes I was very selfish. Because I was so fearful I was selfish. I was afraid I was going to lose things that I already had or I was afraid I wasn't going to get some things that I wanted.

Was I dishonest? Yes I was dishonest. I took things from other people that didn't belong to me. And I was very dishonest. It seemed to me that to be successful in any manner was OK with me. So I was an extremely dishonest person and I certainly didn't know that particularly.
And then I was self-seeking and frightened and inconsiderate of other people for sure. Cause I wanted what I wanted when I wanted it and I didn't make a damn how I got it was the way I looked at my life. And if you got in my way, you just shouldn't have. So I was a very selfish, self-seeking, frightened and inconsiderate individual and I did not know that.

You know it's absolutely a life living on hell whenever you're scared to death that you're not going to get something that you really do want it. And then through dishonesty you go ahead and get it. And then you've got to be scared to death of whatever they're going to do you whenever they catch you. And even if they don't get you, the guilt and the remorse eats you up. And our lives really do become an absolute living hell in trying to satisfy these basic instincts of life and we just really drive ourselves absolutely dingy until we get an opportunity to really truthfully look at these things. Now out there in that fifth column once again we see the exact nature of the wrong. The fears are what's wrong because we find out most of them are incorrect. They're what block us off from God. But what's the actual truth behind them?

Well if we wasn't so selfish, if we wasn't so dishonest, if we were not so self-seeking, frightened, and inconsiderate we wouldn't have to experience near as much fear as we do.

But I'll guarantee you if I stay selfish, dishonest, self-seeking, frightened and inconsiderate, the same old things are going to drive me, I'm going to do the same old things I've always done. Fear, guilt, remorse is going to absolutely eat me up. Sooner or later it blocks me off from God, it causes me to get drunk. So once again what we're doing here in this little inventory sheet. We are doing step 4. This is the fear part of it.

Out in this fifth column we see the exact nature of the wrong for step 5, the defects for step 6, the shortcomings that we're going to ask God to take away in step 7, and then once again many of the names over here in column 1 will be people and institutions we've harmed and we're scared to death of what they're going to do whenever they catch us.

So those names will come off of column 1, they'll be added to the sheet to be used later on for steps 8 and 9. We got some off the resentment sheet; we got some off of the fear sheet also. And one thing that absolutely amazed me is that when I really looked at this truthfully is I begin to see a lot of the names, same names appearing on the fear sheet that I had on the resentment sheet. I had never tied that together in my head before. Barbara was on both sheets. I resented her and I certainly feared her. And I'm still a little bit afraid of that lady today. If she ever finds out everything that I was doing about 30 years ago, she's probably going to file for divorce again. I don't know. I resented the Internal Revenue Service and I feared the Internal Revenue Service. They were also on those sheets and I never really had tied that together in my head.

Now if you think resentments look stupid in your head, wait till you get these things down on paper about fears. Now fears look awful good in your head. But when you get them down on a sheet of paper they really do look double dumb when you see the truth about them. Resentments look stupid; hell fears look even worse then that. And they look so dumb that about 95% of them are going to disappear anyhow when you see the truth about them. Once again there is going to be about 1,2,3,4 or 5 that's been embedded in our minds so deeply that we're probably going to have a little help in order to get rid of some of those. We now come to the second prayer in the big book on step 4 regarding fears.

You know when I prayed for those people that I resented my ideas, emotions and attitudes towards them changed. They didn't change but I did. Now prior to this idea about these fears, my whole attitude and outlook upon life was involved in these fears. And I had fears in every area of my life and didn't know it, because I hadn't had a God in my life either. But I took step 3 and I've got God in my life and now I'm on a different basis. And the book says.

Big Book p. 68, par. 2   *"Perhaps there is a better way, we think so. For we are now on a different basis of trusting and relying upon God. We trust infinite God rather than our finite selves. We are in the world to play the role He assigns. Just to the extent that we do as we think He would have us, and humbly rely on Him, does He enable us to match calamity with serenity.*
We never apologize to anyone for depending upon our Creator. We can laugh at those who think spirituality the way of weakness. Paradoxically, it is the way of strength. The verdict of the ages is that faith means courage. All men of faith have courage. They trust their God. We never apologize for God. Instead we let Him demonstrate, through us, what He can do. We ask Him to remove our fear and direct our attention to what He would have us be. At once, we commence to outgrow fear."

J & C   And you know as I look back at that, my sponsor told me in those early days, he said the most important thing about prayer, the 2 most important things about prayer. One of them is to start and the other one is to continue. And as I look back over my life I can see that every time I prayed I change just a minute amount, just hardly noticeable. The next time I prayed it was just a little bit more. And the next time I prayed it was just a little bit more. And as time goes by I can see a real reliance upon God today in my life. It wasn't that way in the beginning. But when I started trusting and relying upon God rather than myself then those fears begin to come away from me. They weren't as intense as they had been. And they begin to get in the area where God intended for them to be. And at once I commenced to outgrow these fears.

You know we hear always about the promises on page 83-84. We never hear about the promises that are spread throughout the entire book. And I think one of the greatest promises to be found anywhere in the book is what Joe just read.

We ask Him to remove our fear and direct our attention to what He would have us be. At once, we commence to outgrow that fear.

Now we can take these deep-seated fears just like deep-seated resentments. Through prayer on a daily basis, asking God to take this particular fear away from me, direct my attention to what he would have me be instead of that and at once I commence to outgrow that fear. And over a period of days as he directs my attention to what he would have me be and I try to be that, as I ask him to take that fear away, some morning I wake up and that fear is gone. It really, really does work. And I think the reason that it really works is that when we are asking God to take it away and direct our attention to what he would have us be, then that's one of the great xpressions of courage and faith that we human beings can have.

Courage, faith and fear will not exist on the same plain

The fear will be replaced by the courage to do the opposite of that fear and as we begin to change it will be replaced by faith that God really can do these things. And slowly we can remove those fears too.

Now just think, this file cabinet up here in my head that was filled with fears has now been emptied out. That damaged and unsaleable goods called fear is gone at least to the level that God intends for it to be. Once again, God's not going to allow another hole in my head. The fears, if they disappear, they've got to be replaced with the opposite. And the opposite will be faith and courage, the opposite of the fear itself. I found out I didn't have to go to any other fellowships or read any other books to get faith and courage. If God dwells within me, that's always been a part of my makeup, I just never could use it before.

In my chase for money, power, prestige and sex and in my desire to fulfill the basic instincts of life, in my worries in that I wouldn't get what I want and I'd lose what I've got or they're going to catch me at it, faith and courage had to be repressed and I had to operate on that fear level. But now that the fear is gone, faith and courage automatically comes to the surface. Another positive happening. Two thirds of my store now has some peace of mind, serenity and happiness in them and I'm in much less chance of drinking now than I was before I started the inventory process. You see we don't have to wait till step 12 to get something good out of this. Every step brings a positive result. There's nothing negative about anything in our program, period.

Now also just like with a resentment, knowing that fears block you off from God, and that they might get you drunk, if you've got a fear that you don't want to turn loose of, you'd better look at it very, very closely. Because we can also use fear to rationalize and justify not doing something we really would like to do or just as importantly we can use it to justify continuing to do things that we know we shouldn't be doing. And if we've got one of those and we don't want to get rid of it, we'd better look at it very, very closely. Let me give you and example of how you can use fear to rationalize and justify.

How many of you here this morning, and please be truthful with me, how many of you would really like to go back to school and finish your education? Could I see your hands? Oh my God, about half of you at least. Now I'm going to ask you another question. How many of you really do intend to do that? Oh about half of those hands went up this time. I wonder why. Nothing in the world but fear.

Fear that we won't measure up.
Fear of failure.
Fear of hard work.

Actually keeps us from doing things that we really would like to do. Now if we can ask God to take that away and direct our attention to what he would have us be instead then every one of you that wants to go back to school will end up doing it. But until that fear is gone it's going to drive most of us away and keep us away. We use it to rationalize, justify just like we did with resentments. So if we've got one of those, let's look at that closely too.

All my life, I loved to work with my hands, all my life I wanted to be able to build a set of kitchen cabinets. Never would do it because I knew there would be a lot of mistakes, people would laugh and I would be embarrassed. Now after I worked the program for quite some time, one time I got the courage to build a set of kitchen cabinets. Now they don't look very good. There's a lot of mistakes and people laugh at it but I really don't give a damn. It don't bother me anymore see. So we can overcome these things with God's help. It's amazing what we can do with these things.

J & C   OK. Bottom of page 68.

Big Book p. 68, par. 4   *"Now about sex."*

J & C   We're getting ready now to look at the storeroom back here that's filled with guilt and remorse and it seems as though we human beings hurt each other in the sexual area probably faster and easier than we do in any other way. And I think there's a reason for that. You know the other animals here on earth, they have a sexual urge just like we do so that they can and will reproduce themselves. But the difference between their sex life and ours is simply that they don't have this thing called self-will. Most of the other animals here on earth, they don't really have any choice in their sex life. When it comes time for them to reproduce themselves, God usually signifies that by some physical change in the female of the species. The male senses that change, prepares himself, the two join together and it's kind of like bang, bang thank you ma'am. And when it's over with they normally go their separate ways. Not always, but usually they do. Now they didn't think about having sex before they had it. And they didn't think about having sex while they were having it. They couldn't decide when they were going to do it. God made that decision for them. They usually can't decide who they're going to do it with. They can't decide whether they're going to do it with one or more partners. They can't decide how many times they're going to do it. And they can't even decide what position they're going to do it in. So therefore you see very few sexual problems amongst the other animals here on earth. I've never seen a cow on a psychiatrist's couch yet talking about sexual dysfunction. They just don't have those kinds of problems.

We human beings are a little bit different. You see God gives us this thing called self-will. And we can make choices about our sex lives. We can have sex any day of the year that we wish to. We can decide who we are going to have sex with. We can decide whether we're going to have it with one or more partners. We can decide how many times we're going to do it providing we're physically capable of doing so. We can even decide what position we're going to do it in. They tell me there is something like 64 different positions a human being can have sex in. I have no idea what they are. [   ]. And 2 of those damn near killed me. I'm not sure I'm going back to them. So what we are going to look at for just a few minutes this morning is not so much as to how we do sex but as to how we think about sex. Cause how we think about it determines how we're going to do it. And that determines whether we are going to hurt other people or not. And that determines whether we're going to have to be eaten up with fear, guilt and remorse associated with our sex lives. So we are going to look at just a few minutes about how we think about sex.

Big Book p. 68, par. 4 cont.   *"Many of us needed an overhauling there."*

J & C   Now you older fellows don't get your hopes up. We're talking about mental not physical.

Big Book p. 68, par. 4 cont.   *"But above all, we tried to be sensible on this question. It's so easy to get way off the track. Here we find human opinions running to extremes -- absurd extremes, perhaps. One set of voices cry that sex is a lust of our lower nature, a base necessity of procreation."*

J & C   I've heard them all my life. They're the ones that say sex is a dirty thing. You ought to do it one time in one position with one person only. The only reason to do it is to reproduce yourself. And if you enjoy it it's a sinful thing. I've heard them as far back as I can remember. They are to the extremes on one side.

Big Book p. 69   *"Then we have the voices who cry for sex and more sex; who bewail the institution of marriage; who think that most of the troubles of the race are traceable to sex causes. They think we do not have enough of it, or that it isn't the right kind. They see its significance everywhere."*

J & C   Then you hear them today. They're the ones who say that you ought to be able to have sex anytime you want to, anywhere you want to with anybody you want to as many times as you want to. You ought to be able to enjoy it every time and if you don't there must be something wrong with you. And maybe they call that the sexual revolution. Main thing I see wrong with it is it happened 25 years too late for me to participate in it. I know that.

Big Book p. 69, cont.   *"One school would allow man no flavour for his fare and the other would have us all on a straight pepper diet. We want to stay out of this controversy. We do not want to be the arbiter of anyone's sex conduct. We all have sex problems. We'd hardly be human if we didn't. What can we do about them?"*

J & C   And I read that last statement with great relief. Because I knew that this book was getting ready to condemn me for what I had been in the past. I knew it was getting ready to tell me what I was going to have to do in the future. And I'd already made up my mind that I wasn't going to pay any attention to it at all. And I was relieved to find out that we are not going to be the arbiter of anyone's sex conduct. We simply are not going to get into that question. Now this book is meant to be helpful to anybody, anywhere. And we start trying to tell people how they are going to have to conduct their sex lives. We start condemning them for what they've done in the past and surely, surely we're going to alienate people. Besides that, what's sexually acceptable in one part of the world may not be acceptable at all in another part of the world. So we simply are not going to get into that question. What we are going to see is a simple little way to review our own past sex conduct. See what we've been doing with it. See if perhaps we've been using it for the wrong purposes in some cases. Look at those people we've hurt by it. Then try to shape a sex life of the future where we can still engage in it and enjoy it yet at the same time not hurt other people. And if we don't do something about it we continue to hurt other people and feel the fear, guilt and remorse. Sooner or later it will block us off from God and we end up getting drunk over it. Very simple process. Joe.

Certainly I'm not going to be the arbiter of anyone's sex conduct and I needed an overhauling in that area when I arrived at Alcoholics Anonymous. And again we're going to look at the ideas, emotions and attitudes behind these sexual conducts that I had. And I look back in my life and when I was about 12 or 13 years old I got to thinking about this a lot, I mean a lot. Almost gave me brain damage from thinking about it. So I went to my Mom and I said "Mom"…cause of course my Dads in the nut house. I can't be talking to him. So I went to my Mom and I said "Mom, I've been thinking about this sex thing". And she said "Oh my God Benny Joe". Scared her to death. That's my name, Benny Joe. "Oh my God Benny Joe. That's not a good thing to be thinking about. In fact it's a dirty filthy rotten thing to be thinking about." She said. "And you ought to save it for the one you love." Think about that. And she said the only time you are supposed to have sex is when you want to have children. Well let's see she had five children, she had sex five times I figured. Well no wonder my Dad was in the nut house. But somehow I just didn't believe what she was telling me. And we had sex education when I went to school too, but they called it recess. And also in West Tulsa, Oklahoma there was a place called The Jenkins Café and every day and every evening in front of The Jenkins Café there was a gathering of very wise intelligent, experienced men and women of about 15 and 16 years old. And they were more than glad to share with you all they knew about sex. And some of those guys told me that they were having sex with 2 or 3 different partners a night they said. Sometimes they were having sex as many as 10 times a night they said. And you know the fallacy of all that is I tried to live up to that because that's what I thought. I never could but I tried. And I was sober 2 or 3 years in Alcoholics Anonymous before I figured out they were lying to me. At least I hope they were lying. You'd better hope they were lying to you. So certainly I needed an overhauling there. When I got here I had the spiritual knowledge of a 7 or 8 year old boy. I had the coping skills of an 8 or 9 year old boy. And I had the sexual knowledge of a 12 or 13 year old boy. Do you think I needed overhauling in all those areas? How many of you got your sex information pretty much the way I did? I needed to sit down and look at this didn't I? You know I remember the very first time I ever had sex. I was very selfish and self-centred and dishonest and self-seeking. And I was also alone. That's why he's wearing glasses today too. Every time we say that, 2 or 3 of you guys whip your glasses off and put them in your pocket. And gals.

OK let's look at the next paragraph now very carefully. We're going to see here the same set of instructions that we used, to look at sex, that we had for resentments. Only difference here is that they are worded a little differently. Which is Bill's way of doing things.

Big Book p. 69, par. 1   *"We reviewed our own conduct over the years past. Where had we been selfish, dishonest, or inconsiderate? Whom had we hurt? Did we unjustifiably arouse jealousy, suspicion or bitterness? Where were we at fault, what should we have done instead? We got this all down on paper and looked at it."*

J & C   So once again we made up a little sheet to avoid any confusion and it looks just about exactly like the resentment sheet except we call it a review of our own sex conduct. And in this little sheet a review of our own sex conduct we have the same 5 columns.

REVIEW OF OUR OWN SEX CONDUCT

INSTRUCTIONS FOR COMPLETION

Instruction 1 We listed all people we harmed. (Complete Column 1 from top to bottom. Do nothing on Columns 2, 3 or 4 until Column 1 is complete.)

Instruction 2 We asked ourselves what we did. (Complete Column 2 from top to bottom. Do nothing on Columns 3 or 4 until Column 2 is complete.)

Instruction 3 Was it our self-esteem, our security, our ambitions, our sex instinct, which caused the harm? (Complete each column within Column 3 going from top to bottom. Starting with the Self-Esteem Column and finishing with the Sexual Ambitions Column. Do nothing on Column 4 until Column 3 is complete.)

Instruction 4 Referring to our list again. Pulling out of our minds the wrongs others had done, we resolutely looked for our own mistakes. Where had we been selfish, dishonest, self-seeking and frightened and inconsiderate? (Asking ourselves the above questions we complete each column within Column 4.)

Instruction 5 Reading from left to right we now see the harm (Column 1), what we did (Column 2), the part of self which caused the harm (Column 3), and the exact nature of the defect within us that caused the harm, and block us off from God's will (Column 4).

COLUMN 1	COLUMN 2	COLUMN 3 "SELF" AFFECTS MY (Which part of self caused the harm?)											COLUMN 4 What is the exact nature of my wrongs, faults, mistakes, defects, shortcomings:			
		Social Instinct			Security Instinct		Sex Instinct		Ambitions						
Who did I harm?	What did I do?	Self-Esteem	Personal Relationships		Material	Emotional	Acceptable Sex Relations	Hidden Sex Relations	Social	Security	Sexual	Selfish	Dishonest	Self-Seeking & Frightened	Inconsiderate
1															
2															
3															
4															
5															
6															
7															
8															

Column 1 - who did I hurt?

Now I doubt that there is anybody in this room this morning that ever hurt anybody in the sexual area that we don't remember just exactly who that is. That seems to be a form of knowledge that we all have.

There might be some question as to what do we to hurt people in a sexual area. Well certainly we hurt them in many different ways. For instance, if I'm in a married relationship and I go outside of that relationship and I have sex out there and my wife finds out about it. Then surely I've created a problem for her, if not physically then at least emotionally. If that sexual escapade creates a trouble between my wife and I, there are children in my home, and then I've hurt my children also by the same sexual escapade. If the lady I had sex with out there, if it becomes common knowledge, I've hurt her too. If she has a husband and children I've hurt them also. You know, one sex act could many, many different people.

I think sometimes we hurt people in a sexual area by demanding more than our fair share. Maybe our partner isn't too keen about having sex every time we want to. Rather than consider their needs, wants and desires, we selfishly demand that they have sex with us when they really don't want to. Surely that creates a problem for them, if not physically at least emotionally.
I think sometimes we hurt people in a sexual area by demanding that they do things with us physically sexually that they really don't want to do. And once again rather than consider their needs and wants we selfishly demand those things. Surely we create a problem for them, if not physically at least emotionally.
I think sometimes we hurt people in a sexual area just by withholding sex. Maybe we're not to keen to have sex every time our partner wants to and rather than consider their needs and wants we selfishly withhold when perhaps we should give in a little more often. I think we hurt many people in many different ways and we pretty well know what they are.

Column 1 – we list their names.
Column 2 – what did I do to hurt them?
Column 3 – what part of self is affected?

Now you would think that if I hurt anybody in a sexual area that it would be caused by the sex instinct. And probably part of the time that's true. Sometimes in order to get the physical the emotional gratification that comes at the moment of successful completion of the sex act, maybe I'm doing the wrong thing at the wrong time with the wrong person because of the sex instinct. But I think if we will carefully review each situation we're going to find that usually the other 2 instincts are involved just as much as sex and in many cases even more so and sometimes sex really doesn't have a hell of a lot to do with it.

Now I'm going to express an opinion. And I want to make sure that everybody understands that this is my opinion. It's not AA's opinion, not Joe's, not anybody else's, just mine. Today I am convinced that God gave us the sex urge so that we could reproduce ourselves. I'm also convinced he made it a very enjoyable thing so we would do so. I don't think you and I would do the kind of work involved in sex if we didn't get something out of it. Now if we're doing sex for purposes other than reproduction or enjoyment then we might be doing sex for purposes other than what God intended.

For instance, we boys found that at a very early age that you can use sex to build your self-esteem. After all, the more members of the opposite sex you could attract to yourself the greater man you really are, we thought. Now we boys, I don't know what you girls called it, but we boys called it John Wayne-ism. Joe said Jane Wayne. Some of you girls tell me that you used sex for the same purposes. Now if that's what we're using sex for that has nothing to do with reproduction. Really has nothing to do with enjoyment. That's to fulfil a part of the social instinct and sex really doesn't have a hell of a lot to do with it.

Sometimes we use sex to buy a personal relationship. Maybe we're just lonesome. Maybe we just want somebody to pay attention to us. And we found out a long time ago we can give sex and buy back a personal relationship. Now that's not to reproduce, that's not to enjoy. That's also to fulfil a part of the social instinct.
Sometimes we use sex to buy material security. Maybe we're in a sexual situation we really would rather not even be in but we've become so overly dependent upon another human being for our material well being that we give sex to buy back material wellbeing. Has nothing to do with reproduction or enjoyment. That's to fulfil the security instinct.

Sometimes we use sex to get even with another human being. Maybe were in a relationship and our partner has gone out and done something they shouldn't have done and it infuriates the hell out of us we say we'll show them and we'll go out and we'll do exactly the same thing. Fallacy in it is that after we've done it we can't afford to tell them we did it. But certainly we didn't use sex there to reproduce nor to enjoy. We used it to get even with another human being. Sex really doesn't have a hell of a lot to do with that.

You know sometimes we use sex to force our will on another human being. Maybe our partner isn't doing what we think they ought to do and we say we'll show them. We'll just cut them off at the pass. We won't let them have any sex until they come around to our way of thinking. Now we boys aren't too good at that. We only last 2 days at the most. You girls have honed it to perfection. You know exactly how to do that. And I don't blame you I would use it to for that. That has nothing to do with reproduction or enjoyment. That's to force our will on another human being.

I was absolutely amazed as I filled out that third column to see what I had actually been using sex for. Two things happened to me almost automatically. As I filled out the third column, a lot of my guilt began to disappear. I thought I was just a dirty rotten no good SOB. But I found out that I used sex for purposes other than what God intended. Not because I'm a bad human being, but because I'm a sick human being in those areas. And I needed that sex to build the personal relationships and etc. And when I saw that a lot of guilt began to disappear. Tell you another thing that started to happen to me in column 3. I begin to get a handle on this sex thing. You see I always thought I was over sexed and that caused me to do those things. But in column 3 I found out hell I'm not over sexed I'm under secure. And I used sex to build my security and to build my self-esteem. And when I saw what I was doing with sex it began to look pretty stupid to do those things. And a lot of that desire to go did at the wrong time at the wrong place with the wrong people began to disappear and I started to get a handle on the sex thing right here in the third column. I think it's one of the greatest things that we can do for ourselves. Especially we men. We tend to use sex to build self-esteem. And sex doesn't really have anything to do with it. We tend to use it to build our self-esteem. And when I saw that was what I was doing with it then the desire to go do it became less and less.

J & C   Column 4 – what feelings did I create in others?
Did I unjustifiable arouse jealousy, suspicion, or bitterness? What should I have done instead? In column 4 not only are we looking to see those things that we did but we also need to be looking at what should we have done instead? We're trying to shape a new sex life of the future where we can still engage in it and enjoy it yet at the same time not hurt other people.

Column 5 – which character defect is involved?
Same old deal. If I wasn't so selfish I wouldn't be doing some of those things in a sexual area that hurt other people. If I wasn't so dishonest I wouldn't be sneaking around behind my wife's back lying to her all the time anyhow. If I wasn't so afraid of facing life without that sex to build my self-esteem and ego and etc probably wouldn't be doing it in the first place. If I really considered my wife and my children and other human beings ahead of my own needs and wants I wouldn't be doing those things that's going to take a chance on hurting other people. And I'll guarantee you that if I stay selfish, dishonest, self-seeking, frightened and inconsiderate.

I'm going to keep right on doing the same old things.
I'm going to keep right on hurting people in the sexual area.
I'm going to have to be scared to death of what they're going to do to me if they catch me.
The guilt and remorse eats me up.
Sooner or later it blocks me off from God and I end up drunk over it.

It's not a question of right and wrong. It's a question of what can we do and live with it with peace of mind and happiness and be able to stay sober in the future. At the very least we're going to have to so something about some of these things or sooner or later it eats us up. Now once again we're doing step 4. This is the sex part. In the fifth column we see all the information now we need for step 5,6 and 7. Quite naturally all the names in column 1 will come of this sheet and be added to the sheet to be used later on for steps 8 and 9. Again I was amazed to see in many cases the same names appearing on all 3 sheets. Barbara was certainly on all 3 sheets. I even had the IRS on all 3 sheets. I resented them, I feared them and I gave them a pretty good screwing before I got through with them too.

Now let's see what we do with this information.

Big Book p. 69, par. 2   *"In this way we tried to shape a sane and sound ideal for our future sex life. We subjected each relation to this test -was it selfish or not? "*

J & C   And prayer is going to be used three different times in the next page or so. Here's the first one.

Big Book p. 69, par. 2 cont.   *"We asked God to mould our ideals and help us to live up to them. We remembered always that our sex powers were God-given and therefore good, neither to be used lightly or selfishly nor to be despised and loathed. "*

J & C   You see God never did give us anything that was bad.

Big Book p. 69, par. 3   "*Whatever our ideal turns out to be, we must be willing to grow toward it. We must be willing to make amends where we have done harm, provided that we do not bring about still more harm in so doing. In other words, we treat sex as we would any other problem. In meditation, we ask God what we should do about each specific matter. The right answer will come, if we want it.*
God alone can judge our sex situation. Counsel with persons is often desirable, but we let God be the final judge. We realise that some people are as fanatical about sex as others are loose. We avoid hysterical thinking or advice."

J & C   You know this is an area that I don't think we need a whole lot of advice in anyhow. I think all of us deep down inside, we know what we should be doing and what we shouldn't be doing. You know I've never been in a sexual situation that was wrong that I didn't know it was wrong before I ever got into it. Didn't keep me from getting into it. But I never got into one yet that was wrong that I didn't know it was wrong before I ever got into it. And if you start running around asking people for sexual advice, if you ask 6 different people you're going to get 6 different answers. And then you'll have to decide which one of those to follow. And besides that I really can't think of a worse place in the world to get sexual advice than in the fellowship of Alcoholics Anonymous. I think that's a hell of a place to look for it. I think all we've got to do I listen to that little voice inside. I think it pretty well knows. And I think it will pretty well tell us what we should and what we shouldn't do and if we follow it were probably not going to hurt other people.

Big Book p. 70, par. 1   "*Suppose we fall short of the chosen ideal and stumble? Does this mean we are going to get drunk? Some people tell us so. But this is only a half-truth. It depends on us and on our motives. If we are sorry for what we have done, and have the honest desire to let God take us to better things, we believe we will be forgiven and will have learned our lesson. If we are not sorry, and our conduct continues to harm others, we are quite sure to drink. We are not theorizing. These are facts out of our experience.*"

J & C   You know I had a young fellow come to me not long ago he's still in his twenties. And he said, "You know Charlie my sponsor said I couldn't have any sex the first year of sobriety. Is that right?" And I said "No that's not necessarily right. You can have all the sex you want the first year. The second year you can have it with other people." You know sometimes it's hard enough to quit drinking without doing some other things too.

Big Book p. 70, par. 2   "*To sum up about sex: We earnestly pray for the right ideal, for guidance in each questionable situation, for sanity, and for the strength to do the right thing. If sex is very troublesome, we throw ourselves the harder into helping others. We think of their needs and work for them. This takes us out of ourselves. It quiets the [horny condition] imperious urge, when to yield would mean heartache.*"

J & C   Old Bill used some fancy words didn't he?

Ok now we're going to make one other suggestion before we leave the inventory. The book says we have the list for our amends we made it when we took step 4. And we've looked at the people we've hurt on the resentment sheet. We looked at the on the fear sheet. We looked at them on the sex sheet. But there's other people we've hurt in other ways too that perhaps haven't popped up on any of these sheets. Maybe somebody that we've stole money from them. Or maybe somebody we hurt physically. Many ways we hurt people. And any of those names that have come up on at least one of these 3 sheets we suggest we take this fourth sheet, a review of harms other than sexual, and do exactly the same thing with it that we've done with the other sheets.

REVIEW OF HARMS OTHER THAN SEXUAL

Page 10

COLUMN 1	COLUMN 2	COLUMN 3	COLUMN 4	COLUMN 5
WHO DID I HURT:	WHAT DID I DO?	AFFECTS MY: Which part of self caused me to do what I did? Was it caused by the social instinct, the security instinct, or the sex instinct?	WHAT FEELINGS DID I CREATE IN OTHERS? Did I arouse jealousy, suspicion, bitterness, anger, desire to retaliate, fear, etc.? What should I have done instead?	WHERE HAD I BEEN: *Selfish* *Dishonest* *Self-Seeking and frightened* *Inconsiderate*? Which of the above character defects caused me to do what I do to harm another?

Column 1 - who did I hurt
Column 2 – what did I do
Column 3 - what part of self is affected
Column 4 – what feelings did I create in others? What should I have done instead?
Column 5 – which character defect is involved?

And if we'll do that then we've got everything here that we'll need for 4,5,6 and 7, 8 and 9. And when we've done this sheet, when we have completed our inventory we've got everything we need now for 4,5,6,7, 8 and 9 and now then we are ready to get on with our business. Very, very simple procedure. Now let me ask you something.

Did we see anything here to be afraid of?
Did we see anything that was complicated we couldn't do it?
Did we make a list of dirty filthy nasty items?
Did we get any positive results from this?
Is there any reason why we shouldn't go ahead and do step 4?
We don't need to procrastinate any longer now do we?

It is simple enough that we can get with it get on with the program. A little bit of study and a little bit of help from your sponsor and a couple of evenings and you can have it done just that quick. Now the book says

Big Book p. 70, par. 3   *"If we have been thorough about our personal inventory, we have written down a lot. We have listed and analyzed our resentments. "*

J & C   Now some people look at the word analyzed as a bad word. All this is, is another word that means truth. We have takes a truthful, a moral truthful honest analytical inventory. To analyze something simply means to get down to the truth of it. Now he didn't say it but we've listed and analyzed our fears. We've listed and analyzed our sexual harms. We've listed and analyzed harms other than sexual.

Big Book p. 70, par. 3 cont.   *"We have begun to comprehend their futility and their fatality. We have commenced to see their terrible destructiveness. "*

J & C   Now here's some results.

Big Book p. 70, par. 3 cont.   *"We have begun to learn tolerance, patience and good will toward all men, even our enemies, for we look on them as sick people. "*

J & C   My God what a change in personality already. This is a real change taking place here in step 4. We don't have to wait till step 12 to get something.

Big Book p. 70, par. 3 cont.   *"We have listed the people we have hurt by our conduct, and are willing to straighten out the past if we can.*
In this book you read again and again that faith did for us what we could not do for ourselves. We hope you are convinced now that God can remove whatever self-will has blocked you off from Him. If you have already made a decision, and an inventory of your grosser handicaps, you have made a good beginning. That being so you have swallowed and digested some big chunks of truth about yourself. "

J & C   So what are some of the grosser handicaps which we've looked at?
- Resentment
- Fear
- Guilt
- Remorse

What are some of the basic character defects that we've looked at and the basic cause?
- Selfish
- Dishonest

- Self-seeking
- Frightened
- Inconsiderate

We have really looked at those things very carefully haven't we? Now the book recognizes that we will never be perfect. It said these are our grosser handicaps. I think one of the greatest mistakes being made in AA today is everybody is sitting around waiting until they get well so they can do step 4 perfect. You can't do that. Let's get rid of these grosser things. We've got another step later on that we are going to use this process for the rest of our life. We'll be inventorying forever. And it will get better and better. But these are the major things that kill us. We've got them behind us. Now we can get on with our business. You know I think this is all the inventory I need anyhow. As I look back at my lifetime I can't spot an emotional problem I have ever had that didn't revolve around one of 3 things.

- Madder than hell at somebody.
- Scared to death about something.
- Or I've done something I shouldn't have done and the guilt and remorse was eating me up.

As I project my mind in the future I don't see anything that's going to bother me that's not going to revolve around the same 3 things.

- Madder than hell
- Scared to death
- Filled with guilt and remorse

I think this is the perfect inventory for people like us. And we will continue to work on it the rest of our lives anyhow.

Now I don't know if you all have noticed or not but nearly all information in the big book on sex is on page 69. I don't know that that has any significance whatsoever that just happens to be where nearly all the sex information happens to be is on page 69.

You know we heard a story about a young lady who had been in AA about 90 days and she went to her sponsor and she said "Sponsor, I've got a problem." Her sponsor said, "What is it?" She said, "well it's this sex thing. Sober I don't know what to do. Anything I've ever done in the sexual area, tried to attract a member of the opposite sex, or anything else it's always been while drinking. Sober I just don't know how to function. " Her sponsor said "Well go and get out your big book. Read page 69. It will have the answer to any problems you might have. " So the young lady goes home and gets her book out and proceeds to read but she got confused on page numbers. Instead of page 69, she read page 96. Just for the hell of it why don't you go over to page 96 and see what she read.

Big Book p. 96 "*Do not be discouraged if your prospect does not respond at once. Search out another alcoholic and try again. You are sure to find someone desperate enough to accept with eagerness what you offer. We find it a waste of time to keep chasing a man who cannot or will not work with you. If you leave such a person alone, he may soon become convinced that he cannot recover by himself. To spend too much time on any one situation is to deny some other alcoholic an opportunity to live and be happy. One of our Fellowship failed entirely with his first half dozen prospects. He often says that if he had continued to work on them, he might have deprived many others, who have since recovered, of their chance. "*

J & C   I think that's one of the most appropriate things I've ever read. It just goes on and on and on.

J & C   Let's go to page 72, "Into Action". We want to run very briefly now through Steps 5, 6 & 7. So we go to page 72, <u>Into action</u>, now it's not into thinking, it's into action

Big Book p. 72, par. 1
   Having made our personal inventory, what shall we do about it? We have been trying to get a new attitude

J & C   Remember Dr. Jung said   (BB p. 27, line 18) "Ideas, emotions, and attitudes which were once the guiding forces of the lives of these men are suddenly cast to one side, ..."

Big Book p. 72, par. 1
   and a new relationship with our Creator

J & C   And our book said back on page 45 (line 13) that the main object of this book would enable me to find a power greater than myself, which would solve my problem.

Big Book p. 72, par. 1
> and to discover the obstacles in our path.

J & C   And what are some of the obstacles ...   the resentments, fears, harms done to other people

Big Book p. 72, par. 1
> We have admitted certain defects

J & C   And what are these defects, selfish, dishonest, self-seeking, frightened, and inconsiderate attitudes

Big Book p. 72, par. 1
> we have ascertained in a rough way what the trouble is; we have put our finger on the weak items in our personal inventory. Now these are about to be cast out. This requires action on our part, which, when completed, will mean that we have admitted to God, to ourselves, and to another human being, the exact nature of our defects. This brings us to the Fifth Step in the program of recovery mentioned in the preceding chapter.

J & C   We know that Step 5 says, 'We admitted to God, to ourselves and to another human being the exact nature of our wrongs'. But if you'll notice here in the narrative, he said the exact nature of our defects. Now people used to ask Bill about this and we've known two ladies that worked with him/for him for years and they both tell us the same thing. People would say Bill, why did you use the word 'wrongs' in Step 5, yet in the narrative here in the book you use the word defects? And by the way Bill, what's the difference anyhow between a wrong in 5, a defect in 6, and a shortcoming in 7? And they both said that Bill would just rear back and smile and he would say when I took English and Writing courses in college they taught me not to use the same words over and over. It shows how dumb you are. He said there really are no differences in these things. He said,

(a) In Step 4, we find those things that block us off from God.
(b) In Step 5, we're going to talk about them to another human being.
(c) In Step 6, we're going to become willing to turn them loose.
(d) In Step 7, we're going to ask God to take them away.

And he said, you can call them anything you want to, a wrong, a thought, a mistake, a defect, a personality flaw, whatever. We're going to notice on the next couple of pages that's exactly what he does with them. I followed it up in the 12 & 12 thirteen years later. Not only does he do it there, he does it twice as bad as he did in the Big Book. Using these words interchangeably, back and forth, all of them meaning identically the same thing.

Big Book p. 72, par. 1
> This is perhaps difficult - especially discussing our defects with another person. We think we have done well enough in admitting these things to ourselves. There is doubt about that. In actual practice, we usually find a solitary self-appraisal insufficient. Many of us thought it necessary to go much further. We will be more reconciled to discussing ourselves with another person when we see good reasons why we should do so. The best reason first: If we skip this vital step, we may not overcome drinking.

J & C   You take these forms now (Step 4 Inventory pg. 65), and the very, very vital information that we've got here. The book says that the solitary self-appraisal is insufficient. <u>I did the very best I could do filling out these forms with the limited knowledge that I had and experience, but I did the best I could do.</u> Now I take these to another human being and discuss them from left to right all the way across. <u>Someone else who has gone on before me and whose done the inventory according to the Big Book and</u> now <u>that person is going to help me to glean more information out of each of these situations</u> that's going to help me.

I need that information, because a solitary self-appraisal is insufficient. I'll give you an example. Looking around this room today, this weekend, I've noticed two or three character defects. It's real easy for me to look at you and see your defects of character. There's nothing between you and me except air. But

<u>It's very, very difficult for me to look at me and see the truth and see my defects of character
because of years and a lifetime of rationalization and justification of these attitudes.</u>

I need another human being to be able to look at me objectively and help me see things I couldn't see cause I'm starting out on a brand new lifetime engagement here and I need all the information and help I can get to have a very successful life.

<u>And I did the very best I could do on the inventory process,
but a solitary self-appraisal is insufficient.
I need God and another human being to help me see things that I couldn't see.</u>

Now to be sure we have to contradictions here over on page 73, on that first paragraph where it says, "More than most people..." the sentence before that says,

Big Book, p. 73, line 7
> *But they had not learned enough of humility, fearlessness and honesty, in the sense we find it necessary, until they told someone else all <u>their life story</u>.*

J & C   Now there's the statement that got us confused about Step 4.
And we all began to write our life story thinking that would be Step 4. But as we can see 95% of our life story really doesn't have anything to do with our alcoholism.

The fact I was born in 1929 that really doesn't have anything to do with it. But I'll tell you what I have done.
If I've taken the inventory the way the book says, I've shared my life story in those areas that really count.
Resentments didn't come in my head just today. They've been popping in my head as far back as I can remember.
I've shared all my life story - resentment wise.
Fears didn't come in my head just today. They've been coming in my head as far back as I can remember.
I shared all my life story - fear wise.
The harms I've done to other people. I didn't just hurt them yesterday.
I've been hurting people as far back as I can remember.

My mother said to me one day, Charlie, you were the meanest kid I ever say. She said I had a little problem loving you myself. Now when Mama don't love you, you're pretty bad off. As I look at these things today, my whole life is centered anyhow around those three things. Those resentments, those fears, and those harms I've done to others. So I don't have any quarrel with that statement at all any more. <u>If we've done our inventory the way the book says, we've shared our life story</u>. Now here's why we need to share this with another human being.

Big Book p. 73, par. 2
> *More than most people, the alcoholic leads a double life. He is very much the actor. To the outer world he presents his stage character. This is the one he likes his fellows to see. He wants to enjoy a certain reputation, but knows in his heart he doesn't deserve it.*

J & C   A practicing alcoholic is trying to live two lives. You know we've got a conscious. Whenever we're sober we try to live like people are supposed to live. But when we're drinking, since alcohol lowers the inhibitions, we do things we would never think about doing sober. We're living two lifetimes when we are a practicing alcoholic.

Big Book p. 73, par. 2
> *The inconsistency is made worse by the things he does on his sprees. Coming to his senses, he is revolted at certain episodes he vaguely remembers. These memories are a nightmare. He trembles to think someone might have observed him. As far as he can, he pushes these memories far inside himself. He hopes they will never see the light of day. He is under constant fear and tension that makes for more drinking.*

J & C   You know let's face it; we alcoholics have become the world's greatest con artists. You have to be.

You couldn't live as a practicing alcoholic if you didn't learn how to lie, cheat, con, manipulate, steal, whatever's necessary. And I think the one we have to con the most is ourselves. I don't think we could live with ourselves if we had to really see what's going on when we're drinking.

But you see we got a little thing called resentments.
And we use those resentments to transfer blame to others and that way we can live with ourselves.

Now if you've been doing than for 5, 10, 15, 20, 25, 30, 40 years and you come to A.A. and you take Step 4,
you'll be just as honest as you can with yourself - but let's face it, <u>we can't be honest with ourselves</u>.
I now need to take my inventory,
<u>take it to another human being</u>, <u>one who has walked this walk before me</u> who understands 4, 5, 6, 7, 8 and 9 according to the Big Book and <u>have them help me see the things I can't see about me</u>

They're not going to change anything in Column 1, they're not going to change anything in Column 2,
but they'll probably change some things in Column 3.

In one place I said this was caused by the sex instinct and he said nah it isn't,
he said you're just trying to build your self esteem that's all your trying to do.
In the fifth column in one place I said this was caused by fear, and he said this is plain damn dishonesty, that's all this is.

He <u>helped me see things I couldn't see</u>.
    We're getting ready to start a lifetime changing process.
      We need to be sure that we're trying to <u>change the</u> <u>right things</u>,
        so we can have peace of mind in the future<u>.</u>

And we just can't see that by ourselves. I know confession is good for the soul. And I if you belong to a denomination that requires it you ought a go do that. But I still think you ought a take your inventory to somebody in A.A., preferably a good sponsor if you got one that knows the program.

      The main thing is do they really know the program?
      If they do they can help us.
    <u>If they don't then all we are going to get out of it is confession</u>

We need more than that. Page 74 tells people, tells you how to pick somebody. That is not valid today like it was in 1939. In '39 the first person out here in California that got this Big Book, didn't have any other A.A. members or any sponsor and it was difficult for them to find somebody to do Step 5 with. That's what page 74 deals with. But today there's plenty of good people out here in California that understands this program, that have worked this program, that have walked this Step before, that's who we need to select to take Step 5 with. Hopefully it will be our sponsor, page 75 tells us how to do that.

Big Book p. 75, par 1
> *When we decide who is to hear our story, we waste no time. We have a written inventory and we are prepared for a long talk. We explain to our partner what we are about to do and why we have to do it. He should realize that we are engaged upon a life-and-death errand. Most people approached in this way will be glad to help; they will be honored by our confidence.*

J & C   I'll never forget when I called my sponsor Franklin, and I said Franklin can I come over this weekend and do my inventory, do my Fifth Step. He said sure, I'd love to have you come over. So I went to there to Olive Branch, Mississippi and I sat down there with Franklin that evening and I said I've got it all prepared here, you've helped me a lot and I appreciate it. He said yeah I know you do and I'm ready to get started, but first of all let's you and I do the 3rd Step Prayer together. That's the kind of sponsor I had and we asked God to be with us during this process. And we did that and we sat about looking into this inventory process and Franklin <u>helped me see things that I couldn't see</u>. I shared these things with him from left to right, all the way across and he asked me questions and helped me see things I couldn't see, and shared with me some of the things that had happened with him and how he could see things. And it helped me a whole lot, it helped me a lot And then after that weekend was over, like the book says

Big Book, p. 75, par 2

We pocket our pride and go to it, illuminating every twist of character, every dark cranny of the past. Once we have taken this step, withholding nothing, we are delighted.

J & C   Now we see the results. Some more promises.....

Big Book, p. 75, par 2
We can look the world in the eye. We can be alone at perfect peace and ease. Our fears fall from us. We begin to feel the nearness of our Creator. We may have had certain spiritual beliefs, but now we begin to have a spiritual experience.

J & C   We believed in Step two, now we begin to have a spiritual experience

Big Book, pg. 75, par 2
The feeling that the drink problem has disappeared will often come strongly. We feel we are on the Broad Highway, walking hand in hand with the Spirit of the Universe.

J & C   I remember back to when I was drinking how my mind used to race uncontrollably every night. And that's the main reason I drank was to stop it. And after I did this 5th Step and I was on my way home that afternoon.... I used to lay awake nights thinking if I could just get it all even one time, just get it back to zero, back to even, all those situations just one time I'd be okay. And by this time I could see that I could do that, I was looking forward to the next step because I wanted to get things squared away one time ... and I thanked God all the way home for this process up to this point.

Now if you've done (Step) 4 and 5 according to the Big Book you've done a lot of work you're probably tired and need a little rest, the book's going to give us a little rest stop

Big Book, p. 75, par. 3
Returning home we find a place where we can be quiet for an hour,

J & C   Now he didn't say seventy-two days. You see they mean for us to get on with this thing,
between (Steps) 3 and 4 - at once[1]*, now we get an hours rest here but that's all.

Big Book, p. 75, par. 3
We thank God from the bottom of our heart that we know Him better.

J & C   We don't know him yet, but we know him better.

Big Book, p. 75, par. 3
Taking this book down from our shelf we turn to the page (59) which contains the twelve steps. Carefully reading the first five proposals we ask if we have omitted anything, for we are building an arch through which we shall walk a free man at last. Is our work solid so far? Are the stones properly in place? Have we skimped on the cement put into the foundation? Have we tried to make mortar without sand?

J & C   And once again we are referring to the wonderfully effective spiritual structure, the personality change we're building.

Step 1 - Willingness was the foundation (pg. 23, par. 5)
Step 2 - Believing was the cornerstone (pg. 47, par. 2)
Step 3 - Arch that we pass through to freedom - 3 is the keystone (pg. 62, last line)

Now we've put two more stones in place

Big Book, p. 76, par. 1

---

[1] *Big Book pg. 64 line 1*
Though our Decision (Step 3) was a vital and crucial step, it could have little permanent effect unless <u>at once</u> followed by a strenuous effort to face, and to be rid of, the things in ourselves which had been blocking us (Step 4).

If we can answer to our satisfaction, we then look at Step Six. We have emphasized willingness as being indispensable. Are we now ready to let God remove from us all the things which we have admitted are objectionable? Can He now take them all, everyone? If we still cling to something we will not let go, we ask God to help us be willing.

J & C And that's all for Step 6. And if you notice he didn't say a thing about defects of character did he? He did say those things that we admitted were objectionable. Now surely, surely in Step 4 and 5 when we looked out into that fifth column

Column 1	Column 2	Column 3	Column 4	Column 5
I'm resentful at	The Cause	Affects my		

Where had I been selfish, dishonest, self-seeking, frightened or inconsiderate?

and we saw that old selfish, dishonest, self-seeking, frightened, inconsiderate character that we have become, when we saw that those were what cause us to do the things that hurt people. They in turn retaliate, we in turn resent, we're afraid, we're filled with guilt and remorse, causes us to drink then surely those things in the fifth column have now become objectionable to us. Are we ready to turn them lose, if we are we're thru with Step 6. The book recognizes though that self cannot always overcome self. cause it says <u>if we're not ready</u> we ask God to help us be willing to turn these things loose.

Now you would think when we see what they do to us we'd be more than willing, but sometimes we're not. You know we human beings are funny people; sometimes we would rather sit in today's pain and suffering cause we've come to learn how to take care of that.

Sometimes we'd rather sit in today's pain and suffering than take a chance on changing in the future cause we don't know what change will bring.

If I have to <u>get rid of my selfishness and become unselfish</u>, then how am I going to get what I want in the future?

If I'm going to have to <u>get rid of my dishonesty and start operating honestly</u>, then how the heck am I going to make a living? I don't know nothing about honesty when I get here.

If I'm going to have to <u>start getting rid of my self-seeking and frightened character and start operating on courage</u> that scares the hell out of me. I don't know nothing about that.

If I'm going to have to <u>start considering other people and their needs and their wants,</u> then who's going to take care of me?

Sometimes we would rather sit in today's pain than take a chance on changing in the future.

End of Tape 6

And the Book recognized that and said if you're not ready,

Big Book, pg. 76, par. 1
   we ask God to help me be willing.

J & C And with God's help we become willing with (Steps) 3 through 6. When ready we say something like this, (Step 7 Prayer)

Big Book, pg. 76, par. 2
   My Creator, I am now willing you that you should have all of me, good and bad. I pray that you now remove from me every single defect of character

J & C Whoop, whoop. We're at Step 7 now and it said shortcomings[2], but here he calls.... see what he's done to us. He confused the heck out of us didn't he?

Big Book, pg. 76, par. 2

---

[2] Step 7 - Humbly asked Him to remove our shortcomings.

I pray that you now remove from me every single defect of character which stands in the way of my usefulness to you and my fellows. Grant me strength, as I go out from here, to do your bidding. Amen.

J & C   We've then completed Step 7.

Are you ready to have God remove them? (defects of character).   If you are you're through with (Step) 6.
Have you humbly asked him to take them away? If you have you've done Step 7.

But I hope you don't make the mistake I did. I assumed that now that I'm ready, and God being all powerful, that all I've got to do is turn to God and say okay God here I am, warts and all, does that mean give me the $29.95 special and I'll never have to worry about this stuff again. I found out it don't work that way.

God will do for me, what I can't do for myself. I simply do not have the power to remove a character defect - only God has the power.

**God will not do for me, what I can do for myself.
And what I can do for myself is find out the opposite of that character defect,
and then with God's help and all the willpower I can muster,
in every situation it comes up, try to practice the opposite.**

Cause you see God can't take away my selfishness and leave another whole in my head. It's going to have to be replaced with the opposite, which is unselfishness. And when I first got here my mind was a set of mental habits ingrained in 38, 39, 40 yearsr of living. The habitual thing for me was to react selfishly.

The only way to break a habit is to work against yourself.

If I ask God to take away <u>selfishness</u> and I start trying to practice <u>unselfishness,</u>
then slowly the old habit dies and a new habit takes its place.

And over a period of years I have become an unselfish human being. I am not what I was when I first got here.

If I want God to take away <u>dishonesty,</u> then I must do my part, which is to practice <u>honesty</u>

in every situation that comes up and that's hard for me to do. That is so alien to my nature that I can't practice honesty without Gods help. But with God's power and all the willpower I can muster I can force myself to be honest and slowly the old idea dies and a new one takes its place. The habitual thing for me today is to react to any situation with honesty.

If I want God to <u>take away fear</u> then I've got to kick myself in the butt and <u>practice courage</u>.
If I want Him to take away <u>inconsideration</u>, then I must start <u>considering other people and their needs and their wants</u> and slowly the old idea dies and a new idea takes its place.

Big Book, pg. par. 1
    We were reborn.

J & C   I am not what I used to be. Now I'm not completely unselfish, never will be. I'm not always completely honest. Sometimes I'm afraid and other times I'm inconsiderate but the majority of the time I'm an unselfish, honest human being with courage, considering other people first. You know I think you and I are the luckiest people in the world. We have the opportunity through these two little steps right here (6 & 7) two live two lifetimes in one lifetime. Most people out there are sick; most of them are going to their grave sick not even knowing they're sick. We not only know we're sick we know what's wrong with us we found it in Steps 4 & 5.
And in 6 & 7 we can do something about it and we can change it and we become entirely different human beings.

Most people don't get that opportunity. Now be careful, for God's sake be careful, cause if you really accept this as the correct thing and the right thing then that means from this day on **you are responsible for what you are**. I can't blame it on Barbara any longer, I can't blame it on Mother and Dad, I can't blame it on God and I can't blame it on society.

**If I stay selfish, dishonest, self-seeking, frightened and inconsiderate
it's got to be because that's the way I want to be.**

I no longer have the luxury of blaming it on others cause I don't have to be that way. You know what I found out? I found out that when you become <u>unselfish</u> people start kinda liking you a little better than they did before. I found out when you start becoming <u>honest</u> well you feel better about yourself.

That's the way you build self-esteem is to do the right thing for a change

I found out when I practice with <u>courage</u> and I operate on courage instead of <u>fear</u> I do things that makes me fell better and I quit doing things that made me feel so bad.

I found out there's real pleasure in <u>considering other people first and</u> giving to others before you take for yourself.

I didn't know that. How in the hell could I know that, I've never been that way before. This thing really amazes me in what happens to us and the simplicity of this thing if we'll just do what the book says. Joe?

You know there's always a paradox in AA. To give you an idea what a paradox is how many of you have ever called you're sponsor so you could listen. We always call him so we can talk, right? That's the paradox. And the paradox here in these two steps is that they use the Doctors Opinion (p. xxiii) and the first four chapters to do Steps 1 & 2, 3.5 pages for Step 3. 8 pages for Step 4, 4 pages for Step 5, and a whole chapter devoted with "Working with Others". The paradox is that

**two of the biggest steps in all of Alcoholics Anonymous
is on two little paragraphs, (Steps) 6 & 7.
These are the tools of change.
These are the tools of acceptance**.

A lot of people talk about just running around accepting things - I accept this, I accept that. Well I can't do that.

**Acceptance comes after some actions, (Steps) 6 & 7
acceptance comes after the actions of 6 & 7.**

You know there's a story in that other book (Bible) about this guy named Judas.
Judas <u>could not accept</u> what he had done. (Betrayal) So what did he do? He killed himself. That's the importance of acceptance. You can't accept anything unless you take some action. He didn't do Steps 6 & 7 - didn't have them

And the other story is, there's a story in this other book about this guy, his name was Saul. Saul was riding his ass on the way to Damascus. A big bolt of lightening came down and knocked him off his ass, on his ass. That's the way I read it. He gets up and he dusted himself off and this big voice came out of the sky and said, "Saul, can we talk?"
"Yeah, we can talk, what you want to talk about?"
Had to get his attention didn't he. <u>Maybe alcoholism has to get our attention</u>.
"Saul you've been a very selfish individual and you've harmed a lot of people and you're very resentful and angry. And you've harmed a lot of people by those attitudes and I want you to quit doing that?"
And he said, "How do you quit doing that?" He said, "Do these things and if you'll do that then you'll make a change, and when you change then we'll call you Paul. Well he did those things and became Paul.
Now we know that Paul was one of the greatest writers the world's ever known.
And the Corinthians, the town of Corinthians, they asked Paul one day, "Paul, what is this secret to living?"
And he said, "The secret to living is daily dying." The old Saul had to die so the new Paul came alive.

(Steps) 6 & 7. By the time I got to 6 & 7 I could see what I had become as a result of the previous steps and I didn't like what I had become and a little doubt crept in my mind. Can God really change me from what I had become to what he intends for me be? And then I had to reaffirm and rethink about this idea on page 53. It said,

Big Book, pg. 53, par 3
  God either is, or He isn't?

J & C He either can or he can't

Big Book, pg. 53, par 3.
What was our choice to be?

J & C And I chose to believe that he could. The tools of change.

To change from what I had become to what God had intended me to be.

(Steps) 6 & 7 - Two of the biggest Steps in all of Alcoholics Anonymous.

Just before the break I want Joe to tell you one little story about buying some salad to show you practicing this thing. A few years ago I went into a grocery store to buy some salad and some stuff to fix for a salad - that night was having steak. I went in there and bought this stuff and came back up to the register and I was going to pay up and I gave this lady ten dollars and she took the ten dollars and stood right there and counted me out change for a twenty, and I watched her do it. And I picked up that money and I put it in my pocket and I got out to my car and I sat there and I said well you big dummy you sold out for ten bucks. I thought it was worth more than that, I'm glad it wasn't less than that. So I took the money back in there and I told the lady I said you know I'm a member of a fellowship that requires me to be honest and you gave me too much money and I want to give you this ten dollars back. And she said, you know I never heard of a fellowship like that and I said I well I hadn't either till a few years ago, so here's your ten bucks back. The whole point of this story, when I walked out with that ten dollars, and believe I don't need ten dollars; I mean I do not need ten dollars. And I'm walking out I felt about that big, sneaking out the door. You see then I went back in there and gave her that ten bucks back and I walked out and I feel good again. I did the right thing. If you practice that enough times the next time she gives change for a twenty you do it right there you don't even go out the door with it. That's what we're talking about when we change and only we can do it.

Only we can slay ourselves with God's help and become different human beings

**So if you stay dishonest, self-seeking, frightened and inconsiderate
it must be because you want to**

J & C We've completed our first seven steps knowing full well we're going to be working on (Steps) 6 & 7 for the rest of our lives really, <u>trying to change as the **opportunity** comes up</u>. Now we've read in the book where we are

(a) spiritually sick,
(b) mentally sick and
(c) physically sick,

when the spiritual malady is overcome we straighten our mentally and physically (p. 64, par. 4)

and we begin to look at those things and begin to realize that all human beings really are born to live in <u>three dimensions</u> of life.

If **God dwells within each of us**

we're going to have to live with God,
whether we like it or not is beside the point.   (spiritual dimension)
The only question is
do we live with him in harmony or disharmony.

I don't know of anybody that ever got in more disharmony with God than we alcoholics have. We also have what we call the <u>mental dimension</u>.

We've all got a mind, sometimes we act like we don't but we do,
and we have to live with our mind whether we like it or not, is beside the point, we don't have any choice.
And again do we live there in harmony or disharmony?

I don't know of any group of people that ever got more fouled up in their heads than we alcoholics have. For years I thought the <u>physical dimension</u> was my body only. Today I realize

the physical dimension is the world and everything in it

Now we alcoholics don't have any place else to live except here on earth we don't have any choice in the matter whether we like it or not is beside the point. The only question is, do we live on earth with our fellow man in harmony or disharmony?

And I don't know of any group of people that ever got more fouled up in a relationship with the world and everybody in it than we alcoholics have. So we were sick spiritually, mentally and physically. The book talks about a design for living, and it looks to us that

**these steps are designed in such a manner to put us back together and make us well
in all three dimensions of life as God intended for us to be in the first place.**

Steps 1, 2 & 3   We got right with the Spirit. Because <u>we were powerless</u>, we saw the need for the power.

Step 3   We decided to <u>go after that power</u>, and we made a decision that <u>God was going to be the Director</u>. He's the Father, we're the children. He's the Employer, we're the employee (we work for him)

For most of us that's the first time we've had that relationship with God for a long, long, long time. We got the right relationship in (Steps) 1, 2 & 3. <u>That removes self-will</u>, to let us begin to look into our own minds.

Step 4 & 5   <u>We found out those things that block us off from God</u>, that block us off from our fellow man, that creates the resentments and the fears and the guilt's etc.

Steps 6 and 7   <u>we begin to work on those</u> in

We begin to get right in our minds through 4, 5, 6 & 7. That removes just enough self-will, to begin to look at our relationship with the world and everybody in it. Now through 4, 5 & 7 we got rid of these resentments, we got rid of these fears to the level that God intended for them to be. But we haven't really done anything about the storeroom back here that's filled with guilt and remorse associated with the harms we've done in the past.

And if we want to get right in the physical dimension,
our relationship with the world and everybody in it,
it's long been known that the way you do that, is to make restitution for the things done in the past.

Then the guilt and the remorse begins to disappear. I've never yet seen a newcomer come into a meeting and read the steps off the wall and say that I can hardly wait till we get to Steps 8 & 9, that looks like a lot of fun. Nobody likes to do Steps 8 & 9. Nobody that I've ever met, some people might but not that I know. The only question is can we afford not to do that?

<u>It looks like if we don't do that (Steps 8 & 9)
that guilt and remorse in here kind of keeps chewing at us.
After a while it begins to bother our relationship with the world and everybody in it
- we start getting sick in our head.
And after a while that backs up and blocks us off from God
and we end up drunk again</u>

You know when we read the Foreword to the Second Edition it sounds as though Dr. Bob never took another drink after Bill visited with him the first time. That isn't true. Dr. Bob had one more drunk left in him. Not to long after Bill called on him and they began to try to work with people Bob found it necessary to go to a medical convention and his wife Anne begged Bill not to let him go. She said Bill if he goes over there he'll get drunk, he does it every year. And Bill said, let him go. He's got to learn to live in society where there's always going be plenty of alcohol. Bob went to the medical convention, got drunk, came back to Akron, showed up at his nurses home. She called Anne, said come and get him, he's drunk and said get him sobered up he's got surgery in the morning and he's the only doctor on staff right now that can do this particular surgery. Dr. Bob was a proctologist. Whatever your procto is, I'm glad he wasn't working on mine the next morning I know that. They went over and got him and brought him back to Dr. Bobs house and they coffeed him and they walked him and they sobered him to the best of their ability. The next morning Bill took him to the hospital to do the surgery. In the parking lot of the hospital Dr. Bob said, Bill I can't do this surgery. He said I'm sick and I'm shaking and I'm trembling and I'm going to hurt somebody bad. Bill reached in the back seat of the car, brought out a bottle of beer, popped the top on it, said drink this and you'll be okay. Dr. Bob drank the beer, went upstairs, did the surgery and sure enough it came out okay and the only problem is he disappears. Bills waiting on him down in the parking lot. He waits 2, 3, 4 hours. He assumes that the beer's trigger **the allergy** and Bob is off and running. He goes back to Dr. Bob's house and Bill and Anne wait all afternoon. Late, late, late evening Dr. Bob shows up and he's sober. Bill said where in the hell have you been? He said I've been going up and down both sides of the street making my amends to those I've harmed in the past. That bottle of beer was the last drink Dr. Bob took, January 10, 1935 which is AA's birthday. He never would make amends before because he was afraid people would find out that he was alcoholic and he would lose what little practice he had left. He didn't know that everybody already knew he was alcoholic. The day he screwed up the courage, mustered up enough courage to make his amends was the day he took his last drink. Now I would assume if it's good enough for Bob it's probably good enough for me too.

Let's look at 8 & 9 for just a few minutes. We are not going to go through them in great detail, just a few minutes

Big Book p. 76, par. 3 *"Now we need more action, which we find that "Faith without works is dead." Let's look at Steps Eight and Nine."*

J & C   You generally <u>when people go to a Step Study meeting and they begin to talk about Step 8, generally the conversation will get over to how they made amends in Step 9</u>. **But Step 8 is a definite step and it's a step that needs to be done**.

Big Book p. 76, par. 3 *"We have a list of all persons we had harmed and to whom we are willing to make amends. We made it when we took inventory."*

J & C   We simply take all those names off of Column 1 off of those 4 sheets of anyone that we've harmed and we put them on one long sheet. We haven't made any amends yet, we've just made the list. And then the book says,

<u>Resentment Inventory</u>	<u>Fear Inventory</u>	<u>Sex Inventory</u>	<u>Harms Done to Others</u>
Column 1	Column 1	Column 1	Column 1
I'm Resentful at:	I'm Angry at:	Who have I hurt?	Who have I hurt?

Big Book p. 76, par. 3 *"We subjected ourselves to a drastic self-appraisal."*

J & C   We did that in Steps 4 & 5, a drastic self-appraisal.

Big Book p. 76, par. 3 *"Now we go out to our fellows and repair the damage done in the past. We attempt to sweep away the debris which has accumulated out of our effort to live on self-will and run the show. If we haven't the will to do this, we ask until it comes."*

J & C   More prayer, Step 8. And again it's real simple. We make the list, then we become willing to the list, and if we're not willing we ask God to help us to become willing. We haven't made any amends yet. That is Step 8. When we do that, then we've completed Step 8. Everyone one of these action steps recognizes that self cannot overcome self and we have prayer in most of them and here we got it again in Step 8 that if we're not willing, we ask God to help us be willing. I had a lot of difficulty in Step 8 and Step 9 because there's some people that had harmed me just as bad as I'd ever harmed them. And I didn't think it was going to be necessary for me to make any amends to them, I didn't feel like I could and I didn't want to. I told my sponsor about this, he said okay, what I'd like to see you do is take that list that you have and divide it into four lists (columns). He said I'd like to see you put on one list (column)

RIGHT NOW   **LATER**   **MAYBE**   **NEVER.**

He said those that you love and you want to make amends to them **RIGHT NOW** put them on that list
those that you know you're going to do it sooner or later or you're not to keen about, put them on the **LATER** list those that you aren't sure about, you may or may not, put them on the **MAYBE** list

those that you're never going to make amends to, put them on the **NEVER** list

And then he said I want you to start making your amends to the **RIGHT NOW's**.
By the time you're through with that you'll probably be ready to do some **LATER's**.
By the time you're through with the later's list, you'll probably be ready to do some **MAYBE's**.
And he reached in his billfold and pulled out a twenty-dollar bill and said I'm going to bet you twenty dollars
by the time you're through with the Maybe's you be ready to start on the **NEVER's**.

And the old fool was exactly right. I was trying to block myself off entirely from Step 8 & 9 by using three or four names (resentments, etc.) and he didn't let me do that. He gave me a process by which I could become willing to make amends to them all, eventually. And it really did work for me.

So if you've got that problem, or you're working with some whose got that problem, try the Four List. Right Now, Later, Maybe and Never. And it really works.

J& C   Ok. After we've got the list, we're willing, over on page 77 we begin to look at Step 9. Now Step 9 is a definite three-part step. The first part tells us the kind of amends to make.

We made direct amends wherever possible

Direct amends is probably eyeball to eyeball, face to face, one on one. So he tells us the kind of amends to make. **direct amends**
Then he tells us when to make them **wherever possible**
Then he tells us when not to make them

except when to do so would injure them or others.

Now for the next three or four pages he handles each one of these things paragraph by paragraph.
Page 77, that paragraph down in the middle of the page

Big Book p. 77, par. 2   *"We don't use this as an excuse for shying away from the subject of God. When it will serve any good purpose, we are willing to announce our convictions with tact and common sense."*

J& C   The direct amends starts right here with the words

Big Book p. 77, par. 2, cont.   *"The question of how to approach the man we hated will arise."*

J& C   Let's look at this one. I think in the are of the 9th step, especially since were going to go out and make amends for the harms done. I think especially we need to talk to our sponsors and listen to our sponsors in this area to get some information about how we are going to go about making these amends. Cause we can go out in our zeal to make amends and can cause a whole lot more harms than we ever intended or had ever done prior to that just trying to make amends. So check with your sponsor in this area. Lay out how you are going to it and what you propose to do and see what he says. Very, very important.

Big Book p. 77, par. 2, cont.   *"The question of how to approach the man we hated will arise. It may be he has done us more harm than we have done him and, though we may have acquired a better attitude toward him, we are still not too keen about admitting our faults. Nevertheless, with a person we dislike, we take the bit in our teeth. It is harder to go to an enemy than to a friend, but we find it much more beneficial to us. We go to him in a helpful and forgiving spirit, confessing our former ill feeling and expressing our regret.*
Under no condition do we criticize such a person or argue. Simply we tell him that we will never get over drinking until we have done our utmost to straighten out the past. We are there to sweep off our side of the street, realizing that nothing worth while can be accomplished until we do so, never trying to tell him what he should do. His faults are not discussed. We stick to our own. If our manner is calm, frank, and open, we will be gratified with the result.
In nine cases out of ten the unexpected happens. Sometimes the man we are calling upon admits his own fault, so feuds of years' standing melt away in an hour. Rarely do we fail to make satisfactory progress. Our former enemies sometimes praise what we are doing and wish us well. Occasionally, they will offer assistance. It should not matter, however, if someone does throw us out of his office. We have made our demonstration, done our part. It's water over the dam."

J& C   And ever time I read that I think about my cousin Gary. And I was in the area of making amends at this time and I was in this restaurant one day. I had never been in that restaurant before or since and I looked up and Gary was at the door waiting to be seated and I motioned him over. Now he came over very reluctantly. Cause Gary and I had been fighting and fussing, physically and verbally abusing each other all our lives. So he came over very reluctantly. He wasn't quite sure what I might do. And I asked him to sit down and he did reluctantly. And I looked at him and I said "Gary I've found out I'm an alcoholic and I'm a member of Alcoholics Anonymous and I'm trying to straighten out my life and I'm trying to make amends for the harms I've done people. And I've harmed you a whole lot over these years and I want to ask you if you will forgive me for that." And he kind of relaxed like that and he said, "Well you know Joe I want to know if you will forgive me the things I've done to you?" That whole deal went away just like that. And that's a wonderful thing. But the best part about it is that Gary comes to Alcoholics Anonymous from time to time even now. Well he's making progress. He used to be a daily drinker and now he's a periodic drinker. So he's making progress. But he comes to the group that I attend and we'll sit down and we'll visit back and forth a little bit as much as he will allow me to. But had that not happened that many years ago Gary would never have come to Alcoholics Anonymous. Maybe someday he'll get sober. I hope so.

Eyeball to eyeball.
Face to face.
One on one.

I think we've got to remember now the purpose of making the amends is not to get you to like me. I hope you will when I'm through. But the purpose is to get rid of my fear, my guilt and my remorse. If I write you a letter I'm not quite sure how you accepted it. I'm still a little concerned about what you are going to say and do the next time I run into you. I'm not sure I've done my utmost. If I call you on the telephone I've got the same situation. But if I go to you wherever you are, your office, your home or wherever it might be, and we sit down, eyeball to eyeball, face to face, one on one, when I've made my amends I'm through with it. I'll never have to worry about it again. You've done the worst you're going to do to me, right there, and I in turn have done my utmost. No doubt that's the best way to do it.

Another kind of amend is an equal restitution or equal amounts. You know we tended to hurt a lot of people in the material area also. Some of them we stole from them and never did give them their money back. Some of them we ran up bills that we never did pay. We wrote hot cheques that we never did pick up. We tore up automobiles that we never did fix. We've hurt a lot of people in a lot of ways in the material world. What are we going to do about that. It really wouldn't do much good for me to come to you and say "Look, you and I both know that I stole $1200 from you when I was drinking. And I'm sorry about it. Would you forgive me?" You're probably going to say, "I'm sorry about it too. Where's my $1200?" Equal restitution. Bill handles that in the next paragraph.

Big Book p. 78, par. 2   "*Most alcoholics owe money.*"

J& C   Now that's probably the understatement of the year right there.

Big Book p. 78, par. 2 cont.   "*We do not dodge our creditors. Telling them what we are trying to do, we make no bones about our drinking; they usually know it anyway, whether we think so or not. Nor are we afraid of disclosing our alcoholism on the theory it may cause financial harm. Approached in this way, the most ruthless creditor will sometimes surprise us. Arranging the best deal we can we let these people know we are sorry. Our drinking has made us slow to pay. We must lose our fear of creditors no matter how far we have to go, for we are liable to drink if we are afraid to face them.*"

J& C   I think what he's saying to me is this. That if I owe you money for any reason I need to come to you and say, "Look, I know I owe you the $1200 and you know it too. And I'm trying to get my life straightened out. I'm sorry I can't pay you that amount of money today. But what I'd like to do is start paying you $5/week or $10/week." Whatever I can live with. And I start paying you that $5 or $10/week or 20 or whatever we've decided on. And as the weeks go by, some morning I wake up and I say "Hey that suckers paid off." I don't have to worry about that one anymore. The fear and guilt and remorse is gone. I go to the next one. And I say , "Now you and I both know that I owe you a couple thousand dollars. Can't pay you today. But I'd like to start paying you about $20/week." And I start paying you $20/week and some morning I wake up and that sucker's paid off too. And then I go to the next one. And then the next and then the next one and someday I'll wake up and by golly they're all paid off. And the fear and the guilt and remorse is gone. I feel good back here in the back of my head now after that guilt and remorse and fear is gone.

Now a guy came to me one time and we were discussing this. And he said "Charlie if I try to pay them so much a week, do you know how old I would be before I got them paid off?" You'd be the same age that you would be if you didn't pay them off. It don't make any difference. I've lived long enough to know that time is going to pass. I wish I could stop it but I can't. And as time passes I can use it for a worthwhile purpose, do something about these things, or I can keep putting it off and putting it off and putting it off and 5 years or 10 years or 15 years from now still be in the same situation and maybe drunk in the meantime.

We had a good friend that used to live in Tulsa but moved out here to California, he's gone now, he's dead. Name was Dan. When Dan was 29 years sober he said, "Charlie, I paid the last one of them last week." I said "Dan how do you feel". He said, "I feel about 8 foot tall". Now Dan was little bitty fellow about 5'1". He said "This is the first time in my life that I can ever remember that I don't owe somebody something for what I've stolen in the past". He said "I feel pretty good about old Dan". Dan owed a lot of money. When he was drinking he was in the oil business down in Texas. And he hooked them and he hooked them big. Took him 29 years to pay them. But by golly he got it done. I'll tell you what a good con artist Dan was. When he was still drinking in Texas his wife Sara, who later became a beautiful member of Al-Anon, she took him to the state insane asylum in Big Spring, Texas to have him committed for alcoholic insanity. The head psychiatrist interviewed Sara, then he interviewed Dan and after a while Dan left and Sara was locked up. Truth. She stayed there for a year. She learned how to live better electrically and all that goody, goody stuff in there. Dan was a real con artist. Joe.

You know Dan did pay back a lot of money. It's not alot of money out here in California but in Oklahoma it's a lot of money. Hell of a lot of money. You guys have got plenty of money out here. We all know that. But Dan paid them all back and I spent many, many days playing bridge with Dan and Sara and he and my wife and they were teaching us the program alot and sharing with us and they paid a lot of money back. Now you'd of that that the kind of money he paid back would have kept him broke but it didn't. He prospered in other ways. He wasn't rich when he died but he had a very comfortable living throughout all those years and he prospered as a result of doing the right thing with his debts.

And again I hear some of you saying, I can hear awful good. Well Charlie that stuffs probably all right for $1200 or $2000 or maybe $10,000 but what if it's a half a million? What if it's a million? What if it's 2 million? Can we pay that back? I don't know why not, we're smart enough to steal it we're probably smart enough to pay it back if we are willing to do so. You know I think we forget from step 3 on that God is with us. And if we are willing to do these things Gods going to make it possible to do so just like he did for Dan. Dan didn't die a rich man but Dan died a very comfortable man. God saw that Dan had the means to be able to pay these people back. The willingness is what it takes to do this. And it really works for people like us.

On page 79 about the middle of the page it talks about where other people are involved. And we need to really, really consider this now. Sometimes in our zeal to be forgiven for the things we've done in the past we make amends where we end up hurting the one we owe amends to even more. Or possibly hurt somebody else. And if we do that then sooner or later we're going to have to go back and make amends for that too. So we have to be very, very careful where other people are involved. Over on page 80

There we have an example on page 80 where he went to the people involved and got their permission to make the amend before he made it in order to be sure that everything was going to be OK.

Bottom of page 80 he starts talking about domestic troubles.

Page 81 he talks about sex outside of marriage. What are we going to do about those kinds of things? Very carefully he handles just about every conceivable situation that could come up. With the people I work with usually we can find that answer to their amends as to whether they should make them or they shouldn't and how to make it here in the big book. Covers just about all situations. The key thing I think and Joe said it a while ago is get somebody else's advice. I've seen too many people jump into these amends too fast. And not only hurt other people but end up destroying a family, destroying a relationship with another human being completely. You know I think that we should go to our sponsors, get their help, get their advice before we even start making these amends. Especially where it involves maybe hurting other people.

Big Book p. 83, par. 3   "There may be some wrongs we can never fully right."

J& C   You know some of these people are already dead and buried. Some of them to make the amends would hurt them or others. We can't do that.

Big Book p. 83, par. 3 cont.   *"We don't worry about them if we can honestly say to ourselves that we would right them if we could. Some people cannot be seen - we sent them an honest letter. And there may be a valid reason for postponement in some cases.*

But we don't delay if it can be avoided. We should be sensible, tactful, considerate and humble without being servile or scraping. As God's people we stand on our feet; we don't crawl before anyone."

J & C   The one mistake I see us making is we got somebody and try to make our amends and they don't accept it. They didn't always accept mine. Some of them said "Charlie we didn't like you when you were drinking, not too damn crazy about you now, we'd just as soon you get out of here and leave us alone." And when that happens to us it just crushes us. And we tend to want to go back and go back and go back and literally beg those people to forgive us. We don't need to do that. If they don't accept it there's nothing we can do about that. About all we can do is stand in readiness to make it at a later date if the opportunity comes up. But we certainly do not have to crawl before anyone. We are Gods people too.

J & C   As I said here this morning and I became painfully aware, shore fully aware this year, all those situations that I used to have that I thought needed to make amends are all taken care of, I mean every one of them and I'll tell you about two here this morning if you will.

When I was drinking I had a mobile home up north and west of Tulsa, the lake called Lake Keystone, didn't think my wife knew anything about it, nice place. One morning in the middle of the night there's a knock on the door and I finally came to the door and I opened it up and what she did she just broke in Phyllis did. And I really wasn't having a good time, embarrassed me in front of my girlfriend, yeah and our daughter she brought the daughter with her. I was not having a good time. Now Gail, she was affected by my drinking of course. When she was seventeen years old, just a few days after she was seventeen she got married to get away from Phyllis and I cause Phyllis was in the program of Alcoholics Anonymous some twenty-three years she's been sober thank God, but Gail was affected by this. And the book says

Big Book, pg. 83, par. 1   *"A remorseful mumbling [that we are sorry] won't fill the bill at all."*

J & C   Of course I tried to make a few amends verbally to Gail and you know I, she said it's okay but it wasn't until six years ago, I was sober 19 years and talking to Gail on the phone and she was living up in Columbus, Ohio and she said Daddy a thing happened here recently. Her sister in law had died and her husband had died unexpectedly and left two kids for someone else to raise. And she said if something should happen like that to Jim and I would you and Mom take the kids? That's when I knew she really had forgiven me, but it took nineteen years.

Big Book, pg. 83, par. 1   *"A remorseful mumbling [that we are sorry] won't fill the bill at all."*

J & C   Now I'm sober in Alcoholics Anonymous for two and a half years and Phyllis and I get back together and nine years later I'm standing at the back of the room greeting people as they come in to the meeting place that night and I look around and here's the lady of the mobile home incident. Phyllis is at the coffee pot getting coffee and she looked over her shoulder, it all happen just about that quick. I believe you'll get an opportunity to handle all these situations. God makes the wherever possible. And some of the guys were aware of the situation and they asked what did she say and I said she didn't say anything... for about a week. And we were at another meeting and here's this lady and she was trying to get sober and coming to A.A. and again at another meeting there was this lady and Phyllis began to talk ugly to me. They'll do that you know. And I began to pay the price again, began to feel bad about it again. Well after about two or three weeks of this and one night she was settled down, she'd come back down through the ceiling and we were able to talk about this. I said Phyllis you know I've already paid one hell of a price for this I mean I have already paid one hell of a price, physically, morally, spiritually, financially and every way you can pay. And what I'm trying to tell you is I'm not paying anymore. I said it's just like last months gas bill. I paid that one, and I'm not paying that one no more.

They'll let you pay forever if you'll pay. There comes a time when you quit paying.
We don't have to crawl before anyone.
We make our amends to the best of our ability and go on about our business.

If you're right with God in (Steps) 1, 2, and 3 and   (Spiritual Dimension)
If you're right with self in (Steps) 4, 5, 6 and 7   (Mental Dimension)
If you're right with you fellow man in (Steps) 8 & 9   (Physical Dimension - the world and everything in it)

For the first time as far back as we can remember we're well in all three dimensions of life. We're then put back together as God intended for us to be in the first place. If you're well in all three dimensions of life you're going to feel pretty good. I don't think it's by accident the very next thing are **the promises. They come immediately <u>after this program of action</u>.**

Big Book, pg. 83, par. 4   *"If we are painstaking about this phase of our development, we will be amazed before we are half way through."*

J & C   Which phase of our development? Well the (Step) 8 & 9 phase.

Big Book, pg. 83, par. 4
   We are going to know a new freedom and a new happiness.
   We will not regret the past nor wish to shut the door on it.
   We will comprehend the word serenity and we will know peace.
   No matter how far down the scale we have gone, we will see how our experience can benefit others.
   That feeling of uselessness and self-pity will disappear.
   We will lose interest in selfish things and gain interest in our fellows.
   Self-seeking will slip away. Our whole attitude and outlook upon life will change.
   Fear of people and of economic insecurity will leave us.
   We will intuitively know how to handle situations which used to baffle us.
   We will suddenly realize that God is doing for us what we could not do for ourselves.
   Are these extravagant promises? We think not. They are being fulfilled among us, sometimes quickly (spiritual experience), *sometimes slowly* (spiritual awakening). *They will always materialize if we work for them."*

J & C   You know I've had some very horrendous hangovers in my time and I know that you guys have too. I have thrown up sometimes something horrendously, blood and all in my drinking career. But you know those kin of experiences never caused me to want to quit drinking. **What caused me to want to quit drinking was the guilt, shame and remorse that I had as a result of the harm that I did other people.** And these promises began to come about in my life; they came about not in my body but in my mind. I began to experience these things in my mind and I knew of course that the program was working for me and I'm free of those things today thank God. I'm going to read them again, going to add a few words to them and the words that I'm going to add t them refer to the time when I was young, when alcohol was my friend, when I could drink it and be Fred Astaire on the dance floor and the worlds greatest lover in the backseat of a '36 Chevrolet. This is the way alcohol used to make me feel before it turned against me

Whenever I took a drink of alcohol I knew... a new freedom and a new happiness.
Whenever I took a drink of alcohol I did... not regret the past nor wish to shut the door on it.
Whenever I took a drink of alcohol I would... comprehend the word serenity and we would know peace.
Whenever I took a drink of alcohol... no matter how far down the scale I had gone, I could will see how my experience would benefit others.
Whenever I took a drink of alcohol... that feeling of uselessness and self-pity would disappear.
Whenever I took a drink of alcohol I would... lose interest in selfish things and gain interest in my fellows.
Whenever I took a drink of alcohol... self-seeking would slip away.
Whenever I took a drink of alcohol my... whole attitude and outlook upon life would change.
Whenever I took a drink of alcohol... fear of people and of economic insecurity would leave us.
Whenever I took a drink of alcohol I would... intuitively know how to handle situations which used to baffle me.
Whenever I took a drink of alcohol I would... suddenly realize that alcohol was doing for me what I could not do for myself

Think about that a moment. No wonder I loved to drink. When you find anything that will do that much for you immediately become mentally addicted to the use of it, whatever it is. If it had been chocolate ice cream I would have been addicted to chocolate ice cream. If it had been Hostess Twinkies it would have been Hostess Twinkies. If it had been gambling, it would have been gambling. Mine was alcohol. Alcohol did for me what I could not do for myself. It was my friend and it worked for me like magic for years.
But one day alcohol turned against me and **all the things I was afraid would happen to me now began to happen because of the alcohol itself.** I became a very, very confused individual not knowing I was alcoholic, not knowing I would never be able to recapture these feelings from alcohol. I spent the last four, five, six years of my drinking desperately trying to get these things back from alcohol. Almost destroyed me in the process.
I came to A.A. You gave me a book. I found a little program of action in this book. I <u>began to apply it in my life</u>. And one day I woke up and found these promises in my head and I suddenly realized that

> **the first nine steps of Alcoholics Anonymous are doing just exactly for me (promises)**
> **what alcohol used to do for me when alcohol was my friend.**

See that's why I don't drink today. If I hadn't found this somewhere I would still be searching for it. I would probably have gone back to alcohol until it eventually completely consumed me and destroyed me.

> **But I don't need to drink because I found everything good that alcohol gave me**
> **through the first nine steps of Alcoholics Anonymous.** (promises)
> **That's the miracle of Alcoholics Anonymous.**

At the same time I realize it's given me the good I also realize

> **the first nine steps have never turned against me, alcohol did.**

I've never been placed in jail because of the first nine steps
No lady has ever dragged me through the divorce courts because of the first nine steps.
I've never vomited, damn near did a time or two, I've never really vomited because of the first nine steps.
See that's a miracle.

If you read those promises you'll see they all deal with the mind. None of them deal with the body.

> **We came here restless, irritable, discontented,**
> **filled with shame, fear, guilt, remorse, worry, anger, depression, etc.**

> **We work the steps,**
> **we receive the promises.**

Certainly we have undergone a change in our personality. We have undergone a spiritual awakening already.

J & C   Now if that's true then what is the purpose of the last three steps? And many people will tell us that the last three steps are to maintain our sobriety. I will agree that they will help us stay sober. But the word maintenance itself is a misnomer. To maintain something is means to keep it "as is". And another natural law applies.

> Nothing in our universe ever stays "as is".
> Everything in our universe is in a constant state of change.
> It's either growing or it's dying.
> It's progressing or it's regressing.
> It's going forward or it's going back.

Now we've made a tremendous amount of spiritual growth through the first nine steps is we've got the promises. But if we tried to maintain this eventually we start slipping back. And we start having trouble with people. Then with ourself. Then with God. And we end up drunk all over again. Now how do I know that? I see it happen in AA over and over and over and over again. That's what happens when people like us had a good program go back and get drunk again it's because we stopped growing. And we can't stop growing. If you do you start dying. Let's look at the last three steps. Not as just maintenance steps. Not just to keep us sober, but to see if we don't actually continue to grow in our relationship with God, with ourselves and with other human beings.

> Twice in the book Bill has mentioned a fourth dimension of existence.

Once in his story. Once in Chapter 2. A dimension of living far beyond the normal three. You can't explain it. You can't describe it. You can only feel it. And that's what the last three steps do. Move us into another dimension of living. Let's look at them for just a few minutes.

You know one of the things that we did, as a fellowship is we took the steps out of the book and we put them on these little cards and put them on the wall. And if you look at step 10 on this card or on the wall and by the way we left the instructions on how to work the steps in the book. People come into AA and look at the wall and try to work the steps off the wall without instructions. No wonder they get in trouble. Step 10, off the wall or off the cards says

Continued to take personal inventory and when we were wrong promptly admitted it.

And it looked like if we just continued to take a little inventory and if we were wrong promptly admitted it we would be doing the intended step 10. And somehow or other we got the idea that we do that at night. Well the nighttime portion is over in step 11 it's not in step 10. And Charlie and I have discussed this at great detail. We don't get in trouble at night in bed any more. We need a daytime walking around step. So let's look at step 10 in a different light.

Big Book, p. 84, par. 2   "This thought brings us to step ten, which suggests we continue to take personal inventory and continue to set right any new mistakes as we go along. We vigorously commenced this way of living as we cleaned up the past. We have entered the world of Spirit."

J & C   We've had a spiritual awakening.

Big Book, p. 84, par. 2 cont.   "Our next function is to grow "

J & C   To grow, not maintain, not stay where we are, but to grow.

Big Book, p. 84, par. 2 cont.   *"in understanding and effectiveness. This is not an overnight matter. It should continue for our lifetime. Continue to watch for selfishness, dishonesty, resentment, and fear."*

J & C   What step did we use to look at that in the first place. Anybody remember? Step 4? OK.

Big Book, p. 84, par. 2 cont.   "When these crop up, we ask God at once to remove them."

J & C   What steps did we use there? 6 and 7. Alright.

Big Book, p. 84, par. 2 cont.   "We discuss them with someone immediately "

J & C   And what step was that? 5. OK.

Big Book, p. 84, par. 2 cont.   "and make amends quickly if we have harmed anyone."

J & C   What steps did we use there? 8 and 9.

Big Book, p. 84, par. 2 cont.   "Then we resolutely turn our thoughts to someone we can help. Love and tolerance of others is our code."

J & C   It looks to me like it we follow the directions in the book then we will be doing steps 4,5,6,7,8 and 9 every day, on a daily basis, for the rest of our lives. I would defy anybody in this room to do 4,5,6,7,8 and 9 on a daily basis and stay the way you are. You absolutely can not do that. I've got that little inventory sheet right up here in my head. Just as plain as day and you do to. And what I've trained myself to do if I get screwed up at 9:00 in the morning, used to be that I'd wait till I went to bed at night to do something about it. But when I do that I've wasted another day in anger and worry and depression and etc. I finally trained myself that when I get screwed up about 9:00 I get off in the corner by myself. I say OK Charlie

"Who are you mad at?"
"What did they do to you?"
"What part of self is affected?"
"What did you do, if anything, to set it in motion?"
"Which character defect has come back to the surface?"

I can't get upset unless one of those old character defects has come back.

Selfish, dishonest, self-seeking, frightened, or inconsiderate.

I can spot it just like that. I say "OK God you know I don't want to be this way. Please take this away from me." This selfishness or this dishonesty or whatever it is. I try to discuss it with someone immediately, preferably my sponsor. Sometimes I can sometimes I can't but I try to. Then I make amends quickly if I hurt anybody in this process. 10-15-20 minutes it's all gone. The rest of the day is OK. I have wasted all the time that I want to waste in resentments and fear and anger and worry and depression and etc. I don't have to do that anymore. My God I love to feel good. I just don't want to waste any more time, what little I've got left in that other kind of jazz. I've got a tool here that works every time. And as you continue to take personal inventory as you continue to look and see who you are mad at and etc and etc and etc you're going to learn more about yourself. As you ask God to take these things away they become less and less. As you discuss them with another human being, preferably our sponsor, we know more about ourselves. As we make amends quickly our relationship with the world and everybody in it becomes better and better. You can't do step 10 the way the book says and stay the way you are. You just can't. Your relationship with God, with yourself, and with your fellow man will become better and better and better and better. A new dimension of living that we never dreamed existed.

Now be careful. This is just like 6 and 7. This is the other changing step. And if you stay fowled up you can't blame it on anybody else any longer. Cause if you're fowled up and you use step 10 you can get rid of that stuff. But if you stay fowled up and you stay angry and worried and depressed and selfish and dishonest it's got to be because that's the way you want to be. I can't blame it on anybody or God or anything else any longer. And once in a great while I like to be screwed up. There's times I like to be mad. Cause when I'm mad I can romp and stomp and raise hell with everybody around me all day long. And that gives me a comfortable feeling of superiority. And once in a while I just love it. There's times I like to be afraid. Cause I can use that to rationalize and justify not doing what I should do or just as importantly doing something I shouldn't do. But when I do that anymore I don't enjoy it like I used to. Somewhere about the middle of it I catch myself. And I say "OK idiot. You're doing it to yourself again". This thing really does work. And you'll continue to grow.

Now after step 10 you've got another set of promises. Let's look at them for just a moment.

Big Book, p. 84, par. 3. "*And we have ceased fighting anything or anyone—even alcohol. For by this time sanity will have returned.*"

J & C   Remember it said, we came to believe that a power greater than ourselves would restore us to sanity? Well we get our sanity back on page 84 by the way.

Big Book, p. 84, par. 3 cont. "*For by this time sanity will have returned. We will seldom be interested in liquor. If tempted, we recoil from it as from a hot flame. We react sanely and normally, and will find that this has happened automatically. We see that our new attitude toward liquor has been given us without any thought or effort on our part. It just comes! That is the miracle of it. We are not fighting it, neither are we avoiding temptation. We feel as though we had been placed in a position of neutrality--safe and protected. We have not even sworn off. Instead, the problem has been removed. It does not exist for us. We are neither cocky, nor are we afraid. That is our experience. That is how we react so long as we keep in fit spiritual condition.*"

J & C   And again remember way back on page 45 it said that the main object of this book was to enable me to find a power greater than myself which would solve my problem. And somewhere between there and here we have the first 9 steps or 10 steps of the program of Alcoholics Anonymous. And one day into 6 or 7 or 8 months of sobriety and working these steps I looked up one day and I said what happened to that desire of drink that I used to have. It's just gone. I mean it was just gone, seemingly without any effort on my part. I found the power and the power solved the problem. It was just gone. That's the miracle of it.

Now, the next to the last paragraph on page 85.

Big Book, p. 85, par. 2
    Much has already been said about receiving strength, inspiration, and direction from Him who has all knowledge and power. If we have carefully followed directions, we have begun to sense the flow of His Spirit into us. To some extent we have become God-conscious. We have begun to develop this vital sixth sense. But we must go further and that means more action.

J & C   In other words what's happened to us in these steps of 3 through 10 we've removed enough self-will that we are now becoming God conscious. And by now we are beginning to receive some directions from God. Now if the book says that God has all power and all direction and I believe he does the book says so. God dwells within each of us and I believe he does because the book says so. Then it really stands to reason that you and I have within ourselves all the knowledge and all the power that we could ever

need to handle any situation which comes up in the future. It's called a sixth sense of direction. I've got five senses. Everything I know on a conscience level I learned from those. I can see and I can hear I can smell and I can taste and I can touch. But what little bit I've learned through my five sense of direction is just a small amount of knowledge. But if God has all knowledge and all power, if I can tap into him then I can handle any situation in the future with God's help. Whatever it might be. It's long been known. We knew that.
You develop this sixth sense of direction through prayer and meditation.

Most of us when we get here, I didn't know anything about meditation. I though meditation is when you tried to clear you mind of all thought. And I've never been able to do that. When I wake up in the morning that sucker turns on and it will not clear out. I thought maybe it was chanting. Listening to soft music. That's probably some forms of meditation. But I knew nothing about any of it. I knew very little about prayer. Even raised in church. I only knew two prayers. One went like this.
Now I lay me down to sleep. Pray the Lord my soul to keep. And if I die before I wake.
I'm not into that prayer anymore. That's dealing with death and I don't want nothing to do with that. The other prayer that I used and I bet you used it too went like this.
God, if you get me out of this damn mess I swear I'll never do this again.
Now I'm going to have to develop a life of prayer and meditation. Would seem to be impossible wouldn't it. Bill Wilson is faced with the job of teaching people who are spiritually bankrupt how to pray and meditate and Bill Wilson don't know how to do it either. Thank God he didn't. Cause if he had really been knowledgeable he would have written in such a manner that I could never have understood it. But he didn't know enough about it to be able to do that. What he did do is what he's done all the way through the book. He gives us some definite valuable suggestions. And he said if we will use those in our lives today we will develop our own life of prayer and meditation. He couldn't tell us how to pray and meditate but he could tell us how to develop our own. He starts for just a few moments over on page 86 he tells us what to do when we go to bed at night. Here it is now in step 11. He said

Big Book, p. 86, par. 1   "When we retire at night, we constructively review our day. Were we resentful, selfish, dishonest, or afraid? "

J & C   I believe that's step 4 again isn't it?

Big Book, p. 86, par.1 cont.   "Do we owe an apology? "

J & C   That must be steps 8 and 9 again.

Big Book, p. 86, par. 1 cont.   "Have we kept something to ourselves which should be discussed with another person at once? "

J & C   I believe that's step 5 again.

Big Book, p. 86, par. 1 cont.   "Were we kind and loving toward all? What could we have done better? Were we thinking of ourselves most of the time? Or were we thinking of what we could do for others, of what we could pack into the stream of life? But we must be careful not to drift into worry, remorse or morbid reflection, for that would diminish our usefulness to others. After making our review we ask God's forgiveness and inquire what corrective measures should be taken. "

J & C   And there is step 6 and 7 again. So what the book is really suggesting is when we go to bed at night we sit down and kind of take another little inventory. Step 10 was during the day when we're disturbed. Step 11 is before we go to bed at night.

We made up a little sheet here you could use. You can use anything you want to. The main thing is do we inventory or not?

DAILY INVENTORY

When we retire at night,
we constructively review our day.
Were we resentful, selfish, dishonest or afraid?

PERSONALITY CHARACTERISTICS OF SELF-WILL			PERSONALITY CHARACTERISTICS OF GOD'S WILL
SELFISH AND SELF SEEKING	☐	☐	INTEREST IN OTHERS
DISHONESTY	☐	☐	HONESTY
FRIGHTENED	☐	☐	COURAGE
INCONSIDERATE	☐	☐	CONSIDERATE
PRIDE	☐	☐	HUMILITY–SEEKING GOD'S WILL
GREEDY	☐	☐	GIVING OR SHARING
LUSTFUL	☐	☐	WHAT CAN WE DO FOR OTHERS
ANGER	☐	☐	CALM
ENVY	☐	☐	GRATEFUL
SLOTH	☐	☐	TAKE ACTION
GLUTTONY	☐	☐	MODERATION
IMPATIENT	☐	☐	PATIENCE
INTOLERANT	☐	☐	TOLERANCE
RESENTMENT	☐	☐	FORGIVENESS
HATE	☐	☐	LOVE–CONCERN FOR OTHERS
HARMFUL ACTS	☐	☐	GOOD DEEDS
SELF-PITY	☐	☐	SELF-FORGETFULNESS
SELF-JUSTIFICATION	☐	☐	HUMILITY–SEEK GOD'S WILL
SELF-IMPORTANCE	☐	☐	MODESTY
SELF-CONDEMNATION	☐	☐	SELF-FORGIVENESS
SUSPICION	☐	☐	TRUST
DOUBT	☐	☐	FAITH

On one side of the sheet we take the basic character defects, selfish, self-seeking, dishonest, frightened, inconsideration. We took all the other defects in the 12 and 12 which are the offshoots of those first four. We put them on the left-hand side of the sheet and called them the personality characteristics of a self-willed person. We tried to find the opposite and put them on the right hand side of the sheet and called that the personality characteristics of a God willed person. Now all we are trying to do is get from the left hand side of the sheet to the right hand side and I can sit down at night with this little sheet and run down through it making a few check marks that shows me where I've been that day. Shows we what I need to continue to work on. Never do I find myself on either side of the sheet. The check marks change locations from time to time. But I'm beginning to notice that I'm marking more of them on the right then on the left. And slowly over a period of time we continue to become a different human being. Now I've learned one thing about my sobriety. I am going to inventory. I've got one of two choices. I can put it off and put it off and put it off and put it off until I'm so sick that I'm almost drunk. And then I start trying to dig myself out from under the mess. Or I can take just a few minutes each day and by doing it a few minutes each day I keep myself in reasonably good condition. And I'm in much less chance of drinking. I find that it takes less energy to do it on a daily basis then it does to wait till I'm almost drunk and then start trying to dig myself out form under it.

A very definite valuable suggestion.

J & C   OK. The next paragraph tells us what to do in the morning when we get up.

Big Book, p. 86, par. 2   *"On awakening let us think about the twenty-four hours ahead. We consider our plans for the day. Before we begin, we ask God to direct our thinking, especially asking that it be divorced from self-pity, dishonest or self-seeking motives. Under these conditions we can employ our mental faculties with assurance, for after all God gave us brains to use. Our thought-life will be placed on a much higher plane when our thinking is cleared of wrong motives."*

J & C   Most of us get up in the morning and the first thing we do is go to the bathroom. One guy told that the first thing he did was get on a treadmill. I said "Man you've got a better bladder than I've got. I go to the bathroom first". Then we head for the kitchen. And we get a cup of coffee and maybe a little food, and we feed the body. We get the body taken care of and we go back to the bathroom again. And you ladies fix your hair and we men fix our beards or faces or whatever. When we get that part of use done we go to the closet. And we begin to pick out the clothes that's going to cover the body during the day. You make sure they match now. You've got to make sure they match, they're the right color. We send lots of time on our clothes. After we get the body all taken care of, we feed the cat or the dog. We start out the door. We lock the door behind us. We don't want anybody to steal our junk. We go out to the car and we check the air in the tires and we check the fuel in the fuel tank. We turn the switch, start the motor and we take off down the road.

But what did we do about our minds that morning? We took care of all the material things including our body. What did we do about our minds? Our minds are going to run the whole show all day. Did we check the air there? Did we check the fuel level there? Did we feed the mind a little bit? If we would take 5 to 10 minutes in the morning to ask God to direct our thinking throughout the day. Ask God to give us the right thought and action. Before we even start thinking about today, then chances are our thoughts about today are going to be in better shape. If we spent 5 minutes in the morning there coupled with 5 minutes in the evening when we go to bed, there's no telling what we could do with our minds. If we spent as much time on our minds as we do on our bodies, my God we could become anything, couldn't we? If you've spent 5 in the morning and 5 in the evening you've still got 23 hours and 50 minutes to screw the thing up. It only takes a little bit of time. Very definite valuable suggestion.

Big Book, p. 86, par. 3   *"In thinking about our day we may face indecision. We may not be able to determine which course to take. Here we ask God for inspiration, an intuitive thought or a decision. We relax and take it easy. We don't struggle."*

J & C   This is a form of meditation for busy people. We alcoholics don't have time to lay down on the floor and listen to soft music. We don't have time for chanting and all that stuff. We're busy people. The book says when you face indecision, you can't decide what to do, recognize you don't have the answer, turn to God and ask God for the right thought or decision. Don't struggle, relax and take it easy. I think what it means is get your mind off on something else. And the way I get my mind off on something else is I go start mowing the grass, painting the house or washing the dishes. And quite often my mind goes back to that subject and I've got information I didn't have before. It says, "Why don't you call Bill. Maybe he'll know." And I call Bill and Bill's got the answer. I used to say "My wasn't it lucky I called Bill." No, this is a form of tapping into the sixth sense of direction. And if you practice at it, practice at it, practice at it, practice at it, it gets to where it becomes a common thing to do. It's amazing how this stuff works. Very simple suggestions.

Big Book, p. 87, par. 1   *"We usually conclude the period of meditation with a prayer that we be shown all through the day what our next step is to be, that we be given whatever we need to take care of such problems. We ask especially for freedom from self-will, and are careful to make no request for ourselves only. We may ask for ourselves, however, if others will be helped. We are careful never to pray for our own selfish ends. Many of us have wasted a lot of time doing that and it doesn't work. You can easily see why."*

J & C   As I said, I use to use God like an errand boy. Send him out to get this done and that done. It didn't work. He never did come back with nothing. But I learned through doing that, to start praying only for the knowledge of his will for me and the power to carry that out. And today I can't think of anything that would be better than to have God's will done in my life, only. It would be a whole better than anything that I could even dream of. Because as I said here today I am in places today and many, many areas of my life that you can't get to other than by God's grace. It can not be done. You know I was practicing this thing around and one day I was listening to the radio and I heard a song that I had heard all my life and it talks about having a plane of inspiration. I heard this song all my life. It's called "In the garden". Any of you all know that song? And it came to me, "well that's a song about prayer and meditation, isn't it?" In the morning while the dew is still on the roses. That's about prayer and meditation. And I didn't know that. It just came to me. I can read these things and I can see these things today and I know what they mean. And I really do know what they mean. I don't know where that came from either. Certainly it wasn't anything from me. I think it's God working in my life. I believe that.

They said to me "Pray only for knowledge of his will and the power to carry that out" I said "How in the hell is he going to know what I want?" And they said "He don't care what you want." They said "He's interested in what you need" And he knows more about what you need than you know yourself. And that's turned out to be exactly true. If I had written a list of things that I thought I needed when I first came to AA. If I'd have said "God give me these things and I will be satisfied for the rest of my life." I would have cheated myself. God has given me things far, far, far beyond my dreams could possible be before I came to AA. Absolutely amazing the things that take place in our lives by simply, simply trying to follow God's will. People who have been self-willed like us, who have literally destroyed ourselves on self-will, we don't need to be telling God what we want. God knows what we need. And if we do his will he's going to see that we get it. Now who could ever dream years and years ago we could be sitting in this room today, doing what we're doing.

A week ago we were in Reykjavik, Iceland. The place I'd wanted to visit all my life. And by golly I got to tour Iceland. Hell I'm 69 years old now before I got to do it, but I finally got to do it. I couldn't have done that if I'd been drinking. A year or two ago I go to go through the Chunnel under the English Channel. I read something in a magazine when I was a kid about 9 years old. It said, "Sooner or later the English and the French would build that thing." I said then, "If they ever build it, I'm going to go through it" Finally, finally I got to go through the Chunnel and rode that damn Chunnel train doing 200 miles an hour. Sixty years I dreamed that dream. Finally got to do it. Oh yah. God knows what we need. He's not interested in what we want.

Big Book, p. 87, par. 2   *"If circumstances warrant, we ask our wives or friends to join us in morning meditation."*

J & C   About 15 years ago, we were sitting in my living room, my wife over there in her chair and me in mine. And I'm reading my prayer and meditation stuff and she's reading her prayer and meditation stuff. She looked over and "Joe, would you". No she said "Honey?" That's what she said. I'm not ready for that this morning. "No you old silly thing. I want you to read this thing for me and tell me what it says." I said, "Well I can do that." So I read that for her and I told her what it said and I told her a lot more than she wanted to know about it. And the next morning she said "Would you read this and tell me what this says" and I did and we discussed that little bit and that kind of set up a little deal in our house, praying together and sharing together. We hadn't done that before. And I've heard all my life those people that pray together stay together.
Joe, how long has it been since you and Phyllis have had a divorce? 21 years. And I don't ever thought about that. She come up with that.

Big Book, p. 87, par. 3   *"As we go through the day we pause, when agitated or doubtful, and ask for the right thought or action. We constantly remind ourselves we are no longer running the show, humbly saying to ourselves many times each day "Thy will be done." We are then in much less danger of excitement, fear, anger, worry, self-pity, or foolish decisions. We become much more efficient. We do not tire so easily, for we are not burning up energy foolishly as we did when we were trying to arrange life to suit ourselves. It works - it really does."*

J & C   That's a full paragraph right there.

Big Book, p. 88, par. 2   *"We alcoholics are undisciplined. So we let God discipline us in the simple way we have just outlined."*

J & C   If you'll follow these definite and valuable suggestions on page 86, 87 you will develop your own life of prayer and meditation. You'll make your conscious contact. You'll be able to tap in to that sixth sense of direction and it's amazing the things that we can learn by doing that.

J & C   OK we're going to talk now just a little bit about Step 12 and then we'll be done. We don't want to go through this next chapter (Working with Others) we don't have the time, but I do want to look at two or three things in it very briefly. Let's go to page 92. Now this is telling us how to work with other people, how to do our 12-Step call, how to sponsor and etc.   The first paragraph says,

Big Book, p. 92, line 1   "Tell him how baffled you were, how you finally learned that you were sick. Give him an account of the struggles you made to stop. Show him the mental twist which leads to the first drink of a spree. We suggest you do this as we have done it in the chapter on alcoholism. If he is alcoholic, he will understand you at once."

J & C   See this is what Silkworth (Dr.) told Bill to do.

Big Book, p. 92, par. 1&2   "He will match you mental inconsistencies with some of his own. If you are satisfied that he is a real alcoholic, begin to dwell on the hopeless feature of the malady. Show him, from your own experience, how the queer mental condition surrounding that first drink prevents normal functioning of the will power."

J & C   In other words, we share our story and we show him our allergy, our obsession of the mind, our hopeless condition of the mind and body and if he's a real alcoholic he'll match it immediately.   We get his attention that way, we tell him exactly what's wrong with him. Page 93,

Big Book, p. 93, line 2   "Let him ask you that question, if he will. Tell him exactly what happened to you. Stress the spiritual feature freely. If the man be agnostic or atheist, make it emphatic that he does not have to agree with your conception of God. He can choose any conception he likes, provided it makes sense to him. The main thing is that he be willing to believe in a Power greater than himself and that he live by spiritual principles."

J & C   Sharing our story and telling him what happened and we get the idea of the need of a spiritual experience across to him, after we've got their attention, by talking about the problem.

Big Book, p. 94, line 4   "Outline the program of action, explaining how you made a self-appraisal, how you straightened out your past and why you are now endeavoring to be helpful to him."

J & C   <u>Talk to him about the program of action. Take him by the hand and walk with him through the program of action.</u> You see it is suggesting here that we do the same thing the first one hundred did. It's suggesting here we do the same thing the Big Book does. See the Big Book was the Twelve Step in print. They could not go call on that person individually so the book had to tell him the problem, tell him the solution, show him the program of action. Now it's just as valid today working with other alcoholics as it was in 1939. <u>We need have no question about how to 12-Step. We need have no question about how to sponsor. This chapter tells us exactly how to do it.</u> And I said to my sponsor one time,

Charlie: I'm afraid to work with another person, I'm afraid I'll hurt them.
Sponsor: You can't hurt them, they are going to die from alcoholism anyhow. There's no way you can hurt them, and you might help yourself.

                SO IF YOUR NOT WORKING WITH OTHERS YET, FOR GOD'S SAKE START.

The 12th Step has three pieces in it.

(1) Very briefly, the first part is the greatest promise in Book.

        "Having had a <u>spiritual awakening</u> as THE result of these steps..."

I think that promises to me that if I apply the first eleven steps in my life to the best of my ability I will have a spiritual awakening.

Now what is a spiritual awakening? A personality change sufficient to recover from alcoholism

Bill tells us in the 'Twelve and Twelve, there's as many kinds of spiritual awakenings as there are people in AA, but they've all got certain things in common. That is, that we're able to feel, believe and do things that we could never do before on our own strength unaided. (paraphrased from the "Twelve Steps and Twelve Traditions," pp. 106-107) .

I feel things I've never felt before. I feel love, patience, tolerance, compassion and good will toward my fellow man. Before AA I could have cared less about you. Oh yeah you could have some, but I always got mine first. I don't feel that way anymore.

I believe things I never believed before. I believe God is a kind and a loving God. I believe He stands ready to help any human being anywhere in the world <u>the instant they're ready to give up on self will</u> and turn to Him. When I came here I thought He was hell, fire and brimstone. I thought He was a God of justice. Thank God He's not a God of justice. If He was I wouldn't be here today would I? Some of you guys wouldn't be here either if He was. Surely, surely He is pure mercy, pure love, believe that with all my heart.

I can do things I never could do before. By golly, I can stay sober. I never could do that before. And because of the fact I'm sober I'm allowed to do many, many, many things that I never dreamed that I could ever do. Like being here, going to Iceland, driving under the Chunnel going to Paris, France; things that I never could do before. So surely I've had some kind of spiritual awakening.

<u>(2) Now I'm charged though with a responsibility. There really are no free rides; you do have to pay for what you receive.</u>

I am now charged with the responsibility of carrying THIS message to other alcoholics.
- not 'a' message, not 'the' message, not 'some' message, 'THIS' message.

What is THIS message?

      "Having had a spiritual awakening as the result of these steps, ..." .

I'm not like I used to be. Now if you're in AA today and you're all screwed up and you don't feel good;
if you've been doing a little drinking or even thinking about doing a little drinking I know exactly where
you're coming from, that's where I came from too. But I applied these first eleven steps and I had a spiritual awakening and I'm not that way anymore. If you don't want to be that way anymore than you apply the first eleven steps and you wont be that way anymore either, cause you're going to have a spiritual awakening.

      It's the only message that AA's got.

Some of us start fancying ourselves as healers, miracle advisors, spiritual advisors, economic advisors. God I don't know of anybody that's screwed those things up worse than we have. No, we just know one thing. And let me tell you something, the one thing we know, we know it better than anybody alive. You and I know more about alcoholism than anybody alive, we're the only people that's only experienced it. We know more about recovery from alcoholism than anybody alive, we're the only people that's ever done it. I think we're the luckiest people in the world. I think surely, surely, surely God got tired of seeing people like us die back in the 1930's. I think he decided to do something about it, and He's always worked with people through people. I believe He picked Bill and Bob and the first one hundred,. I think he picked Ebby Thatcher and Dr. Jung and Dr. Silkworth, the Oxford Groupers, that whole bunch, and put it together so we could have it today. If that's true, and He picked people then, we've got to realize that those people are dead and gone; they're no longer here. If He picked them then, why surely He's still picking them today. There's not an alcoholic in this room that ought to be here. Everyone of us ought to be dead, some of us two or three times. And we said, my wasn't we lucky last night. I don't think luck had anything to do with it.

      I think God picked you out,
let you suffer your alcoholism so you would learn what he wants you to know.
And then when He got ready to use you, He removed the obsession to drink.
That's the only reason we're here today, to be able to help other alcoholics.

They tell me that 97 out of 100 of us are going to die, never even knowing we're alcoholic. If that's true 3% of us are stumbling in the doors of AA Less than half of us are recovering. We're talking about 1 out of 100. I used to say, God, why am I an alcoholic? Today I say, God why am I not one of those dying from alcoholism.

He's got a job for me; he's got a job for you.
It's only <u>when YOU fit into God's plan for you,</u> that you really become happy.

I think every human being on earth today; God's got a certain purpose for them,
and I think ours is to carry this message of recovery to other alcoholics.

We have the ability to avert death in countless thousands and thousands of people. Very few people have that opportunity. Carrying this message is very simple, just do it like the book says to do it and it always works for those that want it.   If they don't want it we can't do a thing about that

<u>(3) The final thing I have to do is practice these principles in all my affairs.</u>

Now what are the principles? We hear arguments about this all the time. The principle of (Step) 1 is this and the principle of (Step) 2 is that and no, no I think he's referring to the 6th (Step).

He said, "Having had a spiritual awakening as a result of these steps"… he already used 'steps' once in Step 12 so he's not going to use it twice. So this time he'll call them (the Steps) principles. In another place he'll call them 'proposals'. In the front of the Twelve and Twelve he says the 12 Steps of Alcoholics Anonymous are a set of principles. He is referring to the Steps. Now it's easy for me to practice the 12 Steps of Alcoholics Anonymous in AA I love you, I hope you love me and we're going to do our best not to hurt each other. But I'm only in AA at the most an average of one hour a day. What do I do the other twenty-three hours?

Can I practice these principles, these Steps in my home with my spouse?

Can I realize just how powerless I am over that lady? (Step 1)
Can I realize the insanity in trying to control her knowing full well I can't?   (Step 2)
Can I make a decision and turn her will and her life over to the care of God, as I understand him? (Step 3)
Can I inventory me and find those defects of character that keep me trying to control? (Step 4)
Can I talk about that to another human being?   (Step 5)
Can I become willing to have God remove and ask Him to do so and take those away?   (Steps 6&7)
Can I make amends quickly to her when I've harmed her? (Step 8/9/10/11)

There's time when I'm ashamed of me. There are times when I treat absolute strangers on the street with more courtesy than I treat my own wife in my own home. Just think, if I could practice these principles there with her and she with me, why we might pick up ten, twelve hours a day where we could be peaceful, happy and free in our home. If we don't practice them we don't stand a chance, we'll be at each other's throat continually.

Can I practice them with my children? If I can do this with my children what little time I have left with them is good times. If I don't, I try to control, they resist, we'll have no good times at all. I might pick up another hour, two or three a day there.

Can I do it on the job with my co-workers? If I can do it on the job with my co-workers why I might be peaceful, happy and free there for eight or nine or ten hours a day.

Aren't we really saying that

<u>we have a set of tools and if we practice them in all our affairs</u>
<u>we can be peaceful, happy, free and serene</u>
<u>twenty-four hours a day, 365 days a year if we wish to.</u>

My sponsor used to say Charlie, you can be just as happy as you want to be. And I'd say, you old fart you have no idea what you're talking about. Today I hear myself saying,

> God will not do for you, what you can do for yourself - Tape 7

<u>you can be just as happy as you want to be.</u>
<u>You got the tools to do it with.</u>
<u>Now make no mistake, God is not going to do this for you.</u>
<u>Other people are not going to do this for you.</u>
<u>But you, with Gods help and the help of other people, can do it for yourself.</u>

I think we are the luckiest people in the world, I really do. Joe?

Now where does all this stuff come from? It comes from the best of medicine, psychology and religion. There's a story in that other book about this fellow and he was walking around practicing these principles and carrying this message. And one night he told the people there, the things that I do you can do so also, even greater. A couple of guys heard this and they went back to their little village, they had a sick friend there, they brought him to the meeting the next night. Now I like to think they were alcoholics cause they went up o the roof and they chopped a hole in the roof, and they let the guy down in there. And He looked at that guy, and He looked up at them and he said, why it's by your faith that this man was healed. See it was the faith of the people in the fellowship in alcoholics anonymous when I arrived that I was able to hang around 'til I could come to believe, so I could come to take some decisions so that I too could come to have faith. The fellowship of Alcoholics Anonymous is extremely important to me. It was by there faith for me.

Later on He was in a little town called _____ and after the meeting that night and He was leaving the meeting/speaking at the meeting, and after the meeting they were standing around smoking cigarettes and drinking wine I guess, or coffee or whatever they were doing, and they were talking. And they told Him about a fellow they had locked in a cave on the side of a hill, now this might have been the first treatment center I don't know, and He said I want to go up and talk to this guy. They said, no you don't want to talk to this guy, he's harmed a lot of people, we've got him chained to a wall up there so he won't harm himself or other people. You don't want to talk to him, and he said, 'Yeah I do. What's his name? He said his name is Legion for he has many, many defects of character you see. So He went up there and talked to this guy for a little while and turned him loose. Cut loose of his resentment, cut loose of his fear. Cut loose his guilt, shame and remorse and set him free.

He wrote a little step for us right here. The other people that he'd helped, those other twelve guys He'd helped, He took them with Him. And Legion wanted to go with him. He said, can I go with you and do what you do? He said, no Legion I want you to stay here and tell people what happened to you.

I think they call that Pass It On, that's what Bill Wilson said. Is Barbara in the room...

OK. Let's go to page 164.

Big Book, p. 164, par. 3   "Our book is meant to be suggestive only. We realize we know only a little. God will constantly disclose more to you and to us. Ask Him in your morning meditation what you can do each day for the man who is still sick. The answers will come, if your own house is in order. But obviously you cannot transmit something you haven't got. See to it that your relationship with Him is right."

J & C   That's the only relationship this book talks about by the way.

Big Book, p. 164, par. 3/4   "See to it that your relationship with Him is right, and great events will come to pass for you and countless others. This is the Great Fact for us.

    Abandon yourself to God as you understand God.   We did that in Steps One, Two and Three
    Admit your faults to Him and to your fellows.   We did that in Four, Five, Six and Seven.
    Clear away the wreckage of your past.   We did that in Eight and Nine.
    Give freely of what you find and join us.   We do that in Ten, Eleven, and Twelve.

We shall be with you in the Fellowship of the Spirit, and you will surely meet some of us as you trudge the Road of Happy Destiny.

May God bless you and keep you--until then."

Printed in Great Britain
by Amazon.co.uk, Ltd.,
Marston Gate.